D1539007

"Poor, Sinning Folk"

W.  DAVID  MYERS

# "Poor, Sinning Folk"

## Confession and Conscience in

## Counter-Reformation Germany

CORNELL UNIVERSITY PRESS    *Ithaca and London*

Copyright © 1996 by Cornell University

All rights reserved. Except for brief quotations in a review, this book
or parts thereof, must not be reproduced in any form without permission in
writing from the publisher. For information, address Cornell University
Press, Sage House, 512 East State Street, Ithaca, New York 14850.

First published 1996 by Cornell University Press

*Library of Congress Cataloging-in-Publication Data*
Myers, W. David.
  "Poor, sinning folk" : Confession and conscience in Counter-
Reformation Germany / W. David Myers.
      p.  cm.
  Includes bibliographical references and index.
  ISBN 0–8014–3081–X
  1. Confession.  2. Penance—History—Germany—Bavaria.
3. Penance—History—Austria.  4. Counter-Reformation—Germany—
Bavaria.  5. Counter-Reformation—Austria.  6. Bavaria (Germany)—
Church history.  7. Austria—Church history.  I. Title.
BX2263.G3M94  1996
265'.6'094309031—dc20                                        95–46885

Printed in the United States of America

*For Catherine,*

*Mary Alice,*

*Deborah, and Joanne Myers*

AND TO THE MEMORY OF

*Jeanne*

Then it occurs to me, and I think, not without heartfelt sighs, how it was in the world a hundred years ago in Luther's time. Oh unworthy age! Then one could distinguish Catholic from heretic only with difficulty. A person made his confession only once a year and quite reluctantly, without any zeal, or performed such confession only as an outward ceremony and old custom. For commonly, the more seldom we undertake such things, the more negligently and evilly we perform them. This spread such total negligence everywhere, therefore, that one considered it as a special piety when someone went to the Blessed Sacrament more than once a year. At the same time religion and piety stood at their most desperate point, and it was a shame not to want to have fun with the foolish misguided people. This paved the way for the heresy already spreading. What would then come easier to the majority [of people], who beforehand troubled to do it only once a year, than from that point on never again to confess? One can entirely abandon what one seldom does, especially that which brings more pain than pleasure. Now, however, through the kind watchfulness of God, the times have changed, so that I may truthfully say that whoever in our time makes only one confession in the entire year, gives himself away and demonstrates to everyone that they should not consider him to be anything other than a completely cold, half-hearted Christian who, were he not held to it by the commandment [of the Church], would not even once purify his conscience through confession, but would remain jolly with his sins and vices.

—Jeremias Drexel, *Nicetas*, 1625

# Contents

# Illustrations

# Acknowledgments

A long time ago, in a galaxy far, far away, I began at Yale the study out of which this book has grown. I did not realize then that intellectual and personal debts would grow so quickly or mount so high. Now that they crowd about me and clamor for attention, I am tempted like Rabelais to write, "I owe much. I have nothing. The rest I leave to the poor." That will not do, but a few words cannot cover the generosity of institutions and especially the kindnesses of friends. Yale University and the Charlotte W. Newcombe Foundation funded the bulk of the research, with help from the Folger Institute of the Folger Shakespeare Library. Recently Nancy McCarthy and the Fordham University Research Council enabled me to carry out revisions in Germany. I have also been privileged to use some of the world's best libraries, most significantly the Sterling Memorial Library of Yale University, the Library of Congress with its inexhaustible resources, and the Bavarian State Library in Munich. The Folger Shakespeare Library in Washington, D.C., and the Bavarian State Archives in Munich were generous with resources and advice. At Cornell University Press, John Ackerman has overseen the publication process with diligence, tact, and care. Carolyn Pouncy and Kay Scheuer offered incisive criticism and sound advice about my writing.

My experience in the Religious Studies Department of Yale University continues to shape my thinking about religion. The late Sydney Ahlstrom opened my eyes to the varieties of religious experience and the possibilities of studying it. George Lindbeck introduced me to the disciplined, critical study of language. To put it simply, he taught me to think. R. Emmet McLaughlin has read every draft with enormous patience and encouragement. John Stroup's remarkable knowledge of European religion has been of incalculable value. My fellow graduate students convinced me of the

# Acknowledgments

value of religious history through their own work and friendly criticism, and I must therefore mention Ann Braude, Bruce Mullin, Dana Robert Massie, and Bill Silva, along with Ruth Mazo Karras.

Away from Yale, Tom Brady and Gerald Strauss were critical in developing my approach to early modern German history. Many thanks are due them for their advice and to the Folger Institute for allowing me to study with them. A number of friends have helped along the way, among them colleagues at Fordham, especially Tip Ragan and Nancy Curtin. Elsewhere, Richard Stites suggested I contact Cornell University Press. Daniel Sherman has offered support, an occasional cookie, and Flaubert's *Sentimental Education*. Kurt Pfotenhauer and Jenna Dorn provided friendship, bourbon, and welcome relief from personal and academic cares. Cecil Adkins, Alis Dickinson, and the Adkins family made me one of their own, helping me to appreciate the beauty of language and the Texas landscape. The Fitzpatrick family has been unfailing in intelligence and civility, enchanting a desert boy with the light and power of the Atlantic Ocean. In Germany, Graciela Wiegand and Regina Conradt graciously welcomed me into their homes. Above all, Hubertus Jahn and Susan Morrissey have offered a permanent bond of friendship, strengthened by their sharp intelligence and Hubertus's encyclopedic knowledge of Munich, the Bavarian countryside, and beer from Buttenheim to the Tal. When I asked, Hubertus helped me with translations from the German, but the responsibility for any mistakes is mine alone.

And now, the most important and difficult thanks. They go first to a company of smart and courageous women—my sisters and especially my mother. I also thank Elisabeth Adkins, whose careful musicianship taught me the value of patience and craft. I never pass a day or hear music without thinking of her friendship. Last, my deepest thanks go to Tara Fitzpatrick for her critical sophistication and knowledge of literature. Her faith and wit have carried me through good times and bad, and she made me aware of the old island that flowered once for Dutch sailors' eyes. Above all else, though, she knows that life is more than books. Somewhere in it there must be beaches and starlight.

W. D. M.

"Poor, Sinning Folk"

# Introduction

In her autobiography, Dorothy Day described confession in a way familiar to twentieth-century Roman Catholics:

> When you go to confession on a Saturday night, you go into a warm, dimly lit vastness, with the smell of wax and incense in the air, the smell of burning candles, and if it is a hot summer night there is the sound of a great electric fan, and the noise of the streets coming in to emphasize the stillness. There is another sound too, besides that of the quiet movements of the people from pew to confession to altar rail; there is the sliding of the shutters of the little window between you and the priest in his "box."
>
> Some confessionals are large and roomy—plenty of space for the knees, and breathing space in the thick darkness that seems to pulse with your own heart. In some poor churches, many of the ledges are narrow and worn, so your knees almost slip off the kneeling bench, and your feet protrude outside the curtain which shields you from the others who are waiting. Some churches have netting, or screens, between you and the priest and you can see the outline of his face inclined toward you, quiet, impersonal, patient. Some have a piece of material covering the screen, so you can see nothing. Some priests leave their lights on in their boxes so they can read their breviaries between confessions. The light does not bother you if that piece of material is there so you cannot see or be seen, but if it is only a grating so that he can see your face, it is embarrassing and you do not go back to that priest again.
>
> Going to confession is hard—hard when you have sins to confess, hard when you haven't, and you rack your brain for even the beginnings of sins against charity, chastity, sins of detraction, sloth or gluttony. You do not want to make too much of your constant imperfections and venial sins, but you want to drag them out to the light of day as the first step in getting rid of them. The just man falls seven times daily.
>
> "Bless me, Father, for I have sinned," is the way you begin. "I made my last confession a week ago, and since then. . . ."[1]

---

[1] Dorothy Day, *The Long Loneliness* (1952), pp. 9–10.

# Introduction

For Day, as for many others, four features especially marked the experience. One was frequency—weekly confession was so commonplace that she seems to have taken it entirely for granted. It was not a case of sinning mortally and then looking for a confessor, but the other way around: Day accepted the fact of regular confession and prepared accordingly, seeking out sins, large or small, mortal or venial. Second, she had incorporated frequent confession into a general program of piety, self-understanding, and prayer. Indeed, it is not too much to say that the sacrament of confession itself was an object of devotion for her. The third characteristic of Day's experience was privacy. A specially designed booth separated her from fellow penitents, sometimes with a curtain added to intensify the isolation. In any case, though, in the orderly quiet of the church she did not even imagine that other people might want or try to overhear her revelations. The confessional box also marks the fourth feature of her account: anonymity. It was axiomatic that the priest not be aware of her identity or even be able to see her, and any deviation provided a perfectly acceptable reason for changing confessors.

It was the pervasiveness of this practice in modern Roman Catholicism that first engaged my attention. What also seemed striking was its voluntary nature—the long lines of Roman Catholics patiently waiting every week to reveal intimate details of their lives. Even the seeming permanence of confession—a custom already ancient in the sixteenth century and apparently received by Catholics *per omnia saecula saeculorum*—made it and the surrounding controversies an irresistible subject for the scholar of religion. In this book, therefore, I describe the practice of confession beginning in 1500 as customarily experienced in German-speaking territories, primarily in present-day Bavaria and Austria, lands that remained generally loyal (partly through choice, partly through force) to the Roman Catholic Church. The book traces changes in practice, particularly under pressure from the Protestant Reformation, and concludes by discussing the impact of the Catholic Reformation in the first half of the seventeenth century.

Frequent, devout, private, anonymous—these qualities appear to be indispensable elements for confession and forgiveness among twentieth-century Catholics.[2] So permanent and inextricable do they seem that one

---

[2] On the practice of confession in nineteenth- and twentieth-century America, see Jay P. Dolan, *The American Catholic Experience: A History from Colonial Times to the Present* (1985), pp. 226–227, 386.

prominent historian has based his important discussion of late-medieval sacramental penance in part on "my reflections on my own experience as a Roman Catholic raised in the middle decades of this century and thoroughly educated in Catholic schools and in pre–Vatican II Catholicism." He goes on to comment:

> "Such a modern Catholic finds implausible the whole notion of the oppressiveness of the late-medieval penitential system which in its essentials, after all, continued unaltered down to the 1960's, save for the suppression of pecuniary indulgences, the gradual increase in the frequency of confession, and the modern obsession with lust as the only deadly sin."[3]

These memories and reflections may capture the flavor of modern confession, but they deceive the historian seeking to understand its practice in early-modern Germany. By 1500 penance had already undergone a millennium of change, and studying the evolution of this singular system during the sixteenth century provides a key to the development of modern Roman Catholicism itself. In fact, frequent, private, anonymous confession, with its accompanying devotional imagery of lay people creeping quietly into a sealed confessional booth every week to reveal their private sins to a virtually anonymous priest, is a relatively modern event bearing little relation to the experience of pre-Reformation Christians. One could not find a confessional booth in medieval Europe, because this product of the late sixteenth century appeared in Germany only after 1600.[4] Anonymity was thus impossible, and undesirable in any case, for the Church intended that priest and penitent know each other. Privacy was not an issue; by design one's experience was not invisible to fellow penitents. Finally, frequent confession in the modern sense was extremely rare, even abnormal for lay people, and the "gradual increase" in reception reflects a major change in the function and very meaning of the sacrament. Substantial disparities exist between late-medieval and modern practice, with serious consequences for the understanding of both late-medieval and early-modern religious consciousness. Paradoxically, then, understanding sacramental confession begins not with remembering but with forgetting.

[3] Lawrence Duggan, "Fear and Confession on the Eve of the Reformation," *Archiv für Reformationsgeschichte* 75 (1984): 154–155.
[4] The definitive form of the confessional is credited to Carlo Borromeo of Milan. See Chapter 3.

# Introduction

Beyond nostalgia and one historian's curiosity, however, the theoretical importance and pervasiveness of sacramental penance in medieval
and early modern life force scholars to take it seriously. Specifically, how
and when did an inward-looking consciousness emphasizing private and
thorough reflection on the self come to pervade European Christianity?[5]
To answer this, we must trace among European Roman Catholics the
widespread extension of a process of regular and systematic recall, confession, and absolution of misdeeds. Peeling away the surface of sacramental confession should permit us to peer inside the process of making
modern Catholicism.

To investigate this sacrament for sixteenth-century German religious
life requires a shift from earlier approaches. Historians have usually focused on the amount of moral rigor demanded in pre-Reformation confession. Was confession fatally flawed by laxness in absolving sinners, a
sure symptom of late-medieval moral decline demanding the radical prescriptions of Martin Luther as an antidote?[6] Or was the penitential system
rigorous and highly moral, demanding of Christians an intense degree of
true sorrow rooted not in a submoral fear of hell and its punishments but
in charity, the selfless love of God?[7]

Since the 1970s, scholars have shrewdly and provocatively reversed this
early twentieth-century debate, rooting the Reformation in a late-
medieval piety that was not too lax, but rather too rigid. The problem was
not that the medieval Church had done its job badly; it had done it too
well.[8] Here the defense of confession as morally rigorous becomes instead
an indictment arguing that the strict demands of the sacrament fostered a
spiritual anguish resolved only by Luther's emphasis on consolation

---

[5] For a recent and very prominent discussion of this subject, see Jean Delumeau, *La
péché et la peur* (1983), translated into English as *Sin and Fear: The Emergence of a Western
Guilt Culture, 13th–18th Centuries* (1990).

[6] Adolph von Harnack, *History of Dogma* (1898) vol. 6, p. 250, n. 4.

[7] Nikolaus Paulus, "Die Reue in den deutschen Beichtschriften des ausgehenden Mittelalters," *Zeitschrift für katholische Theologie* 28 (1904): 1–36; idem, "Die Reue in den
deutschen Erbauungsschriften des ausgehenden Mittelalters, ibid., pp. 449–485; idem,
"Die Reue in den deutschen Sterbebüchlein des ausgehenden Mittelalters," ibid., pp.
682–698.

[8] Thomas N. Tentler, *Sin and Confession on the Eve of the Reformation* (1977), p. 53.
Steven Ozment, *The Reformation in the Cities: The Appeal of Protestantism to Sixteenth-Century Germany and Switzerland* (1975), pp. 19–22.

rather than judgment. By this account, Reformation theology offered escape from a religious system grown, in Steven Ozment's words, "psychologically and financially oppressive."[9]

More recently, this argument has seemed much less persuasive. For some, such an account appears to be merely a universalization of Martin Luther's own experiences.[10] Other historians have focused on the possibilities, expectations, and practices of late-medieval penance. Questions abound as to the frequency of reception and the ability of the clergy to conduct inquisitions of the conscience. Further, to balance any possibility of over-zealous confessors, some have pointed to the enormous loopholes in the system, which allowed lay people to exercise great control over who heard their confessions and the manner in which they were performed.[11]

This debate over the existence of a "terrorized conscience" induced by burdensome penitential practices has not addressed all the issues involved in the early-modern history of confession. Even if no specifically spiritual difficulties resulted from penance, one might ask whether ensuing social or even economic problems plagued recipients. Conceivably, use or misuse of confession led to public embarrassment or dishonor, even in the absence of any *religious* angst. The standard and much-criticized clerical practice of receiving a fee for performing the sacrament might also have provoked anger or resentment. Just as plausibly, the clergy themselves could have used the confidences exacted in the sacrament to their own worldly or political advantage. In each case, confession could have been onerous even where it did not lead to inherently religious conflicts.

Illuminating as it has been, the debate over the possible fear and misuse of the sacrament has also inhibited our understanding of the way penance actually functioned in pre-Reformation Germany. Historians have not de-

[9] Steven Ozment, *The Age of Reform, 1250–1550* (1980), pp. 50ff., 222. See also Tentler, *Sin and Confession* pp. 349–363.

[10] On this issue in general, see Thomas Brady, Jr., *Ruling Class, Regime, and Reformation at Strasbourg, 1520–1555.* Studies in Medieval and Reformation Thought, vol. 22 (1978), pp. 1–47; and Gerald Strauss, "Three Kinds of 'Christian Freedom': Law, Liberty, and License in the German Reformation," in *Martin Luther Quincentennial Conference*, ed. G. Dunnhaupt (1985), pp. 291–306.

[11] Lawrence Duggan argues convincingly against any widespread psychological burden caused by penance. See "Fear and Confession," pp. 172–173. See also Euan Cameron, *The European Reformation* (1991), pp. 305–308.

scribed what confession was; they have only determined what it was not. Surprisingly, few historians have actually examined sacramental practices for the period after the Fourth Lateran Council in 1215. Most have assumed that after that date, to quote John Bossy, "the sacrament seemed to exist in a timeless and bloodless universe,"[12] with its form, function, and practice permanently fixed. With few exceptions, late-medieval practices have by and large remained terra incognita.[13]

Single-minded emphasis on theology also governs most modern study of the medieval sacrament. Because the *doctrinal* definition of the sacrament—contrition, confession, absolution, and satisfaction—has remained largely intact from the Middle Ages until today, the *practice* of confessing appeared similarly consistent, at least until the Second Vatican Council. Nontheological components have thus seemed irrelevant to an understanding of the workings of confession, which consisted of an individual and secret encounter between priest and penitent. As scholars have typically depicted this intimate experience, other factors, such as setting or ritual, have seemed almost superfluous to the sacrament or its contents.

My goal here is to demonstrate how unwarranted this assumption of continuity is and to change the perspective from which we view confession. Scholars have explored penance from the inside and worked outward, concentrating on the individual encounter to explain the nature and function of confession, thus guaranteeing that late-medieval penance will be understood primarily in doctrinal and psychological terms. In contrast, I examine confession from the outside in, investigating the external trappings of penance and only then working toward the inner character of the experience. I believe we must pull back from the individual encounter be-

---

[12] John Bossy, "The Social History of Confession in the Age of the Reformation," *Transactions of the Royal Historical Society* 25 (1975): 21.

[13] Several exceptions loom large, however. Thomas Tentler's *Sin and Confession* definitively examines the pastoral theology of confession in pre-Reformation Germany. Steven Ozment uses late-medieval manuals and Reformation polemic, while Lawrence Duggan, using different sources, gives the best recent account of confession in the ecclesiastical system of late-medieval Europe. John Bossy's "Social History of Confession" is highly suggestive and provides a general framework for my own thinking. Jodi Bilinkoff has examined confessors and women penitents in sixteenth-century Avila in "Confessors, Penitents, and the Construction of Identities in Early Modern Avila," in *Culture and Identity in Early Modern Europe*, ed. Barbara Diefendorf and Carla Hesse (1993), pp. 83–100. Finally, for an account of seventeenth-century France, see Robin Briggs, "Sins of the People," in his *Communities of Belief* (1989), pp. 277–338.

tween confessor and confessant to observe the workings of penance in the general religious life of the late-medieval Church.

Theologians explicated the definitions of councils in circumstances controlled by the institutional Church. When priest and penitent confronted each other in practice, however, they did so in a setting and at a time determined by religious and social factors extrinsic to the theological definition of the sacrament but central to its significance among the faithful.[14] Because in the twentieth century confession occurs in an almost exclusively private fashion, hidden from nonparticipants, it is easy to forget that the process of confession was and is a sacrament, with a visible ritual attached.[15] To some degree, the entire history of penance until the late twentieth century has been a matter of "moving indoors" and away from public pressure.[16] Until that "move" was complete, however, the public dimension of the liturgy played a role of some importance.

In order to clarify that role, confession, both as a disciplinary measure and as a ritual activity, must be set within the late-medieval religious experience generally. What emerges from this wider view is a sacrament more conditioned by the time, place, and frequency of its reception than by the concerns of pastoral theology. Strikingly, medieval penance proved to be, by design, far less private than modern confession. The confession of sins was secret, but the sacrament of penance was public. Equally notable, for all its official and individual significance, confession was much less prominent in everyday lay religious life than modern historians might suppose.

From an understanding of the medieval point of departure, we can trace the changes effected during the sixteenth and seventeenth centuries. Concurrent with and in response to the Protestant Reformation, these changes in setting, ritual, and performance reconfigured the sacrament, making it

---

[14] "In practice, it was closer to Cranmer's 'ghostly counsel, advice and comfort' than to the anonymous leap in the dark familiar in more modern times . . . It was, that is to say, more a social than a private act." John Bossy, "The Counter-Reformation and the People of Catholic Europe," *Past and Present* 47 (1970): 63.

[15] Pierre-Marie Gy makes this argument forcefully in his "Histoire liturgique du Sacrement du Pénitence," *La Maison-Dieu* 56 (1958): 5.

[16] One reason early-medieval penance became secret was the extreme rigor of public penance, to which sinners would not willingly submit. Ibid., p. 13. See also Henry Charles Lea, *A History of Auricular Confession and Indulgences in the Latin Church*, 3 vols. (1896, repr. 1968).

more conducive to private counsel and interior discipline.[17] Traditional structures gave way, permitting Catholic Reformers to develop the internal and spiritual work of confession. This meant isolating the process from the congregation and making confession essentially an encounter between two individuals. Active encouragement of more frequent penance also brought much more regular contact between the clergy and the lay Christians they sought to discipline and teach. In this setting, Catholicism was far better equipped to inculcate the morals and beliefs of the international Church than had been the case before the Reformation.

A brief look at the issue of privacy shows how a changed perspective widens our appreciation of factors seemingly extraneous to strictly sacramental elements. The modern Catholic Church has certainly gone to great lengths to provide for both priest and penitent a haven from the curiosity of others and the social pressures of the crowd. The medieval Church also placed a premium on secrecy, but this did not necessarily imply privacy. As we shall see, the medieval ritual of penance intentionally involved public display and therefore public pressure on confessor and confessant alike. Secrecy itself proved difficult to achieve.

If one assumes an interview between priest and penitent unmediated by the liturgical season and far from the madding crowd, confession appears to have been an intellectual and moral affair in which the confessant revealed sins as defined by the Church to its judicial representative, the priest. If, however, the setting and timing of confession precluded such a tidy and reflective exchange, other factors may also have influenced the nature, the function, indeed the very content of the encounter.

In wonderfully evocative fashion, Natalie Davis has portrayed a possible Easter scene in a French city:

> During the confession, some have trouble understanding the priest's words and he theirs, since they speak a rural dialect or a foreign tongue; others tell of a sinful event as though it were a wondrous or funny story; others, especially the women, conceal things so they will not appear dishonored before the priest; others lay the blame for everything on someone else; some talk about themselves seriously as the center of an important event. Meanwhile the people in line are pressing forward to overhear what is being confessed ahead and spec-

[17] I am not convinced that "desocializing" confession transformed sin into a matter of psychological disposition, at least not in the seventeenth century. See Bossy, "Social History of Confession," p. 27.

ulating that Pierre is admitting the disobedience to his master he bragged about a month ago at the Three Crowns Inn and that Antoinette is being induced to recount her lascivious behavior with François, currently the subject of gossip on the street.[18]

This imaginative description makes it clear that the role of confession in early-modern society went far beyond the significant psychological function scholars have detected in late-medieval and Reformation theology.[19]

The social and public aspects of penance were exactly what the Catholic Reformation attacked. The Church attempted to bring quiet to the process and remove the crowd. Eventually, making the priest and penitent anonymous meant that potentially embarrassing revelations could occur without fear of social reprisals. Increasing the frequency of confession diminished the force of such revelations by making them almost routine. Regular penance also relieved whatever social pressure and tension accompanied the traditional Lenten shriving. Before examining the spiritual and psychological ramifications of pre- and post-Reformation penance, we must comprehend these changes in the way of conducting and receiving the sacrament.

To achieve such an understanding means looking at sacramental penance first as a ritual process experienced in some fashion by most European Christians. Such an undertaking presents formidable theoretical and practical difficulties. Investigating the rituals of confession seems less potentially fruitful than examining the Eucharist, baptism, or confirmation, each of which operated within the context of a more obvious public ritual.[20] Further, because confession did not arise from the population it served, but rather was legally imposed upon all Christians by the ecclesiastical institu-

---

[18] Natalie Davis, "From 'Popular Religion' to Religious Cultures," in *Reformation Europe: A Guide to Research*, ed. Steven Ozment (1982), pp. 333–334.

[19] "The experience of confession varies and the Protestant rejection of it may depend less on a view of it as always shameful and frightening than on a broader set of social and psychological circumstances that make the priestly role seem unacceptable in any form." Ibid., p. 334.

[20] In addition to John Bossy's work, see also R. W. Scribner, *Popular Culture and Popular Movements in Reformation Germany* (1987); Virginia Reinberg, "Liturgy and the Laity in Late Medieval and Reformation France," *Sixteenth Century Journal* 23 (1992): 526–547; and David Warren Sabean, "Communion and Community: The Refusal to Attend the Lord's Supper in the Sixteenth Century," in his *Power in the Blood: Popular Culture and Village Discourse in Early Modern Germany* (1984). Among earlier German accounts, see Ludwig Andreas Veit, *Volksfrommes Brauchtum und Kirche im deutschen Mittelalter* (1936), and Veit and L. Lenhart, *Kirche und Volksfrömmigkeit im Zeitalter des Barocks* (1956).

tion, it cannot be called a "popular" practice, if by "popular" one refers to religious activities that sprang from the people themselves and remained outside the scope of "official" religion as defined by clerics.[21]

Nonetheless, confession was a religious act in which the entire Latin Christian population of Europe engaged. The institutional Church also hoped to use the sacrament as a focus of religious and moral teaching. Whether imposed from above or spread from below, confession provided a point of contact between priest and penitent, Church and believer, through which the Church hoped to foster in its subjects a specific way of thinking about their own moral lives and their relation to religious and secular institutions.[22] The circumstances and rituals of pre-Reformation confession touched nearly everyone, allowing us to consider experiences and meanings common to most of Latin Christendom.

In order to understand this integration of ritual and pious practice, of ecclesiastical and popular concerns, we must explore confession from a variety of perspectives, utilizing evidence appropriate to each. This book therefore begins with an introduction to the terms and issues of the theology of penance just before the Protestant Reformation. Because scholars have investigated these subjects at length, there is less need to dwell on them than on the setting and circumstances of pre-Reformation confession. The Church outlined its expectations in synods, councils, and ritual books to guide the clergy, and several scholars have explored these to great advantage.[23] In ad-

---

[21] For the numerous possible ways of defining "popular religion", see Davis, "From 'Popular Religion' to Religious Cultures," and John van Engen, "The Christian Middle Ages as an Historiographical Problem," *American Historical Review* 91 (June, 1986): 519–552. A different perspective on the relationship between "popular" and "official" religion is Craig Harline, "Official Religion–Popular Religion in Recent Historiography of the Catholic Reformation," *Archiv für Reformationsgeschichte* 81 (1990): 239–262.

[22] Peter Browe, S.J., "Der Beichtunterricht im Mittelalter," *Theologie und Glaube* 26 (1934): 427–442.

[23] R. W. Scribner recommends the use of synodal materials in his "Ritual and Popular Religion," in *Popular Culture and Popular Movements in Reformation Germany* (1987), pp. 18–19. For Germany, these sources were compiled in the eighteenth century by Josef Hartzheim and Johannes Schannat, *Concilia Germaniae*, 12 vols. (1759–1790), hereafter cited as *CG*, followed by volume and page numbers. Lawrence Duggan has skillfully used these sources in "Fear and Confession." Peter Browe has exhaustively employed these and other similar documents. In addition to "Beichtunterricht," see Peter Browe, *Die häufige Kommunion im Mittelalter* (1938); idem, *Die Pflichtkommunion im Mittelalter* (1940); idem, "Die Pflichtbeichte im Mittelalter," *Zeitschrift für katholische* (1933): 335–383; and idem, "Die Kommunionvorbereitung im Mittelalter," *Zeitschrift für Theologie und Kirche* 56 (1932): 375–415.

dition, contemporary works depicting religious life before the Reformation, satirical accounts of the early sixteenth century, and even autobiographical works from the period will help describe the setting and experiences of the pre-Reformation Church. Individually, these sources tell only a small part of the story from a single perspective. Together, they should provide a multifaceted but clear view of the diverse social and religious contexts in which individual confessions occurred. Only after detailing the ritual and social setting of confession can we ponder the enigmatic world of attitudes and spirituality.[24]

In Chapter 2 I discuss the impact of the Reformation in areas that remained basically Catholic—primarily the duchy of Bavaria, with attention to the bishoprics of Salzburg and Passau and the Habsburg Austrian lands. The Catholic presence remained strong there, in large measure because secular authorities applied enough force either to preclude the establishment of Protestantism (Bavaria) or to suppress it (Passau, Salzburg, and Austria). By the seventeenth century, these territories, especially Bavaria, had become a bulwark of the Counter-Reformation. In them, the impulses of renewed Catholicism could work freely under the auspices of secular power.[25]

The goals of Catholic rulers did not end with the local suppression of Protestantism, however, for Counter-Reformation princes and dukes also seized the opportunity to wield greater authority over Roman Catholicism in their territories, integrating church and state to create a baroque piety at once opulent and austere, stressing obedience and discipline as its highest goals. Instrumental to this renascent Catholic piety was the work of the Society of Jesus. Chapter 3 traces the reform of the ritual and setting of sacramental confession to conform to a uniform and recognizably Roman Catholic standard and to allow catechists and pastors to employ it successfully as a means to piety, education, and discipline. In other words, this section discusses the "confessionalization" of confession.

---

[24] This process might be understood as a "thick description" of a religious culture. Clifford Geertz, *The Interpretation of Cultures* (1973), p. 14. See also Robert Darnton, *The Kiss of Lamourette: Reflections in Cultural History* (1990), p. 343.

[25] This is in contrast to other places such as the Diocese of Speyer, where Protestant strength inhibited the resurgence of Roman Catholicism and fostered a less polemical strain of Catholic Reform. See Marc Forster, *The Counter-Reformation in the Villages* (1992).

# Introduction

Tracing the changes wrought during the late sixteenth century requires a different kind of evidence. Fortunately, to survey religious life in their territory, the dukes of Bavaria conducted extensive visitations, the records of which survive. Confession figured prominently in the visitors' interrogations, and these sources enable us to draw a clear picture of traditional practices under assault from Protestantism. Post-Tridentine Catholicism responded with an outpouring of new official texts, ritual collections and handbooks designed to blunt the new beliefs and to delineate orthodox practice, in effect to define the nature of Roman Catholic practice against its new opponents.

Once we have surveyed these changes in performance and ritual, it becomes possible to ask whether they signaled a transformation of the function of penance as well. Here the rich catechetical and spiritual literature of the late-sixteenth and seventeenth centuries is crucial, and by analyzing it in the light of structural and liturgical developments, we can uncover the significance of confession in shaping the conscience and the sacrament's role in guiding everyday religious life after the Reformation.

Relying on this evidence, this book scrutinizes the ways in which Catholic reformers, particularly the Society of Jesus, famous (or notorious) for its emphasis on confession, used the subtle changes in the sacrament introduced after 1550 to create a widespread Roman Catholic piety focused both on ecclesiastical regulation and on self-discipline and self-awareness. It is my conviction that only with the implementation of this piety did sacramental confession begin to resemble in function and practice the phenomenon so indelibly etched in the minds and consciences of nineteenth- and twentieth-century Catholics. At that point, one story ends, and another begins. This new story, however, is a tale for another day.

# I

## Late-Medieval
## and Reformation
## Confession

# Prologue:
# Theology of Confession
# before the Reformation

Medieval Christian doctrine contained many complex elements, each producing theological debate in its turn. The medieval theology of penance proved particularly susceptible to controversy.[1] Indeed, so abstruse were the discussions and terms involved in the theology of penance that it is tempting to avoid them altogether and concentrate solely on the customs of confessing. However, repentance and forgiveness (of which confession was the mechanism) were so integral to Christian dogma that churchmen sought to guarantee that the practice of the sacrament would accurately encompass these central beliefs. Comprehending late-medieval and Tridentine theology is therefore critical for understanding the particular direction and aims of ecclesiastical reform.

## Definitions

*Confession*

Understanding the technical vocabulary of penance helps sort out the many issues confronting confessors, for the theology of penance did not follow any single path, and all the possibilities that had dominated at one time or another since 1200 still existed as options three centuries later. Three acts of the penitent—contrition, confession, and satisfaction—and an absolution by the priest comprised the late-medieval sacra-

---

[1] Jaroslav Pelikan notes, "The casuistry of penance was notorious for producing differences of opinion." *Reformation of Church and Dogma (1300–1700): The Christian Tradition* (1984), vol. 4, p. 11.

ment.[2] Of these elements, confession is most easily defined. By 1500 it referred to a recounting, made secretly to a priest, with a detailed self-accusation of all sinful acts, their frequency, and their circumstances.[3] Most medieval interpreters argued that only mortal sins must be confessed, but this assertion received no definitive conciliar formulation until the fifteenth century.[4]

*Satisfaction*

Satisfaction meant penal works performed as restitution for offenses against God, neighbor, or Church, remitting through spiritual, physical, or material punishment the temporal or purgatorial debt still owed even after eternal guilt had been absolved in the sacrament.[5] As the medieval centuries progressed, the theological importance of satisfactory works in determining forgiveness declined. By the eleventh century, reconciliation routinely occurred at the same time as the absolution instead of following the expiatory acts. From then onward satisfactory works relieved only earthly punishment and did not directly affect the issue of forgiveness.[6] Indeed, Purgatory came to be defined as a place where satisfactions could be fulfilled even after death for sinners already forgiven and bound for heaven.[7]

*Attrition and Contrition*

The third part of sacramental penance, contrition, became the dominant theological element from the twelfth century onward. Defined most easily as

[2] The three acts of the penitent were taken from patristic authorities. Herbert Vorgrimler, *Buße und Krankensalbung*, vol. 4:3 of *Handbuch der Dogmengeschichte*, ed. Michael Schmaus et al., 7 vols. (1978), p. 145; and Bernhard Poschman, *Penance and Anointing of the Sick* (1964), p. 156.

[3] Pierre Adnes, "Pénitence," *Dictionnaire de spiritualité, ascetique et mystique*, vol. 12, pt. 1 (1984), p. 967 (hereafter, *D. sp.*). See also Karl Rahner, "Penance," *Sacramentum Mundi* (1969), vol. 4, p. 387. In some cases, the Thomists accepted confession to laypeople, but Duns Scotus rejected all claims of efficacy for lay confession. *D. sp.*, pp. 977–978.

[4] Hans Peter Arendt, *Bußsakrament und Einzelbeichte* (1981), p. 267.

[5] Bernhard Poschman, *Penance and Anointing of the Sick* (1964), pp. 157–158, citing Aquinas and Duns Scotus.

[6] Ibid., p. 158. Satisfaction now took place outside the process of justification itself.

[7] The ultimate authority for this view was the pseudo-Augustinian tract *De vera et falsa paenitentia*. E. Amann, "Satisfaction," *Dictionnaire de théologie catholique, contenant l'exposé des doctrines de la théologie catholique, leurs preuves et leur histoire* (1938), vol. 14, pt. 1, pp. 1188–1189 (hereafter, *DTC*).

sorrow for sin, contrition proved anything but simple and was soon broken into *contritio*, which indicated the presence of grace, and *attritio*, which did not.[8] Thirteenth-century scholastics refined this distinction further. Thomas Aquinas understood contrition as a freely willed sorrow occurring simultaneously with the divine implanting of grace in the soul to forgive the penitent, so that it was both a human act and a result of God's love. Attrition, in contrast, was an incomplete or unformed repentance normally preceding and preparing for the infusion of grace.[9] In terms of the penitent's subjective state, the two forms were similar and continuous, but not identical. For Aquinas, supernatural grace transformed attrition to contrition by ordering the soul to its proper end, the love of God, and although this transformation had psychological ramifications, Thomas never explained them fully.[10]

In contrast to Thomas Aquinas, Duns Scotus separated attrition and contrition solely on the basis of infused grace.[11] Subjectively, contrition was indistinguishable from attrition, which therefore constituted a true sorrow for sin.[12] On this basis, Scotus speculated that a Christian could naturally possess an attrition so intense and enduring that God might condescend to accept it and infuse grace to convert it to contrition even without the sacrament, which in these rare cases became unnecessary.[13] The demands of nonsacramental forgiveness were so strict and their result so unsure, however, that Scotus recommended confession as the safe and sure means to absolution.[14]

Fourteenth-century theologians introduced a new schema, in which the critical distinction between contrition and attrition turned on the sinner's

---

[8] Vorgrimler, *Buße und Krankensalbung*, p. 139. Lombard did not know the term attrition, according to P. Anciaux, "Le Sacrament de pénitence chez Guillaume d'Auvergne," *Etudes de théologie et liturgie* (1948): 98.

[9] "Pénitence," *D. Sp.*, p. 972. See also Vorgrimler, *Buße und Krankensalbung*, p. 139.

[10] Gordon Spykman, *Attrition and Contrition at the Council of Trent* (1955), pp. 59–60.

[11] Gordon Spykman writes, "The difference between them [attrition and contrition] is not intrinsic but relational, they lie on opposite sides of the moment of justification." Ibid., p. 75.

[12] Ibid., pp. 78–79, and Poschman, *Penance and Anointing*, p. 186.

[13] Valens Heynck, "Attritio sufficiens," *Franziskanische Studien* 31 (1949): 93–100; Spykman, *Attrition and Contrition*, pp. 76–79. Merit *de congruo* refers to a merit which is itself inadequate for salvation, but which God mercifully accepts, in contrast to merit *de condigno*, which is in itself capable of earning salvation. For a lucid discussion of this distinction and its importance, see Heiko Oberman, *Forerunners of the Reformation* (1981), pp. 123–141.

[14] Spykman, *Attrition and Contrition*, pp. 78–79.

subjective sense of love for God or fear of punishment.[15] Once introduced, the subjective distinction between attrition and contrition became a critical tool for pastoral theologians, who took it further, separating out different levels of attrition to determine a threshold, a minimum standard for valid reception of sacramental absolution. Despite this rising concern for motives in the decision to absolve, however, the main issue was whether or not penitents demonstrated a sorrow resulting in a willingness to confess and amend their lives.

### Absolution

The final element necessary to describe the sacrament had nothing to do with the penitent's subjective state. The absolution pronounced by the priest to effect the working of the "power of the keys," the power to bind and loose, was an "objective" element, outside the acts or disposition of the penitent. As long as satisfaction rendered in a quasi-public forum effected the sinner's reconciliation, the "power of the keys" (based on Matt. 16:18) could mean pardon, excommunication, or exile.[16] When contrition became the decisive element in reconciliation, a question arose: If sorrow effected forgiveness and could do so even prior to confession, what was the purpose of absolution?[17] Through Peter Abelard and Peter Lombard, a "declarative theory" emerged in which the priest merely certified the forgiveness already accomplished through the penitent's own contrition.[18] The Church and confessor, extrinsic to the process of forgiveness, required a full confession only in order to assess wisely and knowledgeably the proper satisfaction.[19]

Uncomfortable with such a limited priestly role, thirteenth-century theologians favored an "indicative theory" in which the confessor actually effected the forgiveness of guilt in the sacrament through the pronounce-

---

[15] This development has been attributed to Richard of Mediavilla. Valens Heynck, "Untersuchungen über die Reuelehre der tridentinischen Zeit," *Franziskanische Studien* 29 (1942): 41. See also "Pénitence," *D. Sp.*, p. 972.

[16] Vorgrimler, *Buße und Krankensalbung*, p. 122.

[17] Poschman, *Penance and Anointing of the Sick*, p. 158.

[18] As support for this theory, theologians referred allegorically to Lazarus and to the healed lepers told to show themselves to the priests. Ibid., p. 160.

[19] See Vorgrimler, *Buße und Krankensalbung*, p. 130.

ment of absolution.[20] This "indicative" theory enhanced the priest's power over the penitent's works and raised a new question: Given the priest's power to forgive, could he absolve an attrite sinner, in the process making him or her contrite? For Aquinas, who considered contrition the normal prerequisite to the sacrament, the answer was a qualified yes, at least for a sinner who in good faith mistook attrition for contrition.[21] For Duns Scotus, confession was the "easy" way to forgiveness. Divine clemency led God to accept the priest's absolution even of unworthy attrite sinners and to infuse the grace necessary to erase the sin.[22] By emphasizing the power of the absolution even to forgive the merely attrite sinner, the Scotist doctrine of penance had enormous influence on theologians of all schools in the fifteenth and sixteenth centuries.[23]

Late-medieval theologians viewed the relationship between contrition and absolution as the critical component of sacramental penance. To distinguish between diverse theological tendencies, one need only trace the inverse relationship between the sinner's sorrow and the power of the priestly absolution. As one waxed, the other waned. Theologians who demanded a "perfect" contrition downplayed or denied the priest's power actually to forgive, while, as a rule, those who championed the sacramental absolution minimized the intensity or nature of sorrow required to obtain forgiveness.

Although Aquinas and Scotus differed, their late-medieval followers generally agreed that even a minimal attrition in conjunction with priestly absolution in confession sufficed. To understand their late-medieval convergence, we need only compare the positions of prominent representatives of each group. Emphasizing as they did the efficacy of the priestly absolution, Scotists of the fifteenth and sixteenth centuries struggled to define the threshold of attrition acceptable for worthy reception. An ex-

[20] Thomas Aquinas employed Aristotelian physics to devise a system in which contrition, confession, and satisfaction constituted the "matter" of the sacrament, which was then "formed" by the grant of absolution. Duns Scotus claimed that the sacrament consisted only of the absolution pronounced by the confessor. See Vorgrimler, *Buße und Krankensalbung*, pp. 131–136.

[21] Ibid., p. 133, and Spykman, *Attrition and Contrition*, p. 61.

[22] "Pénitence," *D. sp.*, p. 975. Heynck defends Scotus himself from the charge of "laxness" by attaching this supposed pre-Reformation decline to later fifteenth-century and sixteenth-century Scotists. See Heynck, "Attritio sufficiens," pp. 100–134.

[23] Poschman, *Penance and Anointing*, p. 184.

treme attritionist perspective emerged, granting absolution whatever the underlying motive as long as at the moment of confession the penitent detested sin and had no desire to persist in sinfulness.[24] In Germany, Johann Von Dorsten and his student Johannes von Paltz adhered to the Scotist double means of forgiveness, recommending confession as easier and surer. In emphasizing the power of priestly absolution, however, Paltz went farther, claiming that virtually no one (*paucissimi*) achieved a sorrow great enough to obviate the need for confession.[25] Paltz divided attrite sinners into three classes, the highest consisting of those who did everything humanly possible to please God and who thus merited forgiveness *de congruo* outside the sacrament. In the second class, to which most Christians belonged, one had not done all one could, but had somehow yearned or worked toward a true repentance. As a result, the power of the sacrament supplied the grace lacking and converted attrition to contrition.[26] The final class included those who had done nothing about their sins, who had remained passive despite being sorry through fear of judgment. For this group not even the power of the sacrament could help, except in the case of extreme need or mortal danger, when even repenting of one's inability to repent sufficed to allow the absolution to work.[27]

Despite the seeming priority of contrition for Thomistic authors, most accepted at least the possibility of regularly absolving those attrite penitents who demonstrated some movement away from sin and toward God.[28] Saint Antoninus of Florence, the author of the most influential late-medieval manual of confession, the *Summa confessionalis*, stressed the importance of contrition.[29] Even so, he accepted the sufficiency of attrition in confession to prepare the way, a view shared by the German Johann Nider in his *Manuale confessorum*.[30] Neither writer ever explained how this

---

[24] Heynck, "Attritio sufficiens," pp. 118–120.

[25] Berndt Hamm, *Frömmigkeitstheologie am Anfang des sechszehnten Jahrhunderts. Studien zu Johannes von Palz und seinem Umkreis* (1982), pp. 280–281.

[26] Ibid., p. 279.

[27] Ibid., pp. 279–280; Adolar Zumkeller, *Erbsünde, Gnade Rechtfertigung und Verdienst nach der Lehre der Erfurter Augustinertheologen des Spätmittelalters* (1984), p. 418.

[28] Poschman, *Penance and Anointing of the Sick*, p. 183. Some theologians hinted that a transformation of attrition to contrition could result automatically from reception of the sacrament. Tentler, *Sin and Confession*, p. 271; "Pénitence," *DTC*, p. 1021.

[29] "Pénitence," *DTC*, p. 1011.

[30] Tentler, *Sin and Confession*, pp. 264–265; see also "Pénitence," *DTC*, p. 1011.

transformation was to occur. The Dominican Sylvester Prierias Mazzolini, also the author of a popular *Summa* for confessors, minimized the required sorrow to the extent that one need only be displeased with sin and desire to gain the grace of God—the ecclesiastical power of the keys provided the rest.[31] For these authors, as for the Scotists they opposed, attrition and contrition were not so materially different that one could not become the other.[32]

Absolving the attrite sinner was also an accepted fact for the preeminent Thomist of the first half of the sixteenth century, the Dominican Tommaso de Vio (Cajetan). He understood contrition as the presence of love for God above all things but divided it on the basis of the presence of grace. Cajetan thus wrote of formed and unformed contrition (*contritio formata* and *informata*). Attrition, in contrast, lacked the sovereign love of God, yet this absence did not preclude forgiveness. Dividing once again, Cajetan referred to an acceptable penitent attrition (*attritio paenitentium*), which included a renunciation of sin that, no matter how vaguely expressed, could be construed as a movement away from evil and toward God. Impenitent attrition (*attritio impaenitentium*), however, included no intent to amend and was thus unacceptable.[33] Absolution could still take place in three of the four situations described.[34]

For both Cajetan the contritionist and Paltz the extreme attritionist, only those who remained totally passive in the face of sin went unforgiven. Whether Thomist or Scotist, most late-medieval thinkers seem to have considered contrition before reception of the sacrament a virtual impossibility. Despite their differences, Paltz and Cajetan each subscribed to a quite conventional definition of the sorrow sufficient to sacramental absolution: repentance and hatred of past sins with the intention of permanent amendment. What consistently mattered most to both was not motivation against sin but action, formed and perfected finally by the presence of infused grace. Love of God certainly counted in defining sorrow, but it was still more a characteristic of the final result than a cause of it. The real dis-

---

[31] Tentler, *Sin and Confession*, p. 271. See also Heynck, "Attritio Sufficiens," p. 125.

[32] Heiko Oberman notes that Prierias actually wrote against the Scotists (*Forerunners*, p. 251).

[33] Vorgrimler, *Buße und Krankensalbung*, p. 144; "Pénitence," *DTC*, p. 1017.

[34] "Pénitence," *DTC*, p. 1017.

tinction to be made in those receiving the sacrament was among various kinds of attrition, and here the dividing line was whether the sinner was moved to renounce sin, to confess, and to make satisfactory amends.

### Ease of Absolution

Laxness is, therefore, an unjust charge to level at even the most extreme attritionist. Rather, these theologians considered themselves far more realistic than their contemporaries in assessing the state of the Christian population. For example, the "laxist" Paltz, facing the question of how a merciful God saved sinners in a decadent age, decided that the solution lay in the objective power of the sacraments, which existed through Christ's saving acts to bring grace to humanity. Without this "new covenant," Christians would be left to their own devices as they tried to produce naturally a sorrow meriting the infusion of saving grace. To Paltz, that would be tantamount to denying the meaning of the New Testament and emptying the Cross of significance.[35] The sacrament displayed the depth of God's mercy by absolving even those—or perhaps especially those—who could not claim in any way to be just or worthy.[36]

Ease of absolution was also important in another way. Minimum requirements for the penitent combined with maximum power in the priest's act to yield a virtual certainty of forgiveness in response to what some historians have described as a late-medieval search for security and sure grace.[37] Theologians argued that although God was trustworthy and had promised that the sacraments gave grace infallibly, weak and sinful human beings could never be certain they had fulfilled the requirements for such grace.[38] To confer a measure of spiritual security, theologians had either to make humankind more certain by demanding greater rigor or to emphasize God's graciousness by diminishing the requirements for grace

[35] Zumkeller, *Erbsünde*, p. 417.

[36] One can see in this the justice of Harnack's claim, attacking Paltz: "There can be no doubt that the doctrine of attritio more and more threatened to become the Church's chief means of producing ease of mind." Harnack, *History of Dogma*, vol. 6, p. 251.

[37] Hamm discusses this issue in detail in *Frömmigkeitstheologie*, pp. 216–247. See also Bernd Moeller, "Religious Life in Germany on the Eve of the Reformation," in *Pre-Reformation Germany*, ed. Gerald Strauss (1972), pp. 12–42.

[38] See, for example, Cardinal Cajetan's response to Luther in Jared Wicks, ed., *Cajetan Responds: A Reader in Reformation Controversy* (1978), p. 54.

and reducing as much as possible the role of the penitent's always dubious motivations.

The Scotists opted for the latter solution, strengthening the role of sacramental absolution as a bulwark against the sinner's potential doubt and transferring the burden of justification from the sinner to the Church so as to make Christian life bearable.[39] In an era of rising concern over the holiness of the priesthood, the power of the sacraments themselves, working independently of their ministers,[40] became an object of trust, for, as Jaroslav Pelikan noted, "there had to be the assurance that it was God who did the absolving."[41] Indeed, for these Scotists, the power of the Church itself was the greatest sacrament, the visible sign of the grace of God, which converted and sanctified sinners regardless of the latter's weaknesses. Despite this objective quality, however, the pastoral success of the Scotist system, like all other penitential theories, ultimately depended on the sinner's trust in the priest or in the sacrament.[42]

Even among the harshest critics of attritionist thinking, its pastoral quality had admirers. The German Gabriel Biel understood the attraction of granting absolution to those barely attrite sinners who had only the will to receive the sacrament and who placed no obstacle in the way of its working.[43] Although Biel believed that a penitent who trusted such a theology could be absolutely sure of grace,[44] he nevertheless believed this thinking to be untenable. Biel represented a third group of late-medieval theologians of penance, who followed in general the thought of William of Ockham[45] and attempted to return to the "ancient" teaching of Peter Lombard.[46] That

---

[39] Spykman, *Attrition and Contrition*, p. 78.

[40] Ibid., pp. 79–80. The sacraments worked *ex opere operato* ("by the work worked"), which refers to the objective power residing in the sacrament simply by virtue of its being performed correctly by a minister with the proper faculties and jurisdiction, regardless of the personal qualities of either the minister or the recipient.

[41] Pelikan, *Reformation of Church and Dogma*, p. 129. See also pp. 92 and 96, on the rise of "Neo-Donatism" and the emphasis on the objective acts and institutions of the Church as a response.

[42] As Jean Gerson and others recognized, however, emphasizing the objective side of penance had limits, for despite the fact that the sacrament worked *ex opere operato*, penance as spiritual counsel also held a special place in the Christian life. Ibid., p. 95.

[43] Heiko Oberman, *The Harvest of Medieval Theology* (1962), pp. 148–149.

[44] Ibid., p. 150.

[45] "Pénitence," *DTC*, pp. 1035–1037; Spykman, *Attrition and Contrition*, p. 85.

[46] Oberman, *Harvest*, p. 155.

teaching included two elements especially significant for Biel. It emphasized contrition to the point of excluding attrition entirely and denied the "indicative" power of absolution *ex opere operato* in favor of the older "declarative" theory.[47] Thus, he decisively rejected not only the Scotists but also the "middle way" of the Thomists.

Biel's thought looked back to a tradition predating the thirteenth century, but with a great difference. This "modern thinker" defined contrition not in terms of a sorrow formed through the infusion of grace, but solely through its motive and direction as, in Spykman's words, a "perfect sorrow, a sorrow directed to the highest end of man's existence, a sorrow driven by love of God."[48] In opposition to Aquinas, Biel claimed that the selfless love of God, required for forgiveness, lay within the realm of natural capacity, not created by grace but enhanced by it.[49] Aware of the potential pastoral difficulties, the anxiety and scrupulosity, that might result from his thinking, Biel turned to a psychological strategy, arguing that confronting the exterior rite of penance could induce contrition in the penitent. This was not a matter of sacramental grace, because contrition constituted a natural act. Rather, the psychology of confession was such that it would foster the love previously lacking in the sinner.[50] Biel's required contrition resembles nothing so much as the forbiddingly rare *attritio sufficiens* required by Duns Scotus for nonsacramental justification.[51] What for Thomas had been supernatural was for Biel natural, and what for Scotus had been rare was now for Biel compulsory.

Not all late-medieval contritionists were nominalists like Biel. Although the influences on the Augustinian Johann von Staupitz have been debated, his view of penance in some ways followed Thomas Aquinas.[52] He stressed both the power of the priest and the necessity of contrition for worthy reception. He also viewed confession as the absolutely necessary path to forgiveness, even though the infusion of grace might occur before

[47] Ibid. See also "Pénitence," *DTC*, p. 1037.

[48] Spykman, *Attrition and Contrition*, p. 85.

[49] Ibid., p. 85; Oberman, *Harvest*, p. 153.

[50] Oberman, *Harvest*, p. 160.

[51] Another correspondence between them lay in the definition of the sacrament itself, which for both Biel and Scotus consists of the absolution. Spykman, *Attrition and Contrition*, p. 87.

[52] David Steinmetz, *Misericordia Dei* (1968), pp. 18–28; Heiko Oberman, *Masters of the Reformation: The Emergence of a New Intellectual Climate in Europe* (1981), pp. 75–91.

actual reception.[53] Staupitz, who influenced Luther, rejected any kind of attrition, whether it stemmed from simple fear of punishment (*timor servilis*, which he likened to a "gallows repentance") or even from a loving fear of God's just punishment (*timor filialis*). For both Staupitz and Biel, the motive must be pure for forgiveness to occur, and this position distinguished them from the other schools.

Unlike Biel, however, Staupitz believed that to be efficacious, sorrow must be grounded, not naturally, but supernaturally, in the sufferings of Christ. In fact, such sorrow reflected God's love of humanity and not humanity's love of God.[54] According to Staupitz's Augustinian views, no human-generated sorrow could forgive even a single mortal sin,[55] and he discounted even the view of Aquinas concerning an attrition honestly mistaken for true contrition.[56] Unless God chose to operate within the soul and produce repentance, sorrow had no effect. The presence of grace assured forgiveness despite continued doubt, tribulation, and suffering, which should make the penitent cling ever more tightly to trust in God's mercy.

This sampling of late-medieval thought makes it clear that, theologically and doctrinally, sacramental penance was far more vague than most historical accounts suggest. Doctrinally, confession had received only meager conciliar attention.[57] Theologically, its very necessity could be disputed, as among the Scotists, and neither terminology nor ideas were precisely defined or universally accepted. Theologians had so far failed to unite the disparate elements in a synthesis that could bind together all the traditional parts and satisfy both subjective and objective demands in a single sacrament. One cannot argue that contritionism was in any way the late-medieval norm, even if some did call for it.[58] In fact, among the contemporary authors of supposedly "practical" *Summae* and *Manuale confes-*

[53] Steinmetz, *Misericordia Dei*, pp. 103–104.

[54] Johann von Staupitz, *Von ainer waren rechten rew* (1517), p. 17, quoted in Steinmetz, *Misericordia Dei*, p. 101.

[55] Ibid., p. 100. For the source of Staupitz's views in Augustinian theology, see Reinhard Schwarz, *Vorgeschichte der reformatorischen Bußtheologie* (1968), pp. 152–153.

[56] Steinmetz, *Misericordia Dei*, p. 101.

[57] Only Lateran IV in 1215 and the Armenian Decree at Florence in 1439 treated confession, and then in disciplinary rather than dogmatic terms. Vorgrimler, *Buße und Krankensalbung*, pp. 152–153.

[58] Tentler, *Sin and Confession*, p. 257.

*sorum,* the contritionist perspective was quite limited. Confusion over the definition notwithstanding, one can safely agree with Gordon Spykman that "it was the attritionism of Scotistic theology which set the penitential pitch of this era."[59]

Confessors could absolve attrite sinners because the responsibility for the sacrament rested not on the penitent, but on the priest and his pronouncement of absolution. Distinguishing between attrition and contrition or defining proper motives was thus not so significant as some have argued.[60] Precise definitions of the sinner's penitential acts carried less weight because theologians were in accord about the objective "power of the keys" to compensate for imperfect motivations or to raise attrition to contrition.[61]

Late-medieval penitential theology has been characterized as either "laxist" or "rigorist" in its emphases, with the proponents of some form of "attritionism" in the former group and those who favored "contritionism" in the latter.[62] This schema, so useful for Reformation and Counter-Reformation polemic, fails to account for the complexity of thinking and views extant during the period. In fact, as this brief survey has shown, no single view can exclusively define the age as a whole, for doctrine and theology remained too fluid and uncertain. For the theology of confession, at least, that time immediately before the Reformation is best described as an age not merely of "doctrinal pluralism"[63] (in Pelikan's term) but of theological and doctrinal confusion.

[59] Spykman, *Attrition and Contrition,* p. 89; Vorgrimler, *Buße und Krankensalbung,* pp. 143–144. Whether or not Scotus himself held this view, statements of his were later interpreted by fifteenth-century disciples to uphold such a less-than-minimal position (Heynck, "Attritio sufficiens," pp. 93–100). Late-medieval contritionists rejected the "fear sorrow" in Scotist teaching while envying its pastoral possibilities.

[60] Tentler, *Sin and Confession,* pp. 262–263.

[61] For Antoninus and also Sylvester Prierias on this issue, see Tentler, *Sin and Confession,* pp. 264, 271–272.

[62] Harnack, *History of Dogma,* vol. 6, p. 250ff. In his series of articles for the *Zeitschrift für katholische Theologie,* Nikolaus Paulus claimed that love of God, not fear, was characteristically demanded in repentance. See "Introduction" above, n. 7. For an interesting use of Paulus's work to justify the Reformation, see Ozment, *Reformation in the Cities,* pp. 21–32.

[63] Pelikan, *Reformation of Church and Dogma,* p. 10.

# I

# "Poor, Sinning Folk": Practicing Confession in Late-Medieval Germany

From the most holy water I came forth again remade,
even as new plants renewed with new leaves pure
and ready to mount to the stars.

—Dante, *Purgatory*

For the ordinary medieval churchgoer religious experience included the elements often deemed "popular religion"—confraternities, pilgrimages, shrines, and tales of saints' lives. Framing these practices, however, were the liturgies and sacraments of the institutional Church, which worked in two ways. First, some sacraments celebrated different stages of the human life-cycle such as birth (baptism), death (extreme unction), and marriage. Second, the rituals and festivals of the liturgical year incorporated religion into the life of the community as a whole.[1] In this way, official religious celebrations addressed human and social concerns.[2] Strikingly, though, most

---

[1] The deepest discussion of these two cycles is Veit, *Volksfrommes Brauchtum.* See also Scribner, "Ritual and Religion," p. 48; idem, "Cosmic Order and Daily Life: Sacred and Secular in Pre-Industrial German Society," in *Religion and Society in Early Modern Europe*, ed. Kaspar von Greyerz (1984), p. 17. Scribner rejects the strict separation of "popular" and "official" religion, describing instead a process of mutual "acculturation" of orthodox and rural Christianity. Scribner, "Religion, Society, and Culture: Reorientating the Reformation," *History Workshop* 14 (Autumn 1982): 14. Others have claimed the essentially pagan character of medieval popular religion. See Jean Delumeau, *Le catholicisme entre Luther et Voltaire* (1979), especially pp. 5–6, and Robert Muchembled, *Culture populaire et culture des élites dans la France moderne (XVe–XVIIIe siècles)* (1978).

[2] "What is essential is that the ecclesiastical forms of worship should take up general human concerns and allow space for independent, though guided, meditation. . . . Seen from this perspective, it is irrelevant whether non-Christian or pre-Christian elements

of the sacraments had little to do with the liturgical year.[3] Christians could be baptized only once, and in theory this was also true of marriage. Extreme unction, of course, operated outside the calendar entirely, and there is good reason to believe that many Christians were hesitant to receive it. In the liturgical cycle, most sacraments had little significance, and for everyday piety, other, nonsacramental means to grace and succor sufficed.

Two sacraments, however, could be repeated and incorporated into the cyclical setting of the liturgical year: penance and the Eucharist. These were the most important sacramental practices touching the lives of lay Christians on a regular basis. On Sundays and feast days, the celebration of the Eucharist, commemorating the heart of Christian belief, was invariably the central event around which all other customs and services revolved, from the ringing of bells to the singing of vespers, from processions to *asperges*.[4] One must distinguish, however, between celebrating, adoring, and receiving the Eucharist, for most Europeans took the Host only infrequently.[5]

Confession too was an important event at many stages of life, particularly the last. Christians were encouraged to confess when in mortal sin, lest unexpected death condemn them to eternal pain. In times of potentially mortal illness, confession eased the conscience and permitted passage to paradise. Pregnant women were routinely counted among the "sick" who were particularly advised to confess.[6] Outside times of personal crisis, for some lay Christians penance held deep personal spiritual importance as a

---

found their way into Christianity or were accommodated within it." Hermann Hörger, "Organisational Forms of Popular Piety in Rural Old Bavaria (Sixteenth to Nineteenth Centuries)," in Greyerz, ed., *Religion and Society in Early Modern Europe*, p. 213.

[3] On the ritual cycle of medieval religious life, see Scribner, "Ritual and Popular Religion," pp. 49–50; J. Pascher, *Das liturgische Jahr* (1963). One can find the sixteenth-century practice in Franz Falk, ed., *Die pfarramtlichen Aufzeichnungen (Liber consuetudinum) des Florentius Diel zu St. Christoph in Mainz (1491–1518)* (henceforth, *Florentius Diel*) (1904); J. B. Götz, ed., *Das Pfarrbuch des Stephen May in Hilpoltstein vom Jahr 1511* (henceforth, *Pfarrbuch des Stephen May*) (1926).

[4] Scribner, "Ritual and Popular Religion," pp. 51–53; Veit, *Volksfrommes Brauchtum*, pp. 79–92. Contemporary accounts can be found in many places, but none so notable as Sebastian Franck's *Weltbuch: Spiegel und bildtniß des gantzen erdbodens* (1533), with its frankly satirical and critical tone.

[5] Virginia Reinburg points out that this was a matter of design on the part of some ecclesiastics ("Liturgy and Laity," pp. 539–541).

[6] Browe, "Pflichtbeichte," p. 348.

central element in guidance and counsel. The mendicant orders, especially the Franciscans, had long dedicated themselves to providing such pastoral care, with considerable significance for their theological views.

Yet to understand fully the meaning of penance for early-sixteenth-century Christians, one must explore it as a regular occurrence within the normal religious lives of most Christians, examining the physical and seasonal factors that conditioned its spiritual impact. These include how often, when, and where it occurred, and whether the medieval sacrament also involved the secrecy so closely associated with modern confession. Thomas Tentler has already examined some of the salient features of late-medieval penance.[7] Reviewing them here allows us to strengthen some conclusions already made while providing a new perspective from which to examine others.

### Confession in Medieval Religion

For medieval Christians, confession was intended as a regular feature of the devout life, and 1215 was a critical date in the sacrament's history. In that year, the Fourth Lateran Council issued the disciplinary decree "Omnis utriusque sexus":

> All the faithful of both sexes, after they have reached the age of discretion, shall faithfully confess all their sins at least once a year to their own priest and perform to the best of their ability the penance imposed, receiving reverently at least at Easter the sacrament of the Eucharist, unless perchance at the advice of their own priest they may for a good reason abstain for a time from its reception; otherwise they shall be cut off from the Church during life and deprived of Christian burial in death. Wherefore, let this salutary decree be published frequently in the churches, that no one may find in the plea of ignorance a shadow of excuse. But if anyone for a good reason should wish to confess his sins to another priest, let him first seek and obtain permission from his own priest, since otherwise he cannot loose or bind him.[8]

The decree exhibits the features of sacramental confession important to medieval religious life: discipline, pastoral care, and worthy reception of communion.

---

[7] Tentler, *Sin and Confession*, pp. 70–95, discusses both frequency and "etiquette" in conducting confession, but they are subordinate to his larger concern with pastoral theology.

[8] H. J. Schroeder, ed., *Disciplinary Decrees of the General Councils* (1937), pp. 259–260.

## Late-Medieval and Reformation Confession

One goal of the Fourth Lateran Council was to acquaint pastors with parishioners and to safeguard against heresy.[9] This intention introduced the possibility that confession was not only a liturgical and spiritual act but a disciplinary one as well, perhaps even a matter of "social control."[10] The sacrament also served as a "lower court" for the discovery of acts that only authorities at the episcopal or the papal level could forgive.[11] Some confessors carried special privileges for absolving these "reserved" sins. The penitent fulfilling the obligation to confess might find his or her priest lacking the authority to absolve.[12] Handbooks and manuals pointed this out to clergy and laity alike.[13] Potentially, an individual confession might quickly cease to be either a private matter or simply a case of spiritual advice. Since it might involve public penance or restitution, which the Church could enforce on its own or through the secular government, receiving the sacrament carried risks for the penitent beyond the forum of confession.

The system of forgiveness differed significantly from purely juridical *fora*, however, by virtue of its spiritual goals; clerical shepherds cared for the souls of their lay flocks. Combining pastoral and juridical concerns produced a paradox. Confession was meant to be a voluntary act, but it was imposed

[9] On the question of detecting heretics, see Gabriel Le Bras, *Institutions ecclésiastiques de la chrétienté médiévale*, vol. 1 (1959), p. 134, and vol. 2 (1964), p. 413. Pierre-Marie Gy, however, advances instead a more pastoral view on the basis of Bonaventure and Thomas Aquinas. Pierre-Marie Gy, "Le précepte de la confession annuelle (Lateran IV, C. 21) et la détection des hérétiques," *Revue de science philosophique et théologique* 58 (1974), pp. 444–450.

[10] Tentler, *Sin and Confession*, pp. 345–347; idem, "The Summa for Confessors as an Instrument of Social Control," in *The Pursuit of Holiness in Late Medieval and Renaissance Religion*, ed. Charles Trinkaus (1974), pp. 103–125. For a response, see in the same volume Leonard Boyle, "The Summa for Confessors as a Genre and Its Religious Intent," pp. 126–130.

[11] Sin can be considered a kind of religious crime, and the ecclesiastical judicial system a parallel to secular courts in medieval Europe, although the relationship between them is ambivalent. See Bruce Lenman, "The Limits of Godly Discipline in the Early Modern Period with Particular Reference to England and Scotland," *Religion and Society*, p. 125.

[12] Lawrence Duggan, "Fear and Confession," pp. 166–167. See also Richard Trexler, review of *Sin and Confession on the Eve of the Reformation*, by Thomas N. Tentler, *Speculum* 53 (1978): 863.

[13] These reserved sins might be either public (theft, murder) or "private" in the modern sense (homosexuality or bestiality). Thus Geiler von Kayserberg's translation of Jean Gerson's *Opus Tripartitum* discussed simony and heresy but also included sodomy and bestiality. Jean Gerson, *Opusculum Tripartitum*, trans. Johannes Geiler von Kaysersberg (1510).

upon the Christian population as an annual obligation, and severe penalties accrued to those who did not comply. In addition to refusing burial on church ground, the Church denied communion to the recalcitrant. In another incongruity, a critical sign of true sorrow was the intention to reveal the sin. Violators of religious and moral law were to police themselves through self-accusation. Having become aware of a sinful act, the sinner then voluntarily submitted to the Church, freely performing the punishment inflicted. Coercion was unnecessary, at least in theory. Confessors could, however, question penitents in order to uncover certain acts of particular concern to the Church, such as usury or heresy, as well as more commonly committed sins.[14]

Although the original intent of the decree was to set confession in the parish, the rise of the mendicant orders immediately brought controversy over who counted as a Christian's own priest—pastors or mendicants. A long competition ensued between regular and secular clergy. Very quickly, the new orders claimed the right to hear lay confessions, and just as quickly secular priests sought to impede them.[15] Pope Boniface VIII's distinction between jurisdiction (which the mendicant orders received) and specific approval (which was left to religious superiors and individual dioceses to decide) was an important step in allowing Christians some choices in confession. Not until 1516, however, did Pope Leo X, in "Dum Intra," finally resolve the issue and give Christians the right to choose their own confessors.[16] Of course, regular clergy were already hearing lay confessions before they received official approbation, and secular clergy continued to hinder them through the eighteenth century.[17] The complaints later leveled by secular priests at the Jesuits had a long prehistory.

[14] For an example, see the *Spiegel des Sünders*, (ca. 1470), in Johannes Geffken, ed., *Bilderkatechismus des fünfzehnten Jahrhunderts* (1855), Appendix, p. 52. Steven Ozment quotes this text at length in *Reformation in the Cities*, p. 25.

[15] Stephan May in Hilpoltstein was very reluctant to allow his parishioners to confess to others. See Götz, *Pfarrbuch des Stephen May*, pp. 86–90.

[16] Lawrence Duggan argues that this possibility sapped the sacrament of its potential rigors, since Christians could always abandon a strict priest for a more tolerant one. See "Sin and Fear," pp. 167–170. On permission to hear confessions, see Anneliese Hilz, *Die Minderbrüder von St. Salvator in Regensburg, 1226–1810*, Beiträge zur Geschichte des Bistums Regensburg, ed. Georg Schwaiger, no. 25 (1991), pp. 31–32.

[17] In early-sixteenth-century Mainz, Florentius Diel was reluctant to allow his parishioners to confess elsewhere without permission or notification and threatened to refuse communion to some. Falk, *Florentius Diel*, pp. 41–42. Even in the eighteenth century, secular clergy still proved recalcitrant.

# Late-Medieval and Reformation Confession

"Omnis Utriusque Sexus" contains two specific demands: the faithful were to confess all sins to their own priest at least once every year, and they were to receive communion at a specific time—Easter, the central season in Christian liturgical and ritual life. The wording of the decree implies that more frequent reception was not only possible but salutary ("at least once a year"), but the Council in fact did not expect this to happen. Requiring annual communion and confession in the early thirteenth century actually represented a decrease from earlier demands for a thrice-annual reception.[18] In light of the disappointing response to earlier calls, Lateran IV, the great council of reform, was in fact adjusting itself to the realities of thirteenth-century lay religious life.[19]

The two demands were closely connected, revealing an important ritualistic and seasonal component deriving from the traditional and ancient role of penance in preparing individuals and congregations for worthy participation in the great feasts of the liturgical year.[20] From the earliest days of the Church, the goal of penance was to purify the faithful for worthy reception of communion. By the eleventh century, this meant that, with very few exceptions, Christians confessed "when and because they received communion."[21] Indeed, most subsequent synods and theologians understood the Fourth Lateran Council's injunction to annual confession as a function of its decree on Easter communion.[22] For this reason, the decree did not have to dictate the time for confessing, which customarily occurred during Lent. Here tradition played a strong role. Lenten fasting followed early shriving, and the congregation as a whole then received a general absolution later in the season, on Holy Thursday or *Gründonnerstag*.[23]

---

[18] According to Peter Browe, some pre-1215 synods stipulated a thrice-yearly communion. "Pflichtbeichte," pp. 342–343.

[19] Browe, *Pflichtkommunion*, p. 43.

[20] Early Christians were permitted penance only once in their lives and so attempted to wait until they were near death. Tentler, *Sin and Confession*, p. 6. By the time of Charlemagne, this had developed into the practice of confessing grave sins before communion. Poschman, *Penance and Anointing*, pp. 136–138.

[21] Browe, "Pflichtbeichte," p. 345.

[22] See Louis Braeckmans, S.J., *Confession et communion au moyen âge et au concile de Trente* (1971).

[23] Browe, *Pflichtkommunion*, p. 24.

# "Poor, Sinning Folk"

## Sacramental Confession in 1500

*The Frequency and Timing of Medieval Confession*

Studying penance as practiced three centuries after the Fourth Lateran Council reveals that the disciplinary and seasonal prescriptions of "Omnis" remained fundamental. Authorities took steps to enforce the decree, not merely by exhortation but by coercion and legal measures. Officials clearly worried that Christians would receive communion unworthily, and their concern may have been less for the individual than for the entire Christian congregation sullied by one person's unworthiness. Yet, while annual confession was theoretically only the minimum, the Church neither demanded nor undertook systematic efforts to spur more frequent reception until the very end of the Middle Ages.[24] Although it was said to be available throughout the year, therefore, sacramental confession remained in practice mostly a Lenten affair, expected, prepared for, and experienced at that season of the Church year.

The late-medieval Church actively enforced the rule of the Fourth Lateran Council.[25] Doing so required efforts to remind and to cajole. Disciplinary decrees also threatened those who did not confess. The Church brought pressure to bear in order to enforce the rule and listed a range of punishments for the recalcitrant. As stipulated by the Fourth Lateran Council, the Synod of Salzburg (1490) denied burial on Church ground to those who neither confessed nor received communion.[26] In Passau (1470) and elsewhere, decrees specified Lent and Easter and ordered those who persistently refused to fulfill their duty denounced to episcopal officials.[27] In each of these cases noncompliance became a matter for the episcopal office. Other synods also threatened disciplinary action against those who failed to meet the annual obligation, although the punishment was not spelled out.[28]

---

[24] Thomas Tentler summarizes the findings of historians on the question of frequency. *Sin and Confession*, pp. 70–82.

[25] Worms (1497), *CG*, vol. 5, p. 665.

[26] Salzburg (1490), *CG*, vol. 5, p. 575.

[27] Passau (1470), *CG*, vol. 5, p. 489; Basel (1503), *CG*, vol. 6, p. 10.

[28] Mainz (1451), *CG*, vol. 5, 411; Worms (1497), *CG*, vol. 5, p. 666; Regensburg (1512), *CG*, vol. 6, p. 115.

## Late-Medieval and Reformation Confession

By 1500 most German Christians were fulfilling their Lenten duty both to confess and to receive communion.[29] Outside Lent, however, reception was rarer, not only in German-speaking lands but throughout Europe, as contemporary accounts indicate.[30] In the upper Palatinate at the beginning of the sixteenth century, receiving the sacraments even three times a year was a curiosity, and according to one pastor, only ten persons received communion outside the Easter season.[31] According to Peter Browe's detailed study of communion receptions, in the fifteenth and early sixteenth centuries, some churches arranged to distribute the host perhaps four times a year, as done at Saint John's in Utrecht,[32] or at most five, as at a filial church of Studenheim in Worms, where the vicar was specifically required to help to administer confession and communion on Easter and at four other high feasts.[33] The parish of Sankt Jakob in Münster gave out communion during the Easter season (on Holy Thursday, Good Friday, and Easter Sunday) and at Pentecost, Corpus Christi, and All Saints.[34] Elsewhere distribution occurred less often. In Ingolstadt during the early sixteenth century, outside the Easter season communion was given only at Christmas, and then only to women and students.[35] At Lorch in Württemberg, priests distributed communion only at Eastertime, deliberately limiting the parish to annual reception.[36]

Clearly, the distribution of communion itself was by design limited. Not everyone needed to receive each time the sacrament was available, and the evidence indicates that most did not. In the church of St. Gandolf in Trier, which noted the number of used hosts annually from the years 1492–1511, an average of twelve hundred people, or most of the parish, received communion at Easter, while at Christmas, only between one and

---

[29] Browe, "Pflichtbeichte," pp. 344–345; Duggan, "Fear and Confession," pp. 159–161.

[30] See Browe, *Häufige Kommunion*, pp. 39–42; Reinburg, "Liturgy and Laity," pp. 539–541.

[31] J. B. Götz, *Die religiöse Bewegung in der Oberpfalz von 1520–1560*, Ergänzung und Erläuterung zur Janssens Geschichte des deutschen Volkes, vol. 5, no. 3–4 (1907), p. 6.

[32] Browe, *Häufige Kommunion*, p. 40, citing the testimony of a deacon there.

[33] Ibid.

[34] Ad. Tibus, *Die Jakobipfarre in Münster von 1508–1523* (1885), pp. 23–31, cited in ibid.

[35] Joseph Greving, ed., *Johann Ecks Pfarrbuch für U. L. Frau in Ingolstadt*, Reformationsgeschichtlichen Studien und Texte, vols. 4–5 (1908), pp. 126, 130. Browe, *Häufige Kommunion*, p. 41.

[36] G. Mehring, "Stift Lorch," *Württembergische Geschichtsquellen* 12 (1911): 188, cited in Browe, *Häufige Kommunion*, p. 41.

four hundred communicated. The church did not distribute at any other time.[37] Saint Christoph in Mainz averaged one to two hundred communions at Easter and only thirty to fifty at Christmas.[38] It is on this basis that Peter Browe claims that "frequent communion" in late-medieval Europe meant perhaps two to four receptions per year.[39]

Restraint in receiving communion reflected both ecclesiastical strictures and lay attitudes. The Church did not encourage frequent lay communion and suspected its advocates both of unorthodoxy and of insufficient respect for the sacrament. In late-medieval Europe neither prelates nor popes recommended more than four communions a year.[40] Those preachers advocating dramatic increases often found themselves confronting official suspicion.[41] Beyond official concerns, however, the preconditions for receiving precluded greater access. The stringent preliminary fast discouraged regular reception of communion, limiting it to seasons in which fasting was enforced by custom and by law, particularly Lent and Advent. The ambivalence of ecclesiastics about sexual intercourse before receiving communion also discouraged many people, especially married lay people.[42]

Given the Church's demands, it is hard to imagine how a religious life grounded in frequent recourse to the sacraments could have thrived outside circles approximating monastic devotion except among lay people (usually women, it appears) of singular piety. That may, of course, have been intentional. For churchmen, some of whom actively opposed the idea of frequent communion, even for the clergy, the inherent temptations and impurities of the lay estate were especially vexing.[43]

Lay thinking also contributed to sparse reception. Lay devotion focused on the Eucharist, and masses and processions of the exposed Host routinely occurred. Yet the very awe with which medieval people regarded the Eucharist also fostered their reluctance to receive it. In medieval Eu-

---

[37] Andreas Schüller, "Messe und Kommunion in einer stadttrierischen Pfarrei vor und nach der Reformation," *Trierisches Archiv* 21 (1913): 65, cited in Browe, *Häufige Kommunion*, p. 41.

[38] Falk, *Florentius Diel*, p. 56, cited in Browe, *Häufige Kommunion*, p. 41.

[39] Browe, *Häufige Kommunion*, pp. 28–29.

[40] Ibid, "Pflichtbeichte," p. 344.

[41] Johann Molitoris, a preacher in Augsburg, advocated daily communion, which was considered a serious abuse. Browe, *Häufige Kommunion*, pp. 36–38.

[42] Ibid., pp. 145–148. On sexual abstinence, see Tentler, *Sin and Confession*, pp. 213–220.

[43] Browe, *Häufige Kommunion*, pp. 152–154.

rope, honoring the Eucharist appears to have worked in inverse propor-
tion to the frequency of reception, as though more regular use might de-
base the Host (this relationship was transformed in the late sixteenth and
seventeenth centuries). Since even "spiritual" reception brought great
benefits, the moral risks of unworthy physical reception may have out-
weighed the advantages. Laypeople also confronted a financial obstacle,
as the clergy normally expected some recompense for their sacramental
services.[44]

Attitudes toward the Eucharist affected confession. The intimate relation
between the two suggests that if communion was by design infrequent, little reason existed to confess more often. The evidence indicates that once
lay Christians fulfilled their duty to confess, the Church asked for little
more.[45] Synods and councils seldom called for more frequent confession,
although this became more common in the fifteenth century. Even then,
synods at Nantes (1410), Paris (1429), Uppsala (1438) and Sens (1485) called
for only three to five confessions a year, close to the number of communions that the most pious might make.[46] In other words, the Church itself
had low expectations for lay reception, although it might hope for more.

Some theologians, however, did urge more frequent lay reception. The
very influential Jean Gerson suggested anywhere from quarterly to
monthly confession, depending on the individual's strength and spiritual
condition.[47] In Italy, preachers and pastoral theologians also called for
more regular confession, as in the case of Saint Antoninus of Florence, author of an influential *Summa confessorum*.[48] Saint Bernardino of Siena, in

---

[44] For Peter Browe, the custom of making a monetary offering for receiving the sacraments helped inhibit the reception of both communion and confession. (Ibid., pp.
134–138).

[45] Duggan, "Fear and Confession," pp. 161–162.

[46] Browe, "Pflichtbeichte," pp. 346–347.

[47] Thomas Tentler discusses Jean Gerson's advice on frequency noting, "His is the
greatest voice in the cure of souls." See *Sin and Confession*, pp. 45–46, 75–78. See also D.
Catherine Brown, *Pastor and Laity in the Theology of Jean Gerson* (1987), pp. 57–58.

[48] Antoninus recommended monthly confession. See Browe, *Häufige Kommunion*, p.
41. Spanish and Italian authors appear to have taken up the call for more frequent confession by the end of the fifteenth century. The lay-oriented Oratory of Divine Love, inspired by Catherine of Genoa and preachers such as Bernardino of Siena and founded
in 1497 in Genoa, required monthly confession as an obligatory minimum. See the
"Rule" of the Genoese Oratory in *The Catholic Reformation: Savonarola to Ignatius Loyola*,
ed. John Olin (1992), p. 24.

the first half of the fifteenth century, sought more frequent confession, but his biographer also remarked that most Christians had previously waited until their fortieth or fiftieth year to confess.[49] Savonarola advocated monthly or even bimonthly reception, noting, however, that in practice lay people usually went to confession only annually and monks every month.[50]

If one focuses on German-speaking lands, however, fifteenth- and early-sixteenth-century synods were more limited in their exhortations. The Observant Franciscan Dietrich Kolde in his brief discussion of confession in the *Christenspiegel* recommended that "all good Christian men should confess at least four times in the year."[51] Johann Eck in Ingolstadt sought to induce Christians to confess four times during the year.[52]

In actual church practice, the dates for distributing communion were also the times set aside for hearing confessions. According to the *Liber consuetudinum* outlining the religious tasks of Florentius Diel, pastor of the Church of Saint Christoph in Mainz from 1491–1518, the clergy made provisions for hearing confessions at three points during the year—Christmas, Lent/Easter, and Pentecost—all great feasts during which some communions might occur.[53] Yet few people received communion on these feasts, nor did many engage in sacramental penance. In the entire diocese of Eichstätt in 1480, only one hundred people confessed outside the required Lenten season.[54] In Hilpoltstein in 1511, only sixty persons from a parish of approximately fourteen hundred confessed outside Lent.[55] It seems probable, therefore, that standards similar to those for receiving

[49] Browe, "Pflichtbeichte," p. 347.

[50] Ibid.

[51] "Item alle goede cristen mynschen sullen tzo dem mynsten veirmail bichten des iairs." Clemens Drees, ed. *Der Christenspiegel des Dietrich Kolde von Münster*, Franziskanische Forschungen, vol. 9 (1952): 164. For a High German translation, see Christoph Moufang, ed., *Katholische Katechismen des 16. Jahrhunderts in deutscher Sprache* (1881), p. xxvi.

[52] A. Brandt, *Johann Ecks Predigttätigkeit an U. L. Frau zu Ingolstadt*, Reformationsgeschichtliche Studien und Texte, vols. 27–28 (1914), p. 151; Greving, *Johann Ecks Pfarrbuch*, p. 125; H. Schauerte, *Die Bußlehre des Johannes Eck*, Reformationsgeschichtliche Studien und Texte, vols. 38–39 (1919), p. 130.

[53] Falk, *Florentius Diel*, pp. 6, 10–28, 34.

[54] Götz, *Religiöse Bewegeng in der Oberpfalz*, p. 6.

[55] Götz, *Pfarrbuch des Stephan May*, p. 88. For the number of souls in the parish, see p. 103.

communion also applied to late-medieval confession. The norm for most Christians was once or twice annually, and four receptions per year indicated strong devotion.

We may guess that women constituted the bulk of the people who confessed and communicated more frequently in Germany, although it is difficult to be sure. As noted above, women and students received communion at Christmastime in sixteenth-century Ingolstadt. This was true in Ulm as well, where, although Easter reception was the norm, no Sunday went by without some pregnant, sick, or pious women taking communion.[56] In Biberach, numerous women received at Christmas.[57]

If annual or semiannual confession was the norm, Lent was the natural time. In its posting of the Lateran decree, its instruction in the act of confessing, and its attempts to punish those who did not comply before Easter, the Church emphasized this season almost to the exclusion of all others. In Bamberg, in 1491, the synod commanded that the statute about annual confession be published every Sunday in Lent, so that no one would have an excuse for missing confession out of ignorance of the Church's law or practice.[58] Preaching, too, played an important role. According to a 1446 statute from Würzburg, pastors were to preach sermons on penance from the first Sunday of Lent onward, diligently inducing all who were capable to make confessions at the "appropriate time" ("tempestive confessions") to a competent priest, in order that they "not be seen to approach the Body of Christ at the Paschal feast with stained (*cruentata*) consciences."[59] Here the need for purity at communion was the explicit reason for requiring confession.

Not only was Lent the season for exhorting people to confess, it was also the one time during the year when instructions about how to receive

---

[56] "Tractatus de civitate Ulmensi," *Bibliothek des litterarischen Vereins in Stuttgart* 186 (1889): 189, cited in Browe, *Häufige Kommunion*, p. 41.

[57] Heinz Schilling, *Konfessionskonflikt und Staatsbildung*. Quellen und Forschungen zur Reformationsgeschechte, vol. 48 (1981), p. 113.

[58] Bamberg (1491), CG, vol. 5, p. 629. The Synod of Regensburg (1512) published the decree at the beginning of Lent: CG, vol. 6, p. 112. Others scheduled it on the first and fourth Sunday of Lent (CG, vol. 6, p. 337) or every Lenten Sunday (CG, vol. 5, p. 411).

[59] "plebes vestras in ambonibus Ecclesiarum moneatis, et omni qua poteritis diligentia inducatis, quod tempestive confessiones suas faciant Sacerdotibus competentibus, ne in conscientis cruentata in Festo Pasche ad Corpus Christi improvide accedere videantur." Würzburg (1446), CG, vol. 5, p. 351.

were given, as at Basel in 1503. At the beginning of the season the clergy were to instruct the populace in ways to confess, inducing even children, if they were old enough to be capable of evil deeds, to the "annual confession." The people were exhorted to approach the priest with all humility and devotion, and not knowingly to hide any mortal sin, lest when they left this life they descend to eternal hellfire.[60] Lenten sermons were supposed to concentrate on explaining sins and the Ten Commandments, as in Eichstätt, where the synod enjoined rectors to take up "at least once in the year the matter of the Ten Commandments and follow it with the appropriate corrections of vices," persuading lay people to penance and reminding them of the Church's law on the matter.[61]

Confession was, therefore, not an event indifferent to the calendar, appropriate at any time during the year. The very efforts necessary to induce Lenten penance indicate its relative absence at other times. Sacrament and season were closely intertwined. This relationship is clear not only in legislative acts, but also in literature depicting everyday religious life in early sixteenth-century Germany. The chronicler of pre-Reformation religion in the imperial city of Biberach noted that Lent was the time for men, women, and all who had reached the age of reason to confess.[62] Lent was also a natural time for the first confessions of children. In Cologne, Hermann Weinsberg made the first of his many confessions during Lent.[63] Early Protestant accounts also assumed such a connection. According to Sebastian Franck's *Weltbuch*, which included a satirical account of the practices of "Roman Christians": "The sixth sacrament is penance, of which an entire Chronicle could be written. Every Christian in danger of death or every Easter time must kneel down before the priest and recite all his secrets to the priest."[64] Later, Franck wrote: "Then

---

[60] Basel (1503), *CG*, vol. 6, p. 9.

[61] Eichstätt (1447), *CG*, vol. 5, p. 364.

[62] A. Schilling, ed., "Die religiösen und kirchlichen Zustände der ehemaligan Reichstadt Biberach unmittelbar vor Einführhung der Reformation," *Freibürger Diözesansarchiv* xix (1887): 115.

[63] Konstantin Höhlbaum, *Das Buch Weinsberg*, Kölner Denkwürdigkeiten aus dem 16. Jahrhundert, vol. 1 (1886), p. 40. I thank Marc Forster for first bringing Hermann Weinsberg's account of confession to my attention.

[64] "Das sechst Sacrament ist die Büß/ davon wer eyn gantz Chronick zuschreiben. . . . Do müß eyn yeder Christ in tods nöten oder all österlich zeit vor den pfaffen nider knien/ und all sein geheymnis dem pfaffen ansagen." Sebastian Franck, *Weltbuch*, p. 129.

follows the sad Fast, in which for forty days they eat no meat, nor milk, cheese, eggs, [or] fat. . . . Then the people confess according to rule, each one all sins and mortal sins. The altars and saints are covered with cloths and a "Fast cloth" is hung, so that the sinful people can not see the idols, nor can the holy pictures see the sinners."[65] For Franck, as for the Church he derided and the chronicler who defended it, confession and Lent were closely connected.

Within Lent, custom and disciplinary reasons led the Church to recommend an early shriving.[66] In general, ecclesiastics sought to have Christians confess before *medium quadragesimae* or *Laetare*, the mid-Lent festival providing a respite from the rigors of the season.[67] Those who confessed by this date also received a papal indulgence, the Golden Rose, as in Biberach where the date and the accompanying indulgence were duly noted.[68] In Osterdorf in 1511, in the Diocese of Eichstätt, the feast of the apostle Matthias (February 24) came during early Lent. As a result the pastor designated it as a day for hearing the confessions of "the old, the infirm, and children."[69]

Disciplinary concerns also made confession before *Laetare* desirable. The possibility of fulfilling the obligation outside one's own parish made some pastors reluctant to give communion without first obtaining some evidence of confession. Also, because numerous sins were reserved to episcopal absolution, such issues had to be resolved before Easter communion could take place. Early penance enabled parish priests to sort out

[65] "Als dann folgt die traurig Fast/ darinn essen sie viertzig tag keyn fleysch/ auch nit milch/ käß/ eyer/ schmaltz. . . . Da beichten die leut nach ordnung eyn yeader all sein sünd bei eyner todsünd. Da verhult man die altar und heyligen mit tüch/ und laßt eyn hungertüch herab/ das die sündigen leut die götzen nit ansehen/ noch die heyligen bilder die sünder." Ibid., pp. 131–132.

[66] Joannes Herolt, *Sermones Discipuli in Quadragesima*, (1606), p. 3. Stephan May in Hilpoltstein urged confession before the middle of Lent. Götz, *Pfarrbuch des Stephen May*, p. 160.

[67] Florentius Diel exhorted his parishioners to confess before *Laetare* Sunday, so that they might rejoice in spirit with the Church. Falk, *Florentius Diel*, pp. 41–42.

[68] Schilling, "Die religiösen," p. 117. On the meaning of *Laetare* or "Rose" Sunday, see Josef Jungmann, "Rosensonntag," in *Lexikon für Theologie und Kirche*, ed. Karl Rahner and Josef Hafer (1957–1967); Franck, *Weltbuch*, p. 132 v.

[69] Karl Schornbaum and W. Kraft, "Pappenheim am Ausgang des Mittelalters in kirchlicher Hinsicht auf Grund des Pfarrbuches des Pfarrers Stefan Aigner," *Zeitschrift für bayerische Kirchengeschichte* 7 (1932): 206. In the city of Biberach, *Invocavit*, or *Weis Sontag*, was the day for children's confessions: Schilling, "Die religiösen," p. 117.

those parishioners confessing elsewhere, those with reserved sins, and those requiring public penance in time to send them to the bishop for appropriate action. Priests could also identify those who must be denied Easter communion.

In the time of fasting and penances that followed, Christians prepared for Easter. On Holy Thursday, the entire congregation made a general confession of guilt and received a general absolution which readied it for communion. The public confession of guilt, which developed from the older tradition of episcopal absolution of public sinners on Holy Thursday (*Gründonnerstag*), appeared in preaching collections as a formula to be recited collectively in the vernacular after the homily. This *offene Schuld*, as it was known, was part of another tradition in medieval Christianity, one especially marked in German-speaking lands: the so-called *Glaube und Beichte* formulas, which constitute some of the oldest relics of the German language.[70] French ritual books of the sixteenth century included a general confession appropriate to the Easter reception, but in Germany the confession seems to have been a regular part of the Mass.[71] Officially this Holy Thursday pronouncement would cover only lesser sins, but it also rounded out and completed the entire cycle of Lenten confession and absolution.

By the sixteenth century, however, despite continued emphasis on early shriving, the practice had changed. Ecclesiastics had by then introduced the major late-medieval innovation to increase the frequency of lay confession. This was the *confessio bina*, or double confession, which required Christians hoping to receive Easter communion to confess twice during Lent. In Biberach, for example, all had to confess during the forty days, but the author immediately pointed out, anyone "who would go to the Sacrament [Eucharist] had to confess once again."[72] Sebastian Franck concurred.[73] In other words, fulfilling sacramental duties in late-medieval

---

[70] On this subject, see Josef Jungmann, *Missarum Sollemnia. Eine genetische Erklärung der römischen Messe* (1962), vol. 1, p. 631; Andreas Heinz, "Die deutsche Sondertradition für einen Bussritus der Gemeinde in der Messe," *Liturgisches Jahrbuch* 28 (1978): 198–199.

[71] Heinz, "Sondertradition," p. 207. When actually receiving communion, Christians made another public and vernacular display of penance. See Jungmann, *Missarum Sollemnia*, vol. 2, pp. 461–462. In Biberach this was also the case. Schilling, "Die religiösen," p. 122.

[72] Schilling, "Die religiösen," p. 115.

[73] Franck, *Weltbuch*, p. 132.

Germany came to mean confessing twice during Lent, once at the beginning and once during Holy Week.

Although recent, this demand for *confessio bina* became widespread, as attested by episcopal orders in Samland (Prussia) in 1471 and by synodal statutes in Swiss territories, Augsburg, and Eichstätt.[74] Ecclesiastics explained the practice in various ways. As pastor in Ingolstadt, Johann Eck defended it (wrongly) as an old and honored custom,[75] but he also considered the practice a guarantee against parishioners receiving the Host while burdened by sins omitted from the first confession through human frailty.[76] Some synods made the same case, urging the *confessio bina* especially for those who confessed only rarely.

Although it increased the expected number of confessions, the Lenten *confessio bina* also strengthened the relationships between season and sacrament and between communion and confession. Lay people's reverence for the Eucharist and their hesitancy about receiving it (other than spiritually) lends support to the idea that any reception of the Eucharist would involve prior confession, with the two coming as close together as possible. This in turn heightened the lay commitment to Lenten penance, with all the rites and sermons designed to evoke sorrow for sin as well as the stringent fast and rules that would help Christians receive both sacraments worthily. Maintaining the custom of reconciliation during Holy Week, the *confessio bina* increased the possibility of "pure" reception of communion both by permitting worthy confessions and by bringing penance as close as possible to communion, so the latter would occur before any new sin could intrude.

The issue, however, is more complicated and goes to the heart of the relation between Lent and sacramental confession. Both the older general confession and the *confessio bina* vestigially recapitulated ancient Christian seasonal rituals involving the expulsion of penitents.[77] Confessing on Ash Wednesday or during the early part of Lent may therefore be viewed as a

---

[74] Browe, *Pflichtkommunion*, p. 25. For Eichstätt, see J. B. Götz, "Die kirchliche Festfeier in der Eichstätter Diözese," *Zeitschrift für bayerische Kirchengeschichte* 9 (1934): 138. See also V. Hoeynck, *Geschichte der kirchlichen Liturgie des bisthums Augsburg* (1889), p. 144.

[75] Schauerte, *Bußlehre*, p. 183. On its relative newness, see Browe, "Pflichtbeichte," pp. 25–26.

[76] Johann Eck, sermon for Passion Sunday (18 March 1526), cited in Brandt, *Johann Ecks Predigttätigkeit*, p. 208. Florentius Diel agreed. Falk, *Florentius Diel*, p. 45.

[77] Gy, "Histoire liturgique," p. 18.

symbolic entrance into the order of penitents, and receiving a general absolution on Holy Thursday allowed for public or communal reconciliation
with the Church and perhaps even within the community. It was no coin-
cidence that Church law and custom designated Holy Thursday as the
time for reconciling public sinners.[78]

This connection may best be understood through a passage found in the
diary of Florentius Diel, pastor in Mainz. After describing the *confessio bina*
in detail, Diel explained, "the first and this second confession are to be
counted as one complete confession of all one's sins."[79] Bracketing Lent
with confession on both ends in effect transformed the entire season into
an extended reception of individual sacramental confession, in which
public congregational acts could induce and reinforce the three sacramental acts of contrition, confession, and absolution. Ideally one confessed,
spent the season reflecting upon and deepening the meaning of that confession, perhaps recalling omitted sins, and then repeated the sacrament,
presumably with greater self-understanding and a more intense detestation of vice. Lenten rites such as sermons and devotions provided a kind
of public and general examination of conscience for a population not
over-supplied with devotional handbooks, penitential manuals, or the
ability to read them. Equally important, the penitent's private reflections
operated within a larger framework of public liturgical acts, such as
preaching, so that individual reflection and self-examination invariably
involved the presence of other people similarly engaged.

Palm Sunday, which celebrated Jesus' triumphal entry into Jerusalem
during the week before his crucifixion, began the most momentous week of
liturgical celebration during the year, a week to which all the events of Lent
pointed. Despite all the exhortations to confess earlier in Lent, this second
confession was clearly the event for which most Christians prepared, and it
appears that many, if not most, tried to skip the earlier shriving.[80] Synods

---

[78] Indeed, the German term for Holy Thursday, *Gründonnerstag*, stemmed from the association of the color green with sinlessness and forgiveness. Ludwig Eisenhofer, *Handbuch der katholischen Liturgie*, 2 vols. (1932), vol. I, p. 513.

[79] "priorem et hanc secundam confessionem pro una plenaria confessione computari
omnium suorum peccatorum": Falk, *Florentius Diel*, p. 45.

[80] H. Schauerte, "Osterbeichte im Mittelalter," *Theologie und Glaube* 12 (1920): 16, citing
H. Klee, *Die Beichte* (1828), p. 278. See also Veit, *Volksfrommes Brauchtum*, p. 88, and
Browe, *Pflichtkommunion*, pp. 25–26.

complained about congregations waiting until the end of Lent, then crowding in all at once, which kept the confessor from careful fulfillment of his duty.[81] Indeed, this procrastination, probably already widespread, may explain the rise of the *confessio bina*, as the Church adjusted to the practices of its members by continuing to encourage early shriving while requiring the one confession Christians actually received.

To prepare for the onslaught of penitents, the clergy made special arrangements. In Biberach, pastors increasd the number of confessors for Holy Week.[82] Elsewhere, priests instructed that confessions take place the day before communion and that penitents at least not wait until the very last minute or until the day of communion.[83] Thus, according to Diel, in Mainz those seeking to receive communion at the Easter vigil were to confess on Good Friday in the afternoon. On Holy Saturday, in anticipation of Easter itself, confessors were to be present from five until seven in the morning and again after one o'clock in the afternoon.[84] Diel continued to be adamant about not waiting until the day of communion, or very late the night before, to confess.

Palm Sunday was generally the first day that one could receive Easter communion.[85] On the principle that confession should occur as close as possible to the time of communion, either that day or the day before would be the logical time to confess. Evidence from Mainz and from Biberach proves that this was indeed the case.[86] Still, Palm Sunday was early for fulfilling Easter duties. The latter part of Holy Week was better, and it appears therefore that Holy Thursday, Good Friday, and Easter Sunday itself were the most popular days.[87] Correspondingly, confessions would

---

[81] Thus, in a synod in Brixen (1449), in G. Bickell, *Synodi Brixinenses saeculi XV* (1880), p. 24. For the text, see Chapter 3. I am grateful to Lawrence Duggan for providing Bickell's documents. In Schwerin in 1521, the parish was to be warned not to put off their confessions until Holy Week, and especially until one or two days before Easter. A. Schönfelder, *Liturgische Bibliothek* (1904–1906), vol. 2, p. 9.

[82] Schilling, "Die religiösen," p. 118.

[83] Falk, *Florentius Diel*, pp. 52–53, 55; Schilling, "Die religiösen," p. 121.

[84] Falk, *Florentius Diel*, p. 54.

[85] The late-medieval standard in Germany seems to have been Holy Week. For changes, see Eisenhofer, *Handbuch*, vol. 1, p. 531; Josef Staber, "Die Teilnahme des Volkes an der Karwochenliturgie im Bistum Freising während des 15. und 16. Jahrhunderts," *Jahrbuch für altbayerischen Kirchengeschichte* (1964): 78; Schilling, "Die religiösen," p. 127; Falk, *Florentius Diel*, pp. 53–54.

[86] Falk, *Florentius Diel*, p. 48; Schilling, "Die religiösen," p. 118.

[87] Schilling, "Die religiösen," p. 120.

take place between Wednesday of Holy Week and Holy Saturday. This is borne out by the evidence available. At Saint Christoph in Mainz communicants on Holy Thursday numbered 150–160. On Good Friday there were perhaps 10 or 12, and on Easter Sunday more than 100, but only in some years as many as 150 or 160.[88] Surprisingly, Good Friday was an acceptable time to receive Easter communion. If one considers the traditional connection between absolution and Holy Thursday, however, those who confessed on that day would naturally consider Good Friday. While authorities were less inclined to allow this by the sixteenth century, the practice remained in effect.

Because people actually confessed not throughout Lent but only on a few days during Holy Week, the event was likely to have an audience. Neighbors, friends, acquaintances, and even enemies were in attendance. Confession was thus not isolated from the larger concerns of local life. The congregation, present at the sacrament, was in a position to exert its influence, silently or aloud. When confessing, the sinner had to consider his or her relations not only with the priest and the Church but also with the community.

The community, however, might be quite narrowly defined. Although a crowd gathered to receive penance, it was not always a miscellany of those found within a particular parish or church. The pastor of Saint Christoph in Mainz noted that those expected to receive communion on Palm Sunday included the young, the sick, and pregnant women. This custom of having children communicate on Palm Sunday was quite widespread. In the Eichstätt diocese, "the young of both sexes" received the Eucharist at that time,[89] and in Biberach they were confessed on the eve of Palm Sunday to communicate the next day. As described by the anonymous chronicler, "Afterwards [after Matins] a signal was made by sounding the great bell and then the young people were given the Holy Sacrament. Perhaps on the Feast of the Annunciation but mostly on the eve of Palm Sunday all confessed."[90] The tendency for people of like condition to receive communion at the same time was true in numerous places. In Osterdorf, a village near Pappenheim in the diocese of Eichstätt, the unmarried received communion on

[88] Falk, *Florentius Diel*, pp. 52, 55–56.
[89] Schornbaum and Kraft, "Pappenheim," p. 206.
[90] Schilling, "Die religiösen," p. 118.

Palm Sunday.[91] In Pappenheim as well as in Ingolstadt, students communicated on Good Friday.[92] As noted, the Easter duty followed soon after the confession. Thus, for example, unmarried people about to receive on Palm Sunday would confess during the vigil, and students would do so on the day before Good Friday. Children who were not old enough to receive communion would also confess early, so as not to interfere with others.[93] They also confessed together, according to whatever instructions the priest and their parents provided.[94] Separation of the sexes during communion (as in Biberach, where women and men went to different chapels to receive communion) may have happened during penance as well. Confraternity members may also have confessed together, and to the same priest, especially if the confessor belonged to a religious order.

All of this made it easier for the confessor to question people according to age, condition, or gender. A well-equipped confessor could refer to a manual or tablet appropriate to those before him, which helps to explain the usefulness of a text such as the "Beichtspiegel" for first confessions in Johannes Wolff's *Beichtbüchlein* of 1478.[95] Intended as a tool for pastors rather than for lay people, the "Beichtspiegel" includes a sample confession with numerous possible sins.[96] It enabled the pastor to guide children or others through the process, perhaps as preparation for the actual reception. The pastor's guide for first confessions may also have helped parents, who were closely involved in the process. In Biberach during Lent, parents prepared their children for confession by discussing in advance what to tell the confessor: "Father and mother led young children there, they being yet small; at home beforehand they taught them to say something, no matter how little, so that they learned to confess and became accustomed [to it]."[97]

---

[91] Götz, "Kirchliche Festfeier," p. 142.

[92] Ibid.

[93] In Osterdorff children confessed earlier in Lent, as noted above, perhaps in order not to interfere with adult receptions later, a reason noted later by the Jesuit Nicolaus Cusanus in a frequently reprinted book that first appeared in 1626, the *Christliche Zucht-Schul/ allen Seelsorgern/ und gemeinem Mann sehr nützlich*, (1675), p. 266. See Chapter 3.

[94] Browe, "Beichtunterricht," pp. 427–442.

[95] Franz Falk, ed., *Drei Beichtbüchlein nach den zehn Geboten aus der Frühzeit der Buchdruckerkunst* (1907), pp. 17–23.

[96] Ibid., p. 14.

[97] "Die Jung Khindt haben Vatter und Muotter ahnhin gefürth, so sie noch Clein seindt gewesen, habens vor dahaimb edtwas gelehrt sagen, wie wenig es ist gesein, damit sie Lehrnent beichten und in brauch Khommen." Schilling, "Die religiösen," p. 115.

The children then confessed on a specific day. Discussing what to say helped prevent anxiety and shame for children. It may also have protected the parents from any unexpected (and unwanted) revelations to the priest.

In another variation on the practice of children confessing together, Hermann Weinsberg of Cologne described his first confession, made during Lent in 1525, when he was seven years old. Hermann's schoolmaster taught his pupils how to confess, "and then all the pupils had to kneel before the priest, one after another, and make their prayer and confess their sins, their penitence, receive their penances, and be absolved according to the Christian customs of the holy church."[98] Such a setting permitted the schoolmaster to employ a text such as Wolff's to prepare his wards for an experience they would undergo together. Yet another possible variation on this confession of children, albeit one later condemned, was admitting groups of childen together to confession, questioning them, and then absolving them in common.[99] These first confessions achieved their purpose of getting children used to confession. Weinsberg himself stated that he "would rather have gone through fire" than confess, but as "year after year I became used to it, it gave me no more trouble, and I thought to myself that it was a praiseworthy thing."[100]

### The Place of Penance

Group experiences such as Weinsberg's seem to have been limited to children; however, even adults confessed in public. Church synods, mindful of the possibilities for scandal inherent in a "private" setting, attempted to define and to specify the place of confession as narrowly as possible. After 1100, the church building became the only acceptable place to hold confessions under normal circumstances,[101] and within the church, confession was to occur in public view. Synodal legislation often repeated these

[98] Höhlbaum, *Das Buch Weinsberg*, vol. 1, p. 40. Steven Ozment has briefly discussed Weinsberg's attitude toward penance [*Protestants: The Birth of a Revolution* (1992), p. 185].

[99] Later, in the seventeenth century, the Jesuit Cusanus condemned the custom of parents coaching their children's confessions.

[100] "Und mich gedenkt, das ich gar noede zu bichten plach; ich wlt lieber dur ein fur sin gangen, dan gebicht haben. Aber wie ich jar vur jar damit in einen brauch quam, do gaff es mir nit zu schicken, und bedunkt mich, das es ein loblich dink ist." Hohlbaum, *Das Buch Weinsberg*, p. 40. See also Ozment, *Protestants*, p. 185.

[101] Cammin (1500), CG, vol. 5, p. 673. Generally the rubric was an *oratorium publicum* or *semipublicum*.

strictures against private venues, especially for women penitents, and forbade clergy from giving sacraments to women in their homes.[102] The same thinking and language appeared throughout the fifteenth and sixteenth centuries, usually but not exclusively applied to women's confessions. In Basel in 1503, confessors were instructed to hear confessions "in public places and with averted faces."[103] Beyond this, the Church did not specify, and a "public place within the church" could refer to many things. The critical feature, however, was visibility by the rest of the congregation.

Confession occurred in an *ad hoc* setting, and late-medieval evidence provides little support for the use of any contraption resembling the modern confessional booth. Unlike the Eucharistic altar and tabernacle or the baptismal font, no structure existed to remind Christians of the necessity or even availability of confession outside Lent. The first "modern" confessionals appeared in Germany only after 1600.[104] Still, although the confessional did not appear until the late sixteenth century, some interesting customs had already developed. The use of a chair or *Beichtstuhl* for the confessor had evolved by the fifteenth century. The earliest examples included neither a booth nor a visual obstacle between the participants, a fact confirmed by examining contemporary illustrations as well as the oldest extant apparatus in German-speaking lands specifically designed for hearing confessions, at Saint Lorenzen ob Murau in Styria, dated 1607.[105] This one-piece contraption consists of a chair for the confessor and a prie-dieu attached at his right side, with a rail upon which the confessor might lean his arm. The side of the chair to which the prie-dieu is affixed also separated confessor and penitent, but this partition does not extend above the chair's arm, so the two would continue to be entirely visible to one another. This portable

---

[102] Eichstätt (1465), *CG*, vol. 5, p. 473; Bamberg (1491), *CG*, vol. 5, p. 630, and Regensburg (1512), *CG*, vol. 6, p. 108.

[103] Basel (1503), *CG*, vol. 6, p. 9.

[104] For a brief history of the confessional itself, see Wilhelm Schlombs, *Die Entwicklung des Beichtstuhls in der katholischen Kirche: Grundlagen und Besonderheiten im alten Erzbistum Köln*, Studien zur Kölner Kirchengeschichte, vol. 8 (1965); Edmund W. Braun-Troppau and Otto Schmitt, "Beichtstuhl," in *Reallexikon zur deutschen Kunstgeschichte*, ed. Otto Schmitt (1948), vol. 2, p. 185. Though flawed by inaccuracy in its citations, Schlombs's account is correct in its general narrative.

[105] A photograph of this chair appears in Braun-Troppau and Schmitt, "Beichtstuhl," p. 185.

*Beichtstuhl* had little to do with Borromean confessionals designed for specific niches in the church.[106]

Synods and ritual handbooks of the Middle Ages discussed reception either in front of the altar (preferable due to its visibility) or behind it.[107] If a chair was used by the confessor, it was usually placed near the altar in the sanctuary of the church. In Biberach, the sacrament took place either in the chapel of Saint Catherine or in the chapel behind the pastor's altar. Sometimes two priests simultaneously heard confession in the Saint Catherine chapel, one behind the altar and the other near the door.[108] Such customs—confessing in a chapel or behind the altar—came under attack from sixteenth-century synods.[109]

In cloistered religious communities, niches in the church or, more particularly, small rooms with latticed windows cut into the church wall provided a means of separating men and women. Most common in Mediterranean lands, these were also occasionally present in Switzerland and Germany.[110] In Nürnberg, the convent over which Caritas Pirckheimer presided also had such *Beichthäuser*, which figured in her defense of Catholicism there during the Reformation.[111] These were not pervasive, however, and appear to have been limited to convents and cloisters. For most lay people, confession meant a face-to-face encounter with a priest sitting in a chair, either in the open church, in a side chapel, or perhaps behind the high altar.

Within most churches no apparatus other than a chair for the confessor was available. If the building was a cold and physically uncomfortable place to spend long hours hearing confessions, the pastor might fabricate devices in order to comply with ecclesiastical regulations. In the Chiemsee (Bavaria) diocese in 1558, for example, the pastor claimed to hear confessions in the church and in a small room, perhaps a lean-to, next to his house.[112]

[106] Ibid., pp. 185–186; Schlombs, pp. 24–27.

[107] Eisenhofer, *Handbuch*, vol. 2, p. 381.

[108] Schilling, "Die religiösen," p. 116.

[109] "Constitutions and Decrees for the Clergy of Regensburg, 1589," *CG*, vol. 7, p. 1065.

[110] Schlombs, pp. 28–36. R. W. Scribner, describing a peasants' revolt in Heggbach, near Biberach, in 1525, recounts an attack on a *"Bichthus"* to discover whether a priest was inside (*Popular Culture and Popular Movements*, pp. 103–104).

[111] Caritas Pirckheimer, *Denkwürdigkeiten*, in *Aus dem Zeitalter des Humanismus und der Reformation*, vol. 4 of *Deutsche Selbstzeugnisse*, ed. Marianne Beyer-Fröhlich (1931), p. 115.

[112] "Er hore . . . in ainem stüblin neben deß pharrhofs peicht." Reiner Braun, *Die bayerischen Teile des Erzbistums Salzburg und des Bistums Chiemsee in der Visitation des Jahres 1558*, Studien zur Theologie und Geschichte, vol. 6 (1991), fol. 226 r., p. 318 (hereafter *Chiemsee*).

# Late-Medieval and Reformation Confession

Like the setting, the physical positions adopted during confession varied. When the priest sat in a chair, a male penitent knelt in front of him, while a woman knelt at his side, so that her face could not be seen. Some sources advised the priest to pull his cowl over his face in order to reduce visibility and therefore the possibility of shame. Others instructed the penitent to sit at the confessor's feet while recounting sins. Illustrations from the period show the sacrament occurring in front of the altar, with the

Late-medieval confession. Rogier van der Weyden, *The Seven Sacraments*, 1445. Koninklijk Museum voor Schone Kunsten Antwerpen. In this stylized painting, part of an altar triptych, no physical barrier separates the confessor in his chair from the kneeling penitent. Here the imposition of hands will signal absolution as another penitent waits nearby.

Late-medieval confession. *Beicht spigel mit vil lere unnd beispilen tzu seligkeyt der selen getzogen auß dem heiligen schrift* (Nürnberg, 1495). Bayerische Staatsbibliothek, Handschriftenabteilung. This woodcut from a late-medieval German confessional manual shows a prie-dieu for the penitent attached to a chair for the confessor, very similar to a device still used at Saint Lorenz ob Murau, dated 1607. In the face-to-face encounter depicted, the confessor cups a hand to his ear, while angels and devils contend for the sinner's soul and bystanders observe the scene.

priest sitting in a chair and the penitent kneeling at his side.[113] These positions enabled the priest to perform the major ritual gesture of absolution, the laying-on of hands, although in the fifteenth and sixteenth centuries this became a controversial issue, demanded by some but discouraged by

---

[113] Schlombs, *Die Entwicklung des Beichtstuhls*; Tentler, *Sin and Confession*, pp. 82–84.

others (notably Saint Antoninus of Florence) as potentially indecent.[114] Even if the imposition of hands did not take place, another visible gesture—the absolution and blessing in the form of the sign of the cross—remained to seal the event.

### Privacy in Confession

The evidence presented thus far about time and place demonstrates that confession in the late-medieval world was not a private affair. The Church sought to guarantee the secrecy of confession itself, which officially involved only penitent and priest. In this sense late-medieval confession was certainly a "private" event.[115] Sacramental penance as a whole, however, was deliberately public. Even the confessions of the sick or dying were to occur with the door to the room open, to be visible to those gathered at the sickbed. Routinely, when Christians made their confessions, other members of the congregation watched, and perhaps hoped to overhear. The penitent had little chance of anonymity. The congregation could also witness refusals to confess, arguments between penitent and priest, denials of absolution, or even excessively lengthy confessions. As a result, distinctions between "private" and "public" penance do not adequately describe the late-medieval situation, which was, curiously, both.

The public visibility of Lenten confession enabled the congregation to affect the process, perhaps even the sins confessed. Conversely, it permitted the absolved penitent to demonstrate to friend and foe alike that the Church had welcomed the sinner back into its fold, a potential advantage to a person seeking to maintain or reestablish his or her honor in a community.[116] Congregational pressure could also be applied to the confessor, who, in addition to representing ecclesiastical justice, also often belonged to the community. A parish confessor, balanced between the demands of Church and congregation, was in a precarious but potentially quite powerful position. He could therefore affect the community in numerous

---

[114] Tentler, *Sin and Confession*, pp. 86–87. This disappeared in the seventeenth century.

[115] Lawrence Duggan emphasizes the prevalence of private confession in late-medieval Europe. See "Fear and Confession," pp. 162–163. Set in the open church, however, and watched by other members of the congregation, most confessions could not be private affairs.

[116] See the illuminating Italian example provided in Guido Ruggiero, *Binding Passions: Tales of Magic, Marriage, and Power at the End of the Renaissance* (1993), pp. 141–147.

ways. For example, requiring public penance had social as well as religious ramifications. It involved public humiliation, especially if the priest mistakenly demanded such punishment for secret acts. If a priest were himself in a dispute or other relationship with one of the confitents, or if scandal and shame accrued to the penitent or to an associate in sin as a result of confession, the balance of relations within the community could be significantly altered.[117]

Public pressure also worked in another way. In parishes there were often people who, whether by their own choice or the Church's, did not take Easter communion, in sharp, visible contrast to those who did.[118] Preventing unworthy reception was a major concern of the Church, demonstrated by the parish book of Florentius Diel in Mainz. On *Judica* Sunday he sketched the conditions under which parishioners must confess to qualify for Easter communion. He also listed the hindrances to receiving it and on Palm Sunday addressed the question of disqualification. Some were prohibited with cause but without blame: these included young children, those without use of reason, or those too sick to be able to swallow the communion host.[119] Others were excluded with cause and blame associated. Defective confessions, especially those not detailing all their sins, figured prominently here, as did those who had confessed to another priest without permission and those who had not performed appropriate penance.[120] A final category excluded people who had committed a sin the absolution of which was "reserved" either to the bishop or to the Pope and must therefore be resolved in episcopal or papal courts.[121] Whatever the nature of the hindrance, persons not receiving Easter communion

---

[117] This is not speculation. Following Gerson, Geiler von Kaysersberg admonished penitents not to confess the sins of others or to bring shame to other people in confession. This question was not theological, but a practical issue of one's own standing in the community.

[118] In the diocese of Brixen, for example, mid-fifteenth-century synods under Cardinal Nicholas of Cusa listed the excluded, among them public adulterers, people refusing to give up concubines, usurers, soothsayers, enchanters, those who cast spells against storms, and people who had eaten eggs during Lent. "Synodus Brixinensis Nicolai Cusani Cardinalis a. 1453," in Bickell, *Synodi Brixinenses*, p. 36.

[119] Falk, *Florentius Diel*, p. 49.

[120] Ibid., p. 21.

[121] Tentler, *Sin and Confession*, pp. 304–318, is a good brief discussion of the topic. At the parish level, reserved sins prevented people from receiving communion on time, and early confession permitted the judicial machinery to function in a timely fashion.

would be quite visible in the parish, and the reasons for exclusion were laid out, if only generally. To this should be added the fact that, especially in smaller churches, acts and offenses among the parishioners, or between them and their pastor, would also be well known.

Also conspicuously excluded was another group of people—those who were undergoing special forms of public penance. This tradition was gradually falling into disuse, but *Rituale* and *Agendae* other than the *Pontificale Romanum* continued to include it. In Bavarian territories the rite endured until the sixteenth century. A Freising synod of 1475 applied it to: "all notorious criminals, whose excesses scandalize the entire parish and who have performed other public penances; some, however, like dogs have returned to their vomit, and to their prior sins: if they are not noble persons, or women, they are to be sent to perform solemn public penance, which is vulgarly called *carena*."[122] *Carena* was for use in extreme and highly visible cases according to the maxim of public penance for public sins. Only in a few books was the ritual actually detailed in the fifteenth century, as it was now in decline, but the Regensburg *Ordo* and the Passau *Agenda* of 1490 describe it.[123]

In the most ancient practice, penitents were expelled on Ash Wednesday and reconciled on Holy Thursday, but in the fifteenth century, *carena* began on Monday or Tuesday of Holy Week. Early in the morning the penitents came barefoot to the church and prostrated themselves in the form of a cross. The priest intoned Psalm 50 (51), the *Miserere*, over them at the same time striking them on the back with a cane. Their hair was then shorn, an admonition preached, and penance laid upon them. The penitents waited at the church door until a procession had completed, and once again the *Miserere* was recited. The surviving ritual does not indicate whether this had to be done at the cathedral or in an individual parish, nor does it say whether the bishop, the pastor, or another priest performed the absolution.[124] It must also be stressed that the rite disappeared from official books in the sixteenth century, perhaps to reserve public penance to a higher authority, or even to prevent its local misuse.

[122] Freising (1475), *CG*, vol. 5, p. 504. On this subject, see Bernhard Mattes, *Die Spendung der Sakramente nach den Freisinger Ritualien*, Münchener theologische Studien, vol. 34 (1967), p. 193.

[123] Mattes, *Spendung der Sakramente*, pp. 194–195.

[124] Ibid., p. 195.

The public setting of confession, and the institution of public penance both made secrecy difficult.[125] Secrecy was further compromised by leaks in the seal binding priests from revealing, explicitly or implicitly, the contents of any confession. The necessity of such a rule was obvious: How could anyone be coaxed into detailing the secret acts of the heart without a guarantee that knowledge of those deeds would remain strictly limited to the Christian, God, and God's representative? Yet this seal proved not to be inviolable. According to Erasmus of Rotterdam:

> No one, however, even though isolated from public life, will dare to rebuke one of these monks, because through the confessional these men acquire the secrets of everyone. To be sure, they believe it a crime to publish these secrets, but they may accidentally divulge them when drinking heavily or when wishing to promote amusement by relating funny stories. The names, of course, are not revealed, because the stories are told by means of implications in most cases. In other words, if anyone offends the monks, the monks in turn will take revenge against the offender. They will reveal their enemies in public sermons by direct implications, so that everyone will know of whom they speak. And they will continue this malicious chatter until bribed to stop.[126]

A breach could occur through clerical drunkenness and lasciviousness. More seriously, trafficking in secrets could also be a deliberate act by power-hungry clergymen, who could thereby acquire leverage over the laity through blackmail or extortion.

Erasmus's complaint about priests was not merely the invention of a master satirist. Before the Reformation the Freising diocese saw the need to remonstrate with its clergy over maintaining the seal of confession. The synodal statutes of 1475 warned priests not to reveal secret crimes in letters or violate the seal of confession in any other way.[127] Later, in 1509, the bishop of Freising criticized his priests for negligently permitting the secrets of confession to be revealed: "many have been incautious about the seal of confession in private among priests and even in public among the laity."[128]

---

[125] See Chapter 3.

[126] Desiderius Erasmus, "The Praise of Folly," in *The Essential Erasmus*, ed. John P. Dolan (1964), p. 150.

[127] Freising (1475), *CG*, vol. 5, p. 504.

[128] "Item multi incauti sunt circa sigillum confessionis tam in privato inter sacerdotes quam etiam in publico inter laicos etc." In "Denkschrift zur Vorbereitung der Freisinger Diözesansynode von Quasimodogeniti [1509]," in Georg Pfeilschifter, ed., *Acta Reformationis Catholicae Ecclesiam Germaniae concernentia saeculi XVI*, 6 vols. (1959), vol. 1, p. 40, ll. 5–6. The document does not specify the reason for this lapse.

# Late-Medieval and Reformation Confession

Breaking the seal of confession, even by accident, had serious personal or social ramifications. Possessing such secrets as might be revealed in confession meant that priests held the power to humiliate and shame their flocks. Only the integrity of the confessor and the discipline of the Church kept such information from being misused. The possible breakdown of secrecy was one reason (among others, of course) that Caritas Pirckheimer in Nürnberg rejected the new Protestant confessors sent to her convent in Lent, 1525. Of the "apostate" confessor, she claimed, "today or tomorrow this monk will take a wife, and that would be a fine thing, that we will support priests and priests' wives and priests' children; then what would one say to someone who worries that what she confesses by day, he says to his wife at night."[129] Pirckheimer's account also reveals why some people preferred to confess to priests in other communities and why many Catholics were reluctant to make complete confessions (noted later in the century).

Because confession, as practiced in the early sixteenth century, was neither frequent nor private, most Christians were precluded from using it for regular counseling and moral correction. Although certainly available for some, "pastoral care" was not the central function of sacramental penance. Worthy reception of communion was the central reason to confess, except in times of illness or death. And because most confessions took place during Holy Week, under serious time constraints, before an overburdened and often unprepared clergy,[130] the confessions themselves had to be short, focused more on absolution than on advice. Indeed, penitents may actually have counted on this pressure to avoid detailed confessions.

Infrequent confession did not, however, indicate religious decline or indifference. The Church might wish for more frequent confession and communion, but in the main it expected only Lenten reception from its subjects. Although it is very clear that the laity showed little enthusiasm

---

[129] Pirckheimer, *Denkwürdigkeiten*, p. 122.

[130] According to Lawrence Duggan, the quality of clerical preparation and education precluded the rigorous use of confession to inculcate anxiety in lay Christians. See "Fear and Confession," p. 157. At the same time, undisciplined and inept confessors could be even more dangerous than their learned counterparts, terrifying gullible penitents without providing commensurate consolation.

for more frequent confession, they did what was expected of them. Within the constraints of its own goals, the system worked.

Nonetheless, the evidence indicates that spiritual anxiety, caused by the penitential system, was not a widespread phenomenon in pre-Reformation Latin Christendom. As Lawrence Duggan has demonstrated, the sacrament was too intermittent, the clergy too unprepared, and the loopholes permitting choice of confessor too great for any widespread spiritual anxiety to occur, although some individuals might develop a "terrorized" conscience of the sort that Luther later excoriated.[131] Confession was too easy, not too hard. Of course, the very infrequency of confession might have made the annual process a daunting affair, filled with concern over having forgotten some failing, which prompted Johannes Eck, among others, to recommend more regular reception in order to facilitate memory. In response, one might argue that, since it was during the fifteenth century that increased exhortations to more frequent reception began, the Protestant Reformers were reacting to recent innovations or demands for them. Overall, however, the practices of confession demonstrate further the relative ease of forgiveness.

But if spiritual anxiety was minimal, other concerns may have proved more burdensome. The lack of privacy and the possibility of exclusion from communion also meant that priest and penitent had to be careful about their questions and revelations. In addition to God and the Church, the confessant had to take into account the congregation viewing the process. Pressure to confess some sins may have been counterbalanced by wariness about the process's potential for scandal or dishonor, especially with a confessor asking probing questions. The potential for spiritual abuse, so important in recent historical accounts, may have been less important than the possible social abuse caused by indiscreet confessors, curious neighbors, and the absence of safeguards in the public process of "secret" auricular confession. Also, the fact that people of like station at times confessed or received communion together added to the possibility of acute embarrassment if an individual were excluded from Easter reception. The Swiss Thomas Platter, who became a Zwinglian in the 1520s, recounted in his autobiography that the denial of absolution by a callous

---

[131] Ibid., pp. 172–173. Euan Cameron agrees: see *European Reformation*, pp. 305–308.

priest caused him to cry inwardly because it prevented him from receiving communion with his fellow students. Fortunately, the laxness of the system, in the form of absolution by a more sympathetic priest, rescued him from shame.[132] For Platter, shame was a central issue. This may help explain the desire of many lay people to avoid confessing to their parish priests.

The sacrament's public character within the Lenten process, however, strengthened its role as a means of purifying individuals who were to receive communion. The imposition of hands signified reconciliation (the decline of the gesture foreshadowed the decline of this deliberately public element of the sacrament) and public, formal recognition of individual forgiveness. When the congregation received the sacrament at the same time and in the same place, some communal reconciliation was also possible. It may be too much to refer to this process as "an annual settling of social accounts,"[133] as Bossy does, but it does indicate that some form of social peace was necessary in order for Christians to receive the Easter sacrament worthily. In this way, penance continued to fulfill its ancient purpose of cleansing the community for Easter. Confession, then, was indispensable to the seasonal ritual life that characterized medieval Christianity, and even to the sense of Spring renewal—a fact evident as much in the festivities of *Laetare* Sunday as in the Easter duty itself.

This highly seasonal and ritualistic character of confession reaches beyond that which a modern historian of popular religion might dub "ritual purification" to an older image. Peter Browe saw medieval Lenten penance as a type of popular mission:

> Together with communion, which, where possible, all were supposed to receive together at the Easter celebration, it [Easter confession] worked almost like a mission, which seized the entire congregation and tore it out of its everyday life. Hate and enmity were given up, harmony and peace in families were reestablished, sinful habits set aside. Thus was the Easter sacramental reception

---

[132] "Thomas Platter (1536–1614)," in Horst Wenzel, ed., *Die Autobiographie des späten Mittelalters und der frühen Neuzeit* (1980), vol. 2, *Die Selbstdeutung des Stadtbürgertums*, p. 159. Platter's life is discussed in Ozment, *Protestants*, pp. 172–181. Paradoxically, although Platter's plight might bear out Ozment's views about religious burdens, they just as easily demonstrate Lawrence Duggan's point that the availability of lax confessors sapped whatever rigor stricter priests might try to uphold ("Fear and Confession," pp. 163–166).

[133] Bossy, "Social History of Confession," p. 25.

the backbone of medieval pastoral care, the starting point for the yearly renewal of the congregation.[134]

Although this may be too sentimental a description of a religious world that was anything but romantic, it expresses well the nature of medieval sacramental confession as an event integrated into a specific seasonal experience. The pressure to confess in Lent was great, and the season could be a highly rigorous period of fast and abstinence. Christians were constantly confronted with specific transgressions and the means to alleviate them. Public Lenten rituals allowed lay people to appropriate the beliefs and customs of the Church as part of their own preparation. The formal practices of Lent provided a mirror in which individuals, in common with family, friends, and foes, could examine themselves and their lives according to the norms of the Church even if they did not wish to engage in rigorous self-examination.

Finally, whatever spiritual or social worries Lenten confession involved, the season and the sacrament, like the mission, were limited, with a clearly defined beginning and end. Confession played an important role, but it was not a continuous source of guilt, fear, worry, or joy. The church building contained no reminder of the opportunity or obligation to confess, since there was no fixed, permanent place to do so. Instead, once the seasonal duty was fulfilled, the absolved Christian could lay it aside for another year, unless grave sin or death intervened. For the remission of "daily" sins, other resources existed, far more available, far easier for the laity to obtain, and relatively independent of the need for contact with the clergy on an individual basis. In German lands, the *offene Schuld* most closely associated with Holy Thursday was in fact repeated in the vernacular on Sundays throughout the year,[135] providing a general and easily understandable absolution for venial sins (although the distinction between venial and mortal may not have been evident to everyone).

The absolved sinner could also tap indulgences, the treasury of merits that would prove so vexing after 1517. Technically, an indulgence required that a person be in a state of grace, and it is not clear whether a new con-

---

[134] Browe, "Pflichtbeichte," p. 344.
[135] Browe, *Pflichtkommunion*, p. 24. See Jungmann, *Missarum Sollemnia*, vol. 1, pp. 631–633; vol. 2, pp. 460–462.

fession was necessary for each new indulgence.[136] Thus, a person who had fulfilled the Easter duty was perhaps able to tap this grace throughout the year. Lent and Easter were good times to pile up indulgences, a fact known to those offering them. The famous indulgence of Munich in 1480 was offered for three consecutive years during Lent, specifically in the week between *Laetare* and *Judica* Sundays. The 65,000 confessions heard during the first week required some 270 priests.[137] In such a crowded atmosphere, many of the conditions affecting Holy Week confessions must have been present as well.

Confession, whether received once or three times a year, was at the center of the machinery of forgiveness, providing the means (the "gravitational pull," one might say) for the effectiveness of many other practices which revolved around it. For most Christians most of the time, these practices were more prominent, although their efficacy resulted from the performance of the central act. Despite its significance, therefore, confession was not a pervasive element in lay religious life. Although this proved acceptable to many lay Christians, to sixteenth-century reformers, both Protestant and Catholic, it was a system that upon inspection required grave changes.

[136] Nikolaus Paulus, *Indulgences as a Social Factor in the Middle Ages*, trans. J. Elliot Ross (1922), p. 15.
[137] Ibid.

# 2

# "The Shorter, the Better": Confession after the Reformation

> "Sister, you are stuck with a store full of repentance
> and no customers. And without sinners to repent,
> what is repentance? It doesn't exist."
>
> —Sky Masterson, in *Guys and Dolls*

In 1564 two Jesuit priests traveled through the territory of Lower Bavaria to assess the religious situation for their superior, Peter Canisius. What they saw left them stunned:

> Only a very few [priests] use the correct form of the Sacraments, especially of absolution. Some absolve their penitents with these sole words, "Misereatur nostri Deus." Others say, "Ego miserator Deus auctoritate et divinitatis Paris et Filii et Spiritus Sancti. Pax tecum." Yet others omit everything except, "Ego absolve te in nomine Patris. . . ." Despite all this they are held for Catholics and so wish to be held, with the result that nearly half the Bavarians in this district no longer care for either God or man.[1]

The Jesuits described an ignorant clergy ineptly caring for a peasant population grown progressively indifferent to the "true" religion. The peasantry around Ortenburg disdained the traditional priests in favor of a Lutheran preacher known for his moral life. They claimed that they would not receive the sacraments from the Catholic clergy until the priests gave up their concubines, married, and led a good life. The Jesuits themselves saw the local clergy as "mighty jesters and drinkers . . . always to be found in pot-houses or at weddings or other celebra-

---

[1] Otto Braunsberger, S. J., *Beati Petri Canisii Societatis Jesu Epistulae et Acta* (1896–1923), vol. 4, pp. 672–673. Cited in James Brodrick, *St. Peter Canisius, S. J., 1521–1597* (1935), p. 606.

tions."[2] The clergy were undoubtedly affected by heretical ideas and referred to Martin Luther, from whose books they culled their sermons, as the "Holy Doctor and precious man of God Martin."[3] Even so, they maintained their "Catholicity" and did not want to be considered Lutherans. Canisius's missionaries were amazed at what they saw, for it was not Catholic in their eyes.

This report, appearing shortly after the high tide of the Reformation in Bavaria, reveals much about the situation of the old Church at mid-century. One notes the dichotomy between two quite different religious identities: the confident, morally earnest Jesuits and their uncertain, loose-living counterparts among the secular clergy. Although part of the same Church, these groups had little in common and were bound to come into conflict. The triumph of the Jesuits (and other new orders, such as the Capuchins) would define the future of Bavaria and Austria as strongholds of reformed Roman Catholicism.[4]

Perhaps the most striking revelation of the missionaries' report is the confusion that existed among clergy and laity alike over the actual definition of the old Church, especially in contrast to its newer competitors. The Jesuits themselves were clear about the differences between Catholicism and Protestantism and stressed these differences ever more strongly, but the historian must answer three questions before agreeing with Peter Canisius and his brethren. First, in what ways did the coming of Protestantism change the practices of confession? Second, what was the actual state of religion in Bavaria and Austria in mid-century, following the onslaught of Protestantism? Finally, to what extent was this situation continuous or discontinuous with pre-Reformation practice? Were the practices that the Roman Church attacked of recent origin, or did they represent elements already present in late-medieval German Christianity? Responding to these questions constitutes the essence of this chapter, which must begin with the Protestant Reformation itself and therefore with Martin Luther.

---

[2] Braunsberger, *Beati* vol. 4, pp. 724–731, cited in Brodrick, *St. Peter Canisius*, p. 607.
[3] Ibid.
[4] This has been studied in depth for the Westphalian city of Münster, in R. Po-Chia Hsia, *Society and Religion in Münster, 1535–1618* (1984).

# "The Shorter, the Better"

## Luther and the Reformation

*The Theology of Penance*

Martin Luther's views on confession paradoxically embraced both the extreme contritionist and the extreme attritionist perspectives. Influenced by Biel and Staupitz, the early Luther emphasized perfect contrition rather than priestly absolution. He agreed that only perfect sorrow could satisfy God's justice. This very demand led him to abandon reliance on it: "Rather you should be assured of this, that after all your efforts your contrition is not sufficient."[5] The penitent must shift the focus from his or her own state and "cast yourself upon the grace of God, hear his sufficiently sure word in the sacrament, accept it in free and joyful faith, and never doubt that you have come to grace—not by your own merits or contrition but by his gracious and divine mercy." For Luther the alternative was a vain attempt at self-generated sorrow, "an ever greater uneasiness of conscience, a vain striving after impossible things, a quest for assurance and comfort that they never find." He did not demand that priests forgo inquiring as to the penitent's state during confession, as long as interrogations did not result in self-deception about one's contrition, "just so no one becomes so bold in the sight of God that he claims to have sufficient contrition. Such an attitude is presumptuous and fabricated, for no one has sufficient contrition for his sin."[6] All honest self-examination must necessarily end with the sinner recognizing and accepting spiritual impotence.

Luther's thinking, however, also echoed the thinking of such men as the attritionist Johann von Paltz. True, Luther scorned "minimal attrition" as great hypocrisy,[7] but like Paltz he ignored the problem of intensity or motive, considered the desire to confess sufficient, and emphasized above all the healing words of absolution. The penitent was to throw him- or herself on the mercy of God's grace in the Cross. Significantly, this did not necessarily bring comfort at first, for a terrified conscience in the form of self-condemnation was integral to the process.[8] For Luther, judgment always

---

[5] Martin Luther, "A Sermon on the Sacrament of Penance," *Luther's Works*, ed. Jaroslav Pelikan and H. T. Lehmann (1955–1986), vol. 35, p. 15 (hereafter, *LW*).

[6] Ibid.

[7] Martin Luther, "Articuli Christianae Doctrinae" (1537), in *Die Bekenntnisschriften der evangelisch–lutherischen Kirche* (1967), p. 440 (hereafter, *BSLK*).

[8] Spykman, *Attrition and Contrition*, pp. 97–101.

preceded consolation: "The hardhearted, however, who do not as yet seek comfort for their conscience, have likewise not yet experienced this tormenting anxiety. To them this sacrament is of no use. One must first soften them up with the terrible judgment of God and cause them to quail, so that they too may learn to sigh, and seek for the comfort of this sacrament."[9] Though present, grace was hidden under the terrible weight of judgment, compassion covered by stern justice,[10] and the sinner despaired of human solutions, ultimately taking refuge in God alone.[11] The genius of Luther's argument lay not in avoiding tribulation but in incorporating the terrors of conscience into the process while continuing to guarantee forgiveness.

For Luther, and later the Lutheran Church, this anxiety was resolved through the certainty and the consolatory power of absolution. As Luther himself wrote:

> When you are absolved from your sins, indeed when amid your awareness of sin some devout Christian—man or woman, young or old—comforts you, then receive this absolution in such faith that you would readily renounce everything else, rather than doubt that you have been truly absolved before God. Since by God's grace it is commanded of us to believe and to hope that our sins are forgiven us, how much more then ought you to believe it when God gives you a sign of it through another person![12]

This was the case regardless of the priest's knowledge of disposition. Luther rejected the Catholic theology of the age by exaggerating its extremes and artfully reconciling contritionist demands with the pastoral concerns of the attritionists by concentrating on the power of the absolution.[13]

---

[9] *LW*, vol. 35, p. 18.

[10] Martin Luther, "Resolutiones disputationum de indulgentiarum virtute" (1518), in *D. Martin Luthers Werke: Kritische Gesamtausgabe* (1883– ), vol. 1, p. 541 (hereafter, *WA*).

[11] "Contritio vera non est ex nobis, sed ex gratia dei: ideo desperandum de nobis et ad misericordiam eius confugiendem." *WA*, vol. 1, p. 322.

[12] "Sermon on Penance," *LW*, vol. 35, p. 14.

[13] Thomas Tentler contrasts Luther's "consoling" doctrine with that of the medieval Church. In doing so, however, he ignores the role that the "terrores conscientiae" played in Luther's own theology. Tentler, *Sin and Confession*, pp. 354–355. Medieval confession often had the same consolatory effect, virtually guaranteeing absolution to those willing to confess and satisfy. Both Luther and the Scotists avoided dependence on the subjective disposition of the sinner and by elevating absolution to an objective level removed it from the debate over purity of motive.

Luther and most of his successors challenged not only contrition but confession and satisfaction. Psychologically and subjectively, they claimed that the contemporary practice of compulsory confession of specific sins to a priest went beyond the law of God and thus burdened the consciences of Christians, who instead of brooding over individual sins ought to have been pondering their general sinfulness and beginning new lives.[14]

The Reformation took place in a religious world demanding annual confession (usually during Lent) according to the decree of the Fourth Lateran Council, which especially aroused Luther's anger: "This I reckon as the greatest plague on earth, through which you have bewildered the consciences of all the world, brought so many souls to despair, and degraded and oppressed all mankind's faith in Christ, for you have said nothing to us of the consolation of absolution, but have made a work out of it, extorted from unwilling hearts with commandments and force."[15] The problem lay in the commandment itself, for the Roman Church had taken the gospel of forgiveness given freely for consolation and entangled it once again in the law.[16] The Reformers denied that secret confession and absolution were divinely mandated or practiced in the early Church. They rejected the idea that confession was a tribunal in which the priest acts as a judge whose power to loose and to bind requires the intimate, detailed knowledge of sinful acts and their circumstances.[17] Detailed enumeration of sins was seen as another unnecessary human demand devised by priests to torment Christians.

Luther's arguments formed the theological and objective basis for subsequent Protestant polemic. A full, detailed confession seemed to rely

[14] Arendt, *Bußsakrament*, pp. 260–262.

[15] "Vermahnung an die Geistlichen, versammelt auf dem Reichstag zu Augsburg (1530)," *WA*, vol. 30, II, p. 287.

[16] "Von der Beicht," *WA*, vol. 8, p. 177. The Council's decree requiring confession was tyrannical insofar as it reversed the principle on which it was founded, and loosed rather than bound (Jean Calvin, *Institutes of the Christian Religion*, trans. Henry Beveridge (1953), III. 4. 17, p. 642, 645). See also E. Roth, *Die Privatbeichte und Schlusselgewalt in der Theologie der Reformatoren* (1952), p. 46.

[17] Melanchthon put it best in his "Apologia der Confession," *BSLK*, p. 273: "For the absolution is simply the command to pronounce the loosing, and is not a new law to investigate sin. For God is the judge and has not commanded the apostles to judge but to administer grace." For Luther, see "Sermon von dem Sakrament der Buße, 1519" *WA*, vol. 2, pp. 716–717; "Von der Beicht," *WA*, vol. 8, pp. 182–183. See also Roth, *Privatbeichte*, pp. 39–42, 51–65, for a discussion on the meaning of absolution for Luther.

more on its own perfection than on the mercy of God, making it a work performed to earn salvation.[18] Also, revealing individual misdeeds obscured the ever remaining, essential sinfulness of which Christians must always convict themselves.[19] The impossibility of complete confession ineluctably yielded an insatiably scrupulous conscience, which led not to faith but to despair.[20]

Satisfaction, the third part of the sacrament, also came under vigorous assault, in fact had touched off the original Reformation controversy.[21] The problem was that satisfaction (in the form of indulgences) diverted the penitent's attention from reliance on the merits of Christ to reliance on his or her own supererogatory works, ignoring in the process the true component of satisfaction—a new life.[22] The Reformers attacked the idea that any penalty remained following forgiveness of sin, which obviated all punishment and becalmed the heart.[23] As frequently happened in his criticism of medieval theology, Luther did not entirely abandon the idea of satisfaction, but his objection to such works lay in their being imposed by law rather than springing freely from a devout, grateful response to the Gospel.

## Confession in Lutheran Practice

So much for theology. To what extent did new conceptions of penance find their way into Lutheran practice? Neither Luther nor Lutheranism abandoned confession; instead they incorporated it into their own pastoral programs. Calvinist changes prove far more drastic, as they essentially eliminated any secret individual encounter between pastor and penitent. Instead, they enhanced the importance of the general confession already present in the medieval mass and made it part of the preparation

---

[18] "Sermo de poenitentia (1518)," *WA,* vol. 1, p. 322; "Confitendi ratio," *WA,* vol. 6, p. 161. See also the "Articuli Christianae Doctrinae," *BSLK,* p. 441.

[19] In addition to the works just cited, see "Rationis Latomianae Confutatio," *WA,* vol. 8, p. 104; "De captivitate Babylonica ecclesiae praeludium," *WA,* vol. 6, pp. 547–548; "Predigt am Osterdienstag (1531)," *WA,* vol. 34, I, p. 302. Calvin's harsh attack on this point is in the *Institutes,* III. 4. 18, p. 643.

[20] "Confitendi ratio," *WA,* vol. 6, pp. 163–164. Melanchthon, "Apologia confessionis Augustanae," *BSLK,* p. 252.

[21] Pelikan, *Reformation of Church,* p. 134.

[22] "Sermon von dem Sakrament der Buße," p. 722.

[23] Roth, *Die Privatbeichte,* p. 69; *WA,* vol. 1, p. 630.

for communion.[24] Some Lutherans employed a general public confession such as that offered by medieval German religious tradition, but in fact Luther's followers frowned upon this practice and retained the possibility of individual confession, which by the end of the sixteenth century became the rule in Lutheran territories. No longer "forced" annually (in the sense of the Fourth Lateran Council), confession remained a necessary precondition for communion in Lutheran churches and in fact virtually never took place without the Eucharist following.[25] Indeed, the two were so closely intertwined that one could explain their relation by stating, "No private confession without communion after, no communion without confession first."[26]

Given this connection, it was logical, as it had been in the medieval Church, to schedule confession as close to the communion date as possible, typically the day before. Saturday therefore became the designated time, usually at the vesper service, which thus became a general penitential service. Afterward, individuals would line up for an interview with the pastor, who would place himself in the confessor's chair (*Beichtstuhl*, reminiscent of the confessionals developing in Roman Catholicism). First came an interrogation over the catechism and articles of faith, during which specific offenses against the Ten Commandments might be discussed.[27] Then came the confession itself, which in Lutheranism sufficed for absolution even though it included no individual sins.[28] Martin Chemnitz, however, argued that the pastor was to determine whether true penitence existed or not. This was to take place, "when people want to go to communion, so that no one knowingly, without true examination, be per-

[24] Arendt, *Bußsakrament*, p. 198. See also Heinz, "Sondertradition," p. 201.

[25] Ernst Bezzel, "Beichte III: Reformationszeit," *Theologische Realenzyklopädie* (1980), vol. 5, pp. 423–424. For an example and early justification of this practice, see Martin Chemnitz, *Handbüchlein der fürnemsten hauptstücke der Christlichen Lehre/ durch Frag und Antwort aus Gottes Wort einfeltig und gründlich erkleret* (n.d.), pp. 296–297.

[26] "Keine Privatbeichte ohne nachfolgendes Abendmahl, kein Abendmahl ohne vorausgegangene Privatbeichte!" Richard Frank, "Geschichte der evangelischen Privatbeichte in Sachsen," *Beiträge zur Sächsischen Kirchengeschichte* 19 (1905): 160. Cited in Hans-Christoph Rublack, "Lutherische Beichte und Sozialdisziplinierung," *Archiv für Reformationsgeschichte* 84 (1993): 129.

[27] Bezzel, "Beichte III," p. 424; Rublack, "Lutherische Beichte," p. 131. Chemnitz justified the practice as a way of ascertaining that the faithful in fact knew the principal tenets of the faith. Chemnitz, *Handbüchlein*, p. 297.

[28] Rublack, "Lutherische Beichte," p. 129.

Reformation confession. Lucas Cranach the Elder, Altar for the Wittenberg Parish Church, c. 1547. Avery Architectural and Fine Arts Library, Columbia University in the City of New York. Johannes Bugenhagen pronounces absolution using the keys of loosing and binding in this stylized representation of Lutheran confession. As in the medieval sacrament, the confessor sits in a chair while a crowd gathers round the event.

mitted to go unworthily, to his judgment. Therefore is each person advised that he ought to examine himself and is instructed how he might examine himself."[29] Lutheran confession thus potentially contained some of the same disciplinary force that medieval penance offered, even without

[29] Chemnitz, *Handbüchlein*, p. 297.

the revelation of specific sins. Apparently, this potential was as little realized as it had been in the medieval Catholic sacrament. As time passed, Lutheran confession increasingly consisted of a ritualized formula, often taken directly from Luther's small catechism.[30] The imposition of hands accompanied the formal pronouncement of absolution, and the penitent was ready for communion on Sunday.

Comparing this to medieval tradition reveals that Lutheranism's most dramatic change in practice was to curtail the required annual confession of specific sins, which corresponded to Luther's theological attack on the very possibility of complete enumeration. While this might imply that investigating and correcting individual faults lay outside the jurisdiction of pastors, such was not the case. Eliminating this function from confession did not itself mean the end of "social discipline" in the Lutheran Church, but simply its displacement to other areas of religious life.[31] Luther's Catechism itself demonstrates just how prominent sins could be, and examinations of parishioners before confession included discussion of the Ten Commandments.[32] Preaching, too, was an opportunity for remonstration and even threat, as the instructions sent to pastors after the Saxon visitation of 1528 made clear: "Therefore they should diligently and frequently preach the Ten Commandments, explaining and clarifying not only the Commandments, but also how God will punish and has often punished in this temporal life those who do not keep them."[33]

In Bavarian and Austrian Protestantism, Lutheranism triumphed. Protestant movements emerged in Bavaria, especially in cities and areas where the nobility and estates sought leverage against the emerging Wittelsbach hegemony.[34] Ultimately, though, the aggressive religious and

[30] Bezzel, "Beichte III," p. 424; Rublack, "Lutherische Beichte," pp. 131–132.

[31] See, for example, Luther's "Instructio pro confessione peccatorum (1518)," *WA*, vol. 1, pp. 258–265.

[32] On this subject generally, see Gerald Strauss, *Luther's House of Learning* (1978), especially pages 203–222. Hans-Christoph Rublack questions the effectiveness of this disciplinary function in "Lutherische Beichte," pp. 135–155.

[33] "Unterricht der visitatoren an die pfarrherrn im kurfurstenthum zu Sachsen, 1528," in Emil Sehling, ed., *Die evangelischen Kirchenordnungen des 16. Jahrhunderts*, 5 vols. (1902–13), vol. 1, p. 152.

[34] On Protestantism in Bavaria, see Hans Rößler, *Geschichte und Strukturen der evangelischen Bewegung im Bistum Freising 1520–1571*, Einzelarbeiten aus der Kirchengeschichte Bayerns (1966), vol. 42. See also Max Spindler, ed., *Handbuch der bayerischen Geschichte*, (1969), vol. 2, pp. 297–405, 626–651. On earlier reactions to the Reformation see Gerald

state policies of the dukes preserved the old Church and bound its success to the triumph of the Wittelsbach family itself.[35] In Austria, the situation was very different, especially in the Archdiocese of Salzburg and the Diocese of Passau. Here the combination of sixteenth-century economic decline, peasant war, and unceasing struggle between the ecclesiastical and the secular estates caused the secular nobility to ally themselves with the Protestant Reformation at an early stage and weakened episcopal rule.[36] Only in the very late sixteenth century, and by force, did emperors and prelates restore Austrian Roman Catholicism.

As early as 1520, both Lutheran and more radical tendencies were evident in Salzburg, and Anabaptists continued to be prominent after the Peasants' War.[37] As a result, sacramental confession came under fire. The visitation of 1528 revealed that a monk in the parish of Saalfeld, with the permission of the parish priest, had preached on *Judica* Sunday (i.e., the second Sunday before Easter) that for those with sorrow (*reue*), the general confession consisted of begging God's mercy through Christ, a practice associated with elements more extreme than Lutheranism.[38] Otherwise, the visitation of 1528 revealed both serious defects and continued fulfillment of religious obligations.[39] The visitation of 1555 showed much more widespread sympathy for the Reformation, but even here it could not be said that the majority of the population had actually become Protestant.[40] This was especially true given the still fluid definitions of the various churches. The demand for communion in both kinds was a long-standing Protestant

---

Strauss, "The Religious Policy of Dukes Wilhelm and Ludwig of Bavaria in the First Decade of the Protestant Era," *Church History* 28 (1959): 350–375.

[35] Georg Schwaiger claims that because of ducal religious policy, the Reformation could not establish deep roots in Bavaria and never threatened the existence of the old Church in the territory. Georg Schwaiger, ed., *Geschichte des Erzbistums München und Freising*, 2 vols. (1989), vol. 2, p. 495.

[36] Franz Ortner, *Reformation, katholische Reform und Gegenreformation im Erzstift Salzburg* (1981), pp. 11–32. On the nobility's exploitation of religious unrest, see Erich Zöllner, *Geschichte Österreichs von den Anfängen bis zur Gegenwart*, 8th ed. (1990), p. 194. See also Hugo Hantsch, *Die Geschichte Österreichs* (1959), vol. 1, pp. 241f.

[37] Zöllner, *Geschichte*, p. 192; Hantsch, *Geschichte*, p. 245; Ortner, *Reformation*, pp. 55–58.

[38] Ortner, *Reformation*, p. 63.

[39] Ibid., pp. 58–66.

[40] Ibid., p. 73. This opinion is in contrast to the views of Hans Widmann, *Geschichte Salzburgs*, 3 vols., (1907), vol. 3, p. 86, and Gerhard Florey, *Geschichte der Salzburger Protestanten und ihrer Emigration 1731/1732* (1977), p. 44.

one, but since at various times in the 1540s and 1550s the emperor and other Catholic rulers granted its use, did its presence in the visitation necessarily identify people as Protestants, especially if in other respects they continued to believe and practice as before? Still, the situation of the old Church had become more precarious, evident in the decay of ecclesiastical property and especially in the lack of priests.[41]

In Passau, much of the territorial nobility adopted Lutheranism after the Peasants' War as a spiritual means of quelling unrest while usurping ecclesiastical prerogatives.[42] They succeeded so well that Passau became the center of the Augsburg Confession in Austrian lands.[43] The visitations carried out in 1544 and 1555 demonstrated the dire straits of Catholicism in Inner and Lower Austria, with cloisters abandoned, priests married, numerous parishes without pastors, indeed without any priests at all, and church properties falling into disrepair.[44] In Styria, the Protestant presence was less public, but still prominent.

Thus, in both Bavaria and Austrian lands, but especially in Salzburg and Passau, Protestantism, particularly Lutheranism, had gained considerable influence by the time of the Augsburg Interim of 1548, and at the Peace of Augsburg in 1555 some local rulers officially adopted Lutheranism. This was already true in some areas. In 1549, the Salzburg ecclesiastical province held a synod that closely followed the statutes of the Interim, including the affirmation of individual confession and the enumeration of specific sins.[45] Both the clergy of the province and various secular estates formulated complaints (*gravamina*), either in preparation for or in response to the synod, and from them it is possible to understand some of the issues involving confession. The same synod also illustrates the difficulty of deciding whether a community was Protestant or Catholic.

---

[41] Ortner, *Reformation*, pp. 73–74.

[42] Ibid., p. 255. The classic account of the politico-religious conflict in upper Austria is Karl Eder, *Glaubensspaltung und Landstände in Österreich ob der Enns 1525–1602*, Studien zur Reformationsgeschichte Oberösterreichs, vol. 2 (1936).

[43] Ortner, *Reformation*, p. 253.

[44] Ibid., p. 157. See also Eder, *Glaubensspaltung*, pp. 57–63.

[45] For documents relating to this synod, see Johann Loserth, "Die Salzburger Provinzialsynode von 1549: Zur Geschichte der protestantischen Bewegung in den österreichischen Erbländern," *Archiv für Österreichische Geschichte* 85 (1898): 131–357.

The synod upheld the traditional practices of confession, especially the individual and specific enumeration of sins.[46] The Styrian estates responded by agreeing that penance was a sacrament and affirming "the custom in the church, that Christians, before the priest, in secret, confess their burdens and obligations, namely, that they have sinned and thereby angered God the Almighty, and also themselves and others through which they have inflicted great shame and earned just punishment." Nonetheless, they argued in explicitly Lutheran fashion that it was a misunderstanding to believe such a custom meant, "that one ought and must, even at the loss of the soul's health, to recount and indicate to the priest in the above-mentioned confession all sins that a person has committed, which is neither grounded nor commanded anywhere in Scripture." The best requirement for absolution was not the recounting of sins, "but a contrite heart and Christian improvement of an entire life along with strong faith."

Because specific confession was unnecessary, the practice of reserving sins for public penance or episcopal action was also unwarranted and was not based in Scripture. Thus, no minister required special "jurisdiction," and the clergy's main duty was to preach the forgiveness of sin and the preaching of the gospel. Discipline and good morals were not the task of the church, but belonged instead to the secular government, as God had ordained.[47] This claim not only undermined the old Church, but also served to strengthen the secular power of local rulers at the expense of prince-bishops.

The theme of secular responsibility for punishing transgressions also figured in the response of the Carinthian estates, who were much less inclined to Protestantism. Like the Styrians, they too emphasized the power and rights of secular governments and attacked the practice of public penance for serious sins, arguing that this belonged to secular rather than religious authority.[48] They went on to state: "And it ought not to be, that the clergy should publicly humiliate and for their pleasure make a specta-

---

[46] Ibid., p. 154.

[47] "Auf der geistlich Saltzburgisch provincial statuta deren von Steyr antwortet (1549)," in Loserth, "Salzburger Provinzialsynode," pp. 276–277.

[48] "Antwort der Kärntner 'auf der Geistlichen Beschwär-Artikel,' " in Loserth, "Salzburger Provinzialsynode," p. 333. The issue of ecclesiastical versus secular jurisdiction over punishment of public offenses is itself an interesting question, which unfortunately cannot be addressed here. In this instance the foremost issue is the question of public penance itself.

cle of people they want to pursue, although they confess such sins in confessions, which in part would be more suitable to slanderers."[49] Here the clergy were directly accused of using the penitential system to bring public disgrace to Christians.

Although this response addressed the important question of whether ecclesiastical or secular governments should have the power to discipline criminals or sinners, its ramifications for the sacrament of penance were also significant. The complaint accused the clergy of using sacramental confession, by which was probably meant reserved sins requiring public penance, to cause public humiliation. In this case, the clergy were being accused of using secret sins as the basis for public penance. The manner in which even serious private offenses were brought to light could have disturbing implications for all confessions and further clarifies the reluctance of individuals to enumerate and recount their offenses to the clergy. As Erasmus had noted earlier, confession could potentially be damaging, perhaps not spiritually, but socially and even legally.

The Carinthians had other complaints about Catholic penance, more practical than doctrinal, and less Protestant-sounding. According to them, the clergy used the occasions of deathbed confession to convince men and women that their souls would benefit greatly if they would only leave half their earthly goods to the church, especially to the confessor's religious order.[50] Another basic criticism was that members of the clergy were lazy, even cutting short some confessions of Christians who lay sickened or in danger of death and begged for the sacrament, thus denying them proper spiritual attention.[51] Especially on holy days, "the clergy do not want to visit their parishioners in these cases; they give as reason that the holy days are also commanded of them, on which they have to rest, for on these same days they have to study and

---

[49] "Und solle kaineswegs sein, dass die geistlichen die menschen, ob sy solche sundt in der peicht pekennen, darumben offenlich zu schanden machen und irs gevallen damit schauspil, welche zum thail den nachrichtern pass zimbten, treiben wollten." Ibid., p. 333.

[50] "Etliche beschwärungen wider die geistlichkeit in Khärnndten," Loserth, "Salzburger Provinzialsynode," p. 351. This, of course, was an old theme, satirized by Erasmus. See "The Funeral," in *Ten Colloquies*, trans. Craig Thompson (1957), pp. 92–112.

[51] Loserth, p. 349.

preach."[52] It is not hard to imagine the same clergy's reluctance to undertake the tedious task of hearing confessions except when strictly necessary.

The Carinthians were not necessarily Protestant. Certainly many received communion under both species, and they had numerous complaints against the old Church. They themselves, however, explicitly rejected many of the clerical accusations and upheld numerous customs as praiseworthy. The most Protestant characteristic of their response was their stated willingness to decide some religious matters for themselves. But with the sacraments, the Carinthians were far more Catholic than were the Styrians, and except for demanding the communion under both species, they appear to have accepted traditional customs.[53]

The Peace of Augsburg, the desire to end confusion among Austrian Protestants, and the sympathy of Emperor Maximilian II, resulted in some Austrian lands adopting (briefly, it turned out) the Augsburg Confession. Thus in 1571 there appeared a Protestant *Agenda*, which upheld private absolution, "through which the wholesome quickening of grace and general preaching of the Gospels about the forgiveness of sins is proclaimed and applied to each person individually. Therefore, each person, individually, who is absolved from sin by the servant of Christ, can believe certainly and should not doubt, that his sins certainly are forgiven by Christ himself." In this document, the Protestant estates upheld confession and private absolution.[54] According to the Augsburg Confession, this meant no forced annual confession, but only an individual encounter before receiving communion (or when conscience dictated), and no recounting of specific sins.

How these new beliefs fared was another matter. In practice, the situation was quite murky, a fact demonstrated by the Lutheran visitation

---

[52] "Und sonderlichen wellen die geistlichen die underthanen an den feyertagen in disen fällen nicht besuechen, geben die ursachen fuer, als seyen inen die feyertag auch gesetz, daran sie rehen sollen, dann sy auf dieselbigen tag studiern und predigen muessen." Ibid.

[53] Loserth, "Salzburger Provinzialsynode," p. 216.

[54] "Christlich Kirchen Agenda, wie die bey den zweyen Ständen der Herrn und Ritterschafft im Ertzherzogthumb Österreich unter der Enns gebraucht wirdt," in Ernst Tomek, *Kirchengeschichte Österreichs*, 3 vols. (1949), vol. 2, pp. 342–344.

[55] For the results of this visitation, see Tomek, *Kirchengeschichte*, vol. 2, pp. 356–389, where they are methodically detailed.

in Lower Austria in 1580.[55] Some newly Lutheran parishes professing the Augsburg Confession had abandoned individual penance altogether. One pastor had to be warned "to hear each separately";[56] others, along with their parishes, received a similar admonition.[57] The Evangelical visitation showed that numerous Lutheran pastors continued to use private confession and absolution.[58] In doing so, however, some followed the old Catholic customs as far as the time of reception, to the dismay of Lutheran visitors. The pastor of Trautsmanstorff administered private confession and absolution, but only at Easter time, which violated the Lutheran idea that the sacrament should not be restricted to any one time of the year.[59] Another pastor claimed that he would conduct the sacrament privately but for the fact that so many people arrived from near and far to receive it.[60] In these cases, one may, paradoxically, infer greater popular support both for tradition and for more radical new practices than adherents of the Augsburg Confession wanted to admit.

Lutheran practice quite clearly meant giving up the specific enumeration of sins and the various satisfactions meted out by confessors. These were significant changes. Otherwise, however, Lutheran confession in some areas actually brought less change from medieval patterns than one might suspect.[61] True, Lutherans abrogated the Fourth Lateran Council's demands for annual reception, but confession was still necessary for receiving communion. Medieval Christians themselves seldom confessed unless also preparing for communion. The presence of the *Beichtgeld* [Penance money] offered to the priest also continued a medieval practice much lamented by the authorities, as did the idea that the money offered was a fee of sorts for guaranteeing absolution. Indeed, interpreting Lutheran confession as a social ritual rather than a pastoral event empha-

---

[56] "einen jedweden insonderheit zu hören." Ibid., p. 354.

[57] In Zöger, Oberhöflein, Buch, and Seifritz. Ibid., pp. 355–356.

[58] Ibid., p. 375.

[59] "nur zur Oster Zeit stellete er dieselbe [Beicht] ein; welches ihm aber verweisen und auferlegt ward, selbige zu jeder Zeit zu halten." Ibid., p. 368.

[60] Ibid., p. 376.

[61] On the relationship between Catholic and Lutheran practices see Ernst Walter Zeeden, *Katholische Überlieferungen in den lutherischen Kirchenordnungen des 16. Jahrhunderts*, Katholisches Leben und Kampfen im Zeitalter der Glaubensspaltung, vol. 17 (1959), p. 17f.

sizes its continuity with the medieval world.[62] As strange as it may seem, Lutheran customs may actually have been too close to medieval usage. The possibility that the processes might look similar, separated in the main by the absence of specific enumeration, forced Catholic authorities into diligent efforts to identify and distinguish Catholic ritual from Protestant.

### Catholic Practice at Mid-Century

Sacramental confession came under sharp attack from the Protestant Reformation, but did the Reformation affect practice in Catholic territories as a result? How did the practice of penance in 1560 differ from that of 1500? These are by no means simple questions to answer. The numerous descriptions, reports, and complaints from Jesuit, territorial, or episcopal emissaries may reveal a decline in penance caused by Protestantism and peasant rebellions, but they may also describe problems arising in a traditional religion no longer acceptable to Catholic Reformers seeking to inculcate a new understanding of Catholicism. For example, concubinage may have demonstrated the clergy's turpitude, but its pervasiveness preceded the Reformation. Similarly, the inability of priests to pronounce the proper formula of absolution may indicate Protestant incursion, but might it not also demonstrate the lack of clerical education, variety of local customs, the irregularity of episcopal control, and the absence of a single, comprehensive ritual formula? If confessors accepted only a general confession instead of the specific accounting of sins demanded by authorities and theologians, Lutheran contamination may be suspected, but the practice also implies a priest's tacit compact with his parishioners in difficult circumstances.

The task of identifying innovations and separating the new from the traditional requires precise descriptions of religious practice over a wide territory. While such accounts are relatively rare for the medieval Church, the use of sixteenth-century ecclesiastical and territorial visitation records allows us to examine the external, public part of religious life in great detail.[63]

---

[62] See Rublack, "Lutherische Beichte," pp. 153–154, and Bezzel, "Beichte III," p. 424.

[63] Gerald Strauss has recommended visitation records and discussed their difficulties in *Luther's House of Learning*, pp. 249–267. See also August Franzen, ed., *Die Visitationsprotokolle der ersten nachtridentinischen Visitation im Erzstift Köln unter Salentin von Isenburg* (1960), pp. 1–3.

# "The Shorter, the Better"

In Bavaria the first visitations, carried out between 1558 and 1560, received active support from territorial rulers and thus had a force and comprehensiveness lacking elsewhere.[64] These records therefore permit us to describe the religious situation at a particularly delicate moment.[65] While the visitation themselves provide the bulk of information here, they are corroborated in important details by reports by papal nuncios, the statutes of reforming diocesan synods, and individual descriptions. These sources provide a basis of comparison with earlier practices.

The visitations carried out in the dioceses of Freising, Passau, Regensburg, and the Chiemsee sought specific information about the conduct of confession. The doctrinal section of the questionnaire asked three questions about penance:

> 1) What kind of general confession and absolution the pastor uses; 2) Whether he admonishes the people, that they confess at least once in the year, what he thinks about auricular confession and the specific recounting and confessing of mortal sins, or whether he teaches that the general confession suffices and specific recounting is not necessary; 3) Whether he rejects penance and satisfaction, as given in confession, and teaches that this is against the satisfaction of Christ.[66]

Another section inquired about the individual sacraments, including the following concerning confession:

> Where and in what manner does he hear confession? Does he absolve penitents after general confession, without specific recounting of sins? How does he absolve and with what words, or does he absolve all communicants generally? Does he impose a penance on penitents after completing confession, or why does he omit it? Does he know what the reserved cases are, or how does he think about them? Does he confess himself, how often and to whom? How does he think about public penance and how it is practiced?[67]

[64] See Strauss, *Luther's House of Learning*, pp. 288–289; idem, *Law, Resistance, and the State: The Opposition to Roman Law in Reformation Germany* (1986), pp. 260–262.

[65] On the circumstances of these visitations, see Anton Landersdorfer, ed., *Das Bistum Freising in der bayerischen Visitation des Jahres 1560* (1986), pp. 32–65, hereafter referred to as *Freising*; also *Chiemsee* and Paul Mai, *Das Bistum Regensburg in der Bayerischen Visitation von 1559*, Beiträge zur Geschichte des Bistums Regensburg, ed. Georg Schwaiger, vol. 27 (1993), hereafter referred to as *Regensburg*. These editions of the Bavarian visitations serve as the basis for much of this chapter.

[66] *Freising*, pp. 43–44. A closely related version of these questions can be found in Florianus Dalham, ed., *Concilia Salisburgensia Provincialia et Dioecesana*, (1778), p. 591.

[67] *Freising*, pp. 46–47.

The visitors justified their interrogation as a way to assess the degree of Evangelical influence in Bavarian territories. Four concerns appeared most significant: first, administrators worried about ecclesiastical discipline—compliance with the precept to confess annually, knowledge of reserved cases, and the priest's own practice. Second, authorities tried to establish clear boundaries between Catholic and Evangelical, in two ways: by questioning pastors about requiring the private confession of specific sins rather than either individual or group absolution following a general confession, and by asking whether confessors imposed satisfactions for sins. These questions had already been answered theologically for each group, the Catholics maintaining the necessity of satisfaction and the Protestants claiming that assigning penances detracted from the sufficiency of the one sacrifice of Christ.[68]

The third major concern of the visitors was both disciplinary and pastoral. The Jesuits cited at the opening of this chapter lamented the variety and inadequacy of absolution formulae used by the parish clergy. The investigators reasoned that such illicit formulae might render the sacrament invalid, especially since great emphasis was placed upon the efficacy of absolution pronounced *ex opere operato*. Also, in the chaos of competing churches, variety might mask suspicious inclinations and allegiances. A final concern among officials was that the secular clergy's poor performance also proved them to be incompetent at providing pastoral care.

Armed with episcopal authority and secular military protection, the visitors made their exhaustive survey. What they learned about the state of sacramental penance certainly reveals the effects of the Evangelical movement, but their gleanings also permit comparison with pre-Reformation practices. So that we can examine their findings, the results will be divided into the general categories used in describing medieval confession, with added attention to the innovations of the first forty years of the Protestant movement. The visitation reports provide answers to the questions of frequency, time, and place, but the records also permit detailed discussion of the manner in which the sacrament was conducted with reference to the formula of absolution and confession of specific sins.

[68] See chapter 1.

# "The Shorter, the Better"

## Frequency of Catholic Confession during the Reformation Era

*Lay Confession*

As seen in the previous chapter, the medieval Church demanded that its subjects confess their sins at least once a year; whatever exhortations to greater frequency ecclesiastical officials made, they limited their expectations to annual Lenten penance and little more. The sole novelty of the fifteenth and early sixteenth centuries was the introduction of the *confessio bina*. The coming of the Reformation did not change these expectations. For most of the sixteenth century, Catholic authorities were relieved that people continued to confess at all. Plagued by a shortage both of clergy and of the means to pay them, officials in some places lamented the numbers of Christians who had not confessed for years.[69] The timing of penance only compounded the problem, for Lenten confession placed the reduced clergy under great strain. Despite these failings, however, mid-sixteenth-century practice reveals continuity more than collapse. Catholics in Bavaria confessed as did their grandparents, no more but—significantly—no less. Among the clergy there was greater variety, a fact troubling to ecclesiastical authorities who realized that they had exercised only ineffective supervision of clerical morality, knowledge, and orthodoxy. However, even the clergy did not deviate significantly from medieval expectations. Ultimately, Catholic authorities worried not only over the pernicious results of the Reformation but also about the traditional practices of the Church they were committed to defending.

In Freising, the most securely Catholic diocese, the records show that almost half the laity received the sacrament only once a year. This was the case whether or not a particular church had experienced a Protestant movement. In no church, parish or monastic, urban or rural, is there evidence of lay people confessing more than twice annually. Indeed, to the visitors, twice-annual confession proved a parish's diligence.[70] Ten churches throughout the Freising diocese unqualifiedly affirmed the

---

[69] "Instruktion für die von Ferdinand angeordnete Visitation der niederosterreichischen Länder Österreich ob und unter der Enns, Steiermark, Kärnten und Krain (November 1543)," in *Acta Reformationis Catholicae*, vol. 4, p. 338.

[70] "Peichten im jar zway mal und suechen den gotsdienst gar vleisig heimb." *Freising*, p. 310.

Lenten *confessio bina*.[71] Unreserved acceptance of the *confessio bina* was not the norm, however, for some degree of reluctance was often evident. Pastors did attempt to introduce double Lenten reception, often unsuccessfully, as in the parish of Güntzelhoven, where "his parishioners for the most part confess only one time per year, regardless that he earnestly admonishes them to it [the *confessio bina*]."[72] The same explanation was heard in Jesenwang, Viehkirchen, and Aubing.[73] Elsewhere the single Lenten performance was simply noted, without remark. Most commonly, "older people" confessed only once a year while "the young" went twice.[74] Pastors urged "older people" to double reception, but to no avail.[75] In Kholbach, the report implied that the practice was generally accepted, except among the old.[76] It must be remembered that the call to *confessio bina* was of relatively recent origin, did not constitute a part of Church law, and was only gradually gaining acceptance in parishes. Catholics in some areas may have considered it a worthwhile practice for disciplining the young but unnecessary for adults.

In some cases refusal to confess indicated Evangelical leanings. In the village of Höchenberg, for example, the new Catholic priest suffered still from the previous pastor's Protestant innovations and complained that even with the help of the secular authority, no one would confess more than once.[77] This was, however, only infrequently the case in the Freising diocese, and the need for secular assistance did not necessarily indicate Evangelical influence.[78] The temptation to ascribe Protestant sympathies to these cases is tempered by evidence from traditional parishes, un-

[71] Ibid., pp. 312, 313, 315, 321, 360, 365, 411, 419, 421.

[72] "Sein pfarrvolckh peicht maist thails nur ain mal im jar, unangesehen, das ers treulich dartzu verman." Ibid., p. 338.

[73] Ibid. In Viehkirchen, "Sein pfarrvolckh kund er jerlich vor der communion uber ain peicht nit pringen" (p. 303). The same was true in Jesenwang (p. 346) and in Aubing (p. 416), where most simply waited for Holy Week, as was normal.

[74] As in Sultzmoß, where "Das junk volckh peicht noch zwai mal, die allten zum thail nur ain mal." Ibid., p. 335. See also Mammendorf (p. 350); Gröffling (p. 341); Egenhoven (p. 345); Berkirchen (p. 323), and Kholbach (p. 317).

[75] Ibid. In Egenhoven (p. 345) and Einspach (p. 352).

[76] Ibid., p. 317.

[77] "Khünd sein volckh zwaimal zubeichten nit pringen, dann wo sy mit inen fur die obrigkait kommen, finden sy schlechten beistandt. Doch ain mal miessen sy peichten." Ibid., p. 471.

[78] See the parish of Lengrieß, where the priest had detected no evangelical influence, but who nonetheless required the authorities to enforce annual confession. Ibid., p. 478.

tainted by resentment or Evangelical teaching, in which the norm of single confession prevailed and the pastors saw nothing amiss.[79]

Elsewhere, in the Chiemgau and the diocese of Regensburg, the same pattern of reception held, but evidence of Protestantism was greater. In fact, only half the pre-Reformation Regensburg diocese remained in Catholic hands to be visited.[80] The evidence of Protestant influence increased as one came closer to the evangelical city of Regensburg itself, and the town of Straubing was also affected. Despite this, however, the diocese generally remained Catholic in practice, according to visitors, pastors, and the government.[81] As in Freising, the *confessio bina* was not pervasive, and the visitors were disappointed. In most churches annual confession was the norm, even where priests claimed that they had urged their congregations to the sacrament.[82] It was also true in churches noted to be diligent and thoroughly Catholic,[83] although there were places where the people obeyed only reluctantly.[84] The *confessio bina* was less extensive, and the visitors' viewed it as a sign of a good, traditional priest and congregation.[85] In another variation also evident in Freising, young people were sometimes expected to confess twice annually, but adults went only once.[86]

In the Freising diocese, then, for the most part, the customary practice remained in place for the laity. Examining territories belonging to Passau and Salzburg reveals the same pattern, except that recalcitrance was

---

[79] Täning may have typified the old Church's problems. In this completely Catholic parish, unaffected by Protestantism, the pastor knew nothing of confirmation or last anointing. His parishioners confessed once a year, but he knew neither the parts of penance, the reason for granting absolution, the formula of absolution or of general absolution, nor the reserved sins. Ibid., p. 469.

[80] Mai, *Regensburg*, pp. 27–28. The imperial city, of course, was not visited, having become Protestant.

[81] Ibid., p. 45.

[82] This was the case in Geisling, Tegernhaim, and Obertraubling. Mai, *Regensburg*, pp. 13, 29, 38.

[83] In Hädersbach, the visitors noted of the parishioners, "omnia bene et Catholic, allein peichten sy nur ain mal." Ibid., p. 57. The same was true in Nidernästern. Ibid., p. 188.

[84] For example, in Prechenpach. Ibid., p. 237.

[85] Neuhausen is one good example. Ibid., p. 243. Another is Steinbach, where the visitors remarked upon the cleanliness of the church, the diligence of its liturgies, and the fact that the congregation confessed twice annually. In the church, therefore, everything was as of old ("alles wie vor alter"). The only blot on this Catholic congregation was the priest's "cook" and child. Ibid., p. 101.

[86] In Hüttenkofen, Schatzkofen, and Jachsenhausen. Ibid., pp. 327, 382, 485.

greater in each, commensurate with the greater inroads made by Protestantism. As in the Bavarian core, Evangelical forms concentrated in pockets—in individual towns, communes, or territories—rather than sweeping through the region. The custom of making an offering to the clergy upon receiving the sacraments also proved a hindrance to many people. As the value of stipends and benefices declined in Salzburg during the sixteenth century, *Beichtgeld* became more important, demanded by the clergy as a means of support and withheld by the laity in protest, anger, or frugality.[87] This conflict is quite visible in preparations for the Salzburg synod of 1549, in which the lay *gravamina* against the priests complained that the clergy demanded an offering for performing the sacraments and refused to administer them without one.[88]

Visitation records reveal that in the middle of the century the precept of annual, Lenten confession remained firmly in place. In indisputably Catholic territories (the dioceses of Freising, Chiemsee, to a lesser extent Regensburg and Passau), one finds general acquiescence and even some evidence of accepting the *confessio bina*, despite lay resistance. Of course, enforcing the *confessio bina* would have had the effect of strengthening the association of penance with Lent and with preparation for communion. Religious or social tumult in Catholic territories such as Salzburg and inner Austria could mean the loss of even minimal compliance. A final factor in understanding the nonreception of the sacraments, especially Eucharist and penance, was the lack of priests. This did not apply to the Freising diocese or other Bavarian territories, but in Salzburg and inner Austria the lack of priests proved a serious problem for which the authorities could find no solution. Officials visiting parts of the Salzburg province were appalled at finding parishes to which no priest could be tempted and in which for years, sometimes a decade, neither communion nor confession had been received. These officials believed that in these cases, bad priests were better than no priests at all.[89]

[87] Ortner, *Reformation*, pp. 15–17, 42, 59–63. P. Browe contends that this had always hindered more frequent confession. See "Pflichtbeichte," pp. 356–357.

[88] On this point see "Etliche beschwärungen wider die geistlichkeit in Khärnndten," Loserth, "Salzburger Provinzialsynode," p. 349.

[89] See, for example, the arguments of Austrian ecclesiastics in the 1540s (*Acta Reformationis Catholicae*, vol. 2, p. 676). See also vol. 2, pp. 359 and 562 for discussions of the clergy's problems.

# "The Shorter, the Better"

## Clerical Confession

If ecclesiastical authorities were resigned to minimal compliance by the laity, their attitude changed when they considered the clergy, among whom wide disparities in reception surprised and concerned officials. Traditional worries about morality were compounded in the later sixteenth century by the fact that irregular, infrequent clerical confession also hindered supervision of education and orthodoxy: if a priest were to disseminate heresy in his parish, how would authorities know of it? How could one compel the laity to comply with church regulations when the clergy themselves proved remiss?

Once again, visitation records provide a way of measuring practice, and evidence from a Catholic "stronghold" again reveals the tenacity of tradition despite the encroachment of the new faiths. The sporadic compliance revealed by the records points up the inconsistency of clerical discipline in the old Church and the discrepancy between monastic and secular clergy. In general one may say that the clergy confessed more often than the laity, but this was not uniformly the case. Little correlation exists between the degree of "Catholicity" and the frequency of confessions among the clergy—in numerous cases the thoroughly orthodox pastor of a completely "Catholic" parish received the sacrament only once a year.

Some clergy did confess frequently, as often as once a week, but these were few. Out of one hundred responses about clerical frequency in the Freising visitation, only three clerics claimed to receive the sacrament on a weekly basis. One of these was a monk, and the others were secular priests serving the Holy Ghost parish in Munich.[90] Two others claimed to confess every other week.[91] In the Chiemsee, only one priest claimed a weekly confession, while two others claimed to confess six or seven times a year.[92] For Regensburg, no secular priest claimed to confess on a weekly or semiweekly basis, and in that diocese, even a monthly confession was exceedingly rare.[93]

[90] *Freising*, pp. 402 and 505.
[91] Ibid., pp. 428, 388.
[92] *Chiemsee*, pp. 265, 206, 203.
[93] The very devout pastor in Inkhofen confessed monthly, while a priest in Aschau went nine times a year. *Regensburg*, pp. 80, 138.

At the other extreme, very few would admit to less than annual confession. According to the Freising visitation, a priest in the parish of Aubing in eight years had failed to confess five times.[94] In Eschelbach, the pastor himself had failed to confess three times during the previous ten years.[95] One cannot claim here a strong correlation between new teachings and noncompliance with church strictures. Although Eschelbach was riven by Evangelical sentiment, especially among the peasantry, Aubing was a Catholic parish in which no Protestantism had been detected. Each priest was described as quite unlearned, and this seems the only connection between the two cases.[96]

Although extremes of frequency did exist, most of the clergy either fulfilled the general obligation of annual confession or went somewhat beyond it. Despite the relative paucity of statistical evidence, one may make some tentative conclusions about clerical frequency. Three patterns of reception emerge from the visitation records: the most common custom among the parish clergy was to confess four times a year, followed by simple annual confession, and lastly by monthly reception. In Regensburg, some priests confessed four times annually, but more often they admitted only to one or two receptions a year, mirroring the laity.[97] In the monasteries, where answers about frequency were admittedly few but expectations higher, annual confession still prevailed. It is striking that some of the most frequent confessions took place in women's cloisters, as in Regensburg, where in one cloister the nuns confessed nineteen times annually.[98] In the Chiemsee diocese, authorities were especially struck by the intermittent confession of the clergy, and at the end of the visitation remarked on the fact that so few priests confessed more than twice annually.[99]

---

[94] *Freising*, p. 416.

[95] Ibid., p. 707.

[96] For Eschelbach, ibid., p. 707. For Aubing, p. 416.

[97] In Pfaffenberg and Holtztraubach, the pastors confessed four times. *Regensburg*, pp. 43, 83. In Schierling and Reissing, the pastors went twice a year, as did Melchior Theininger in Straubing, a priest who appears to have been both learned (he knew the reserved sins) and devout. Ibid., pp. 64, 154, 119. The learned pastor in Grauentraubach, a man who possessed numerous Catholic books and no heretical tracts, and who preached regularly, nonetheless admitted to a single confession annually, as did others. Ibid., pp. 89, 149.

[98] Ibid., pp. 318–319.

[99] "so befind sich in examine vaßt bey allen priestern, daß sy gar wenig und selten ainer deß jars uber 2 mal peichten." *Chiemsee*, p. 430.

Therefore, even though observers rightly attacked their moral, spiritual, and intellectual condition, many priests did confess more often than the laity, sometimes significantly more. For the secular clergy, moreover, traditional expectations meant that they did not need to distinguish themselves particularly from their congregations in religious practice. Nonetheless, although on the whole the clergy did confess more frequently than the laity, their compliance depended on individual choices. In the absence of visitations or a sure mechanism to enforce discipline, it was as it had always been—a haphazard, largely unsupervised process.

Despite the logical connection between clerical frequency, piety, and learning, no such relationship is evident empirically. One can find in thoroughly Catholic parishes apparently devout pastors who confessed only annually, while some priests who confessed more frequently proved to be almost scandalously unlearned. Nor did confession, for most of the clergy, indicate Martin Luther's problem; an anguished conscience driven to but unsatisfied by repeated penance simply did not exist as a significant issue. Officials recognized that the problem was quite the opposite: priests did not receive the sacraments frequently enough. Nor were the inhabitants of monasteries unduly troubled in conscience. It is, however, possible that by mid-century, clerics with terrorized consciences had already become Protestant.

Nonetheless, by this time the Roman Church clearly viewed increased clerical reception as a necessity. Irregular confession by the clergy was a serious problem, because it meant that a significant number of priests lived without spiritual supervision and that disciplining clerical morals, universally acknowledged as lamentable, was difficult if not impossible. Without regular confession to someone in a position to counsel and to correct, the Church could not hope to exert control over the clergy's beliefs or behavior. The 1569 Synod of Salzburg recognized this: "This especially is not to be passed over, but given the greatest consideration, that many priests who daily offend God gravely, scandalize their neighbors, perpetrating many iniquities, omit the confession of their sins, or confess them only once a year."[100] Church officials reasonably linked infrequent clerical confession to moral laxity, but the visitations do not contain enough evi-

---

[100] Salzburg (1569), *CG*, vol. 7, p. 349.

dence either to corroborate or to reject this view. In any case, more frequent penance would have enabled officials to supervise and to correct
priestly morals, to attack heresy, and to check the clergy's knowledge of
the faith—although, as has been noted, frequency neither implied education nor guaranteed perfect orthodoxy.[101]

The sporadic nature of clerical confession had another implication recognized by concerned officials. Once again, the Salzburg synod stated the
issue:

> If the laity, through the precept *saltem semel per anno*, are obliged to confess, in
> order to please God, and counsel their consciences, and satisfy the church; how
> much more ought priests [confess], who daily should pray to God for them-
> selves and the people, and often handle Divine mysteries, not only once in the
> year, but whenever they know themselves to have offended God mortally, and
> they should comprehend they are to do this that they might spotlessly assist
> Almighty God.[102]

The clergy's exalted position in the church demanded a greater degree of
purity from them than from the laity, and this entailed more frequent recourse to penance. The reverse might also hold: if the clergy were not purer
than the laity, if indeed the two were indistinguishable in their behavior,
how could priests justify or claim special status? This issue surfaced, for
example, in the Bavarian report to Peter Canisius, when peasants in lower
Bavaria refused the sacraments from Catholic clergymen who remained in
a state of moral turpitude and preferred a morally fit Lutheran.

A similar issue was raised by evidence of infrequent confession in
monasteries. If monks had only occasional recourse to this sacrament,
then how could monastic life be construed as superior to lay life? How
could monks claim their place as professional holy men praying for society and for individuals? Clerical morality was a matter not only of discipline but of the religious worth of traditional Christian institutions under
assault from Protestant innovations.

---

[101] One pastor accustomed to confessing twice a month, quite frequent for the sixteenth century, proved himself learned in all things except that he "absolves without
special enumeration" ("absolviert sine speciale enumeratione") of sins. *Freising*, p. 439.
Yet another, who confessed on a monthly basis, was described as "an unlearned priest,
knowing almost no word of Latin" ("ain ungelerter priester, schier kain wort latein").
Ibid., p. 341.

[102] Salzburg (1569), *CG*, vol. 7, p. 349.

Determining the overall frequency of reception in the mid-sixteenth century in part reveals the state of affairs between the old Church and its subjects, lay or clerical, as well as the relations between clergy and laity. While it cannot be doubted that some individuals might have frequent recourse to the sacrament, the visitation records show that, by and large, confession was not a close spiritual encounter between priest and confessant with great significance for lay religious life or piety. The same records also show that the Church had continued to accept this situation. By mid-century, authorities in Germany were only beginning to encourage a dramatic increase in the frequency of lay reception, and as long as the laity accepted the *confessio bina*, the Church seemed content. Authorities reacted differently to the pattern of sporadic clerical reception, however, which they plainly found intolerable.

### General Confession at Mid-Century

The Council of Trent made its will perfectly clear on the question of whether sins could be confessed generally or must be declared specifically and in detail:

> From the institution of the sacrament of penance as already explained, the universal Church has always understood that the complete confession of sins was also instituted by the Lord and is by divine law necessary for all who have fallen after baptism; because our Lord Jesus Christ, when about to ascend from earth to heaven, left behind Him priests, His own vicars, as rulers and judges, to whom all the mortal sins into which the faithful of Christ may have fallen should be brought in order that they may, in virtue of the power of the keys, pronounce the sentence of remission or retention of sins. For it is evident that priests could not have exercised this judgment without a knowledge of the matter, nor could they have observed justice in imposing penalties, had the faithful declared their sins in general only and not specifically and one by one. From which it is clear that all mortal sins of which they have knowledge after a diligent self-examination, must be enumerated by the penitents in confession, even though they are most secret and have been committed only against the two last precepts of the Decalogue; which sins sometimes injure the soul more grievously and are more dangerous than those that are committed openly.[103]

Trent concentrated on defending the individual, secret revelation of specific faults. In order to be valid, the sacramental formula must be pro-

---

[103] H. J. Schroeder, ed., *Canons and Decrees of the Council of Trent* (1978), 14.5, pp. 92–93.

nounced over individuals, not generally over a group or congregation, and only after the specific listing of mortal sins, not after mere general confession. For the medieval Church, this constituted the sacrament of penance. Although other *fora* for penance and absolution existed in late-medieval practice, scholastic theologians, as has been seen, had long since agreed that they lacked all sacramental character and were only efficacious in releasing venial sins. General or public confession and absolution received scant attention at the Council.[104] This was true as well of the revered custom of a general confession and absolution pronounced on Holy Thursday and of the German tradition of *offene Schuld*—the vernacular public confession regularly declaimed by the congregation during Sunday Mass.[105]

The vernacular general confession said during the mass was a long-standing German tradition. Thus, while Trent itself ignored the question of general confession and absolution, the situation in German lands was very different indeed. In 1576, the papal nuncio in southern Germany, wrote to the curia describing the pitiable state of the old Church in the Diocese of Augsburg. Among the abuses, he noted, "through the ignorance of the parish priest, confessions in the diocese, if they are made, are mostly in general." He remarked further that no one cared for "reserved cases" and that "all are absolved commonly." Similarly, in a 1577 description of religious practice in his diocese, Bishop Urban of Passau wrote that "personal confession is neglected by many. There is only general confession and absolution without differentiation and without confession of different sins individually."[106]

Observations such as these from scandalized ecclesiastics disclose aberrations in the traditional practice of confessing sins, but where this problem occurred in the penitential process remains unclear. As a topic for Catholic Reformers in the sixteenth century, "general confession" might

---

[104] Arendt, *Bußsakrament*, p. 198.

[105] Ibid., p. 197. See also Josef Jungmann, *Die lateinischen Bußriten in ihrer geschichtlichen Entwicklung* (1932), p. 289f.

[106] *Nuntiaturberichte aus Deutschland*, cited in Josef Oswald, "Der päpstliche Nuntius Ninguarda und die tridentinische Reform des Bistums Passau (1578–1583)," *Ostbaierische Grenzmarken. Passauer Jahrbuch für Geschichte, Kunst und Volkskunde* 17 (1975): 20. See also Karl Schellhass, *Der dominikaner Felician Ninguarda und die Gegenreformation in Süddeutschland und Österreich 1560–1583* (1930), vol. 1, p. 269.

involve simple refusal to detail sins, but it also might refer to the traditional, public (and general) confession of sins, either in the Mass or on
Holy Thursday, which might be mistaken for, or converted into, an actual
absolution. The practice was retained by Protestants in reforming the Eucharistic celebration. It must be added here that, since the open confession
was acknowledged even in Catholic circles to forgive *venial* sins, any confusion about the difference between mortal and venial sins either by
clergy or congregation could also blur the distinction between the *offene
Schuld* and sacramental penance. Performed as it was, in the vernacular,
the general confession was especially susceptible to use by Evangelicals.

Examples of all these possibilities surfaced in the latter sixteenth century. Protestant practice and visitors' observations confirm the complaints of bishops and nuncios. The "Interrogatoria circa doctrinam" in
the visitation questionnaire asked pastors what kind of public confession
and absolution they used. Placing this inquiry amid questions about the
Mass and customs surrounding the sermon suggests concern for *offene
Schuld* pronounced at the same time.[107] Another question from the same
section addressed specific enumeration of sins, asking: "What does he believe about auricular confession and specific recounting and confession
of mortal sins, or does he teach that the general confession is enough and
that the specific [recounting] is not required?"[108] Later, in sections specifically treating the sacraments, the visitors asked whether the confessor
absolved penitents (*peichtkhinder*) after a general confession, without specific enumeration; they also probed the clergy's beliefs about public
penance and its practice.[109] The clergy generally answered that they held
Catholic beliefs on the subject, but time and again were unable to pronounce the general confession properly. Visitors' reports were filled with
responses such as "does not know well" or "he cannot respond in a
Catholic fashion."[110]

The problem seems not to have been that the *offen peicht* was adapted
to heretical purposes and converted into a general absolution. The real
problem, according to the visitation, was that many people attempted to

[107] *Freising*, p. 73.
[108] Ibid., p. 44.
[109] Ibid., pp. 46–47.
[110] Ibid., pp. 653, 656.

receive absolution without recounting specific sins, although they maintained the traditional process in most other respects.

In Bavarian territories, such practices seem to have been rare. The visitation for Freising, as well as the Chiemsee and Regensburg, indicates that in most parishes, specific enumeration was demanded by the clergy and provided, however reluctantly, by the laity. Despite dire claims by ecclesiastical officials, practices in mid-sixteenth-century Bavaria appear on the whole to have been continuous with pre-Reformation customs. Throughout the Salzburg ecclesiastical province and in other parts of Austria, in contrast, the visitation records suggest that significant numbers of people were unwilling to detail their sins during confession. Naturally enough, this occurred in areas and parishes influenced by Protestant beliefs. However, in a surprisingly large number of cases, even in securely Catholic parishes, many refused to detail individual sins but continued to hope for and receive absolution from their pastors.

Geographical areas in which the new beliefs dominated or achieved a significant, visible presence resisted attempts to enforce specific confession. In Neukirchen, the pastor was thoroughly Catholic.[111] His parishioners, however, were another matter:

> [They] do not want to sing the old Catholic songs any more. . . . When on Saturday he goes around, he has no one who will add to the offering. . . . His parishioners die without the sacrament, rather than receive it under one species. He announces the procession, but no one goes with him. He permits no sects to baptize children, therefore they take the children out of the parish to another place. . . . The pastor and mass priest go to the processions but no one else. The sectarians do not go to mass, but to the sermon, and that seldom.[112]

In the village parish of Au, near the Protestant-influenced town of Rosenheim (in eastern Bavaria), the new Catholic pastor contended with the work of his Protestant predecessor.[113] As a result:

---

[111] Ibid., p. 523.

[112] "Sein pfarrleuth wellen die alten catholischen gsang nit mer singen. . . . Wann er am sambstag umbgeet, hat er niemandt, der im den weichkessel nachtrueg. . . . Seine pfarrleuth sterben on das sacrament, ehe sys sub una specie wellen nemen. Verkündt die creutzgeng, aber niemandt get mit. Last kainen sectischen kinder höben, derhalben die kinder aus der pfarr an andere ort getragen. . . . Zum creutzgengen get pfarrer und meßner, sonst schier gar niemandt. Die sectischen geen nit zu der meß, aber zu der predig, und das sellten." Ibid., p. 524.

[113] According to Hans Rößler, the leading historian of Protestantism in the diocese, the previous pastor was Johann Salzhuber, a Protestant. See ibid., p. 557, and Rößler, *Geschichte und Strukturen*, pp. 148–151, 159–162, 168.

His parishioners sing German psalms against his will, and when he begins Catholic songs, they are silent. The parishioners eat meat on forbidden days and hold the mass to be nothing. When on Sundays he blesses with salt and water, no one will carry the holy water at the procession. On Palm and Candlemas Days they bring neither palms nor candles to consecrate, and what the Catholics want to bless, the others drive out with mockery. . . . There are 1500 communicants, among whom only 250 receive under one specie; the others go without the sacrament. From the previous priests in the parish, they began [to receive] under both species and to consecrate outside mass. Many peasants have seductive, erring books.[114]

Not surprisingly, in parishes such as these, adopting the new beliefs clearly meant denying specific confession. In Neukirchen, "The parishioners will not confess other than generally. Thereupon, if he will not absolve them, they leave."[115] It should be noted that the pastor attempted to question his parish over their sins, using the *Summa Angelica*.[116] In Au, "the populace shrinks from specific enumeration of sins out of pure stubbornness."[117] In Protestant parishes recalcitrance meant active resistance.

Similar conditions existed in parishes where Protestant influences were significant but did not dominate. In Aibling, a town close to the Protestant center of Rosenheim, response to the old Church was decidedly mixed. Although he had in his possession some Lutheran books, the pastor nonetheless seemed Catholic enough to the visitors. The parish itself exhibited the same tendencies. Some parishioners had Lutheran books at hand, the people were "undisciplined" (*unzichtig*) in church, they fled from the mass, and refused to provide for the pastor. Nonetheless, rejection was not total, for of the 1500 communicants, all but 60–75 acquiesced to receiving communion in one form only. Here again, the pastor lamented that the people "abhor" specific confession.[118]

Professing the new faith in Bavaria obviously meant rejecting the specific enumeration of sins. What is surprising is that even in securely Catholic areas where there was little or no hint either of Protestant influ-

[114] *Freising*, pp. 556–557.
[115] "Pfarrvolckh well nit anderst peichten dann generaliter. Will er sy darauf nit absolviern, so lauffen sy hinweckh." Ibid., p. 523.
[116] "Examiniert sy doch auf die articl summae angelicae." Ibid., p. 523. This examination may have contributed to their recalcitrance.
[117] "Populus refugit specialiem enumerationem peccatorum ex mera pertinacia, nihilominus tamen absolvit illos." Ibid., p. 557.
[118] Ibid., pp. 540–541.

ence or even dissatisfaction with the old Church, some people either refused to confess their sins specifically or were not required by their pastors to do so. Three kinds of nontraditional situations existed: first, entirely Catholic parishes where the priest did not demand specific confession; second, entirely Catholic parishes where the parishioners simply refused to confess specifics; and third, parishes basically Catholic, but in which minor evangelical influence may be detected to serve as the basis for refusal.

Of the first situation, in which the pastor or priest did not demand specific confession, only a few cases appear. In the Augustinian monastery of Peyrberg (modern-day Beuerberg), a priest who cared for the village of Degerndorff (Tegerndorf) responded well and in an orthodox fashion to all questions of doctrine and practice, with one exception—his confessants did not enumerate their sins in the sacrament. A striking incongruity existed: here was a monk who had spent twelve years in the order, five of them as a priest, and who not only answered all questions of dogma and practice well, but preached every Sunday from Catholic books. In the same way, the parish he served, which had some two hundred communicants, was completely Catholic and innocent of alien religious views.[119] Yet he did not require complete, specific confession. The same situation was found in Oberhaching, just south of Munich. In this parish of about one thousand and eighty communicants, all the priests were found to respond well and in a Catholic manner. Even so, one assistant, who had been a priest for ten years, absolved without any special enumeration.[120]

The education of these priests did not appear to have been defective in any way, for each answered all other questions well. This, of course, was not always the case. In the parish of Aubing, under the jurisdiction of Saint Peter's in Munich, one priest proved unable to respond to questions about the Mass, although he did understand the veneration of saints and knew the seven sacraments and the correct relation between faith and works. He was a priest who seldom heard confessions; when he did, penitents did not explain sins in detail but only generally. Upon hearing this

[119] Ibid., p. 494.
[120] Ibid., p. 439.

the church visitors forbade him to hear confessions, not because he was a Protestant, but because he was ill-educated.[121]

In these three cases the clergy, although Catholic, did not demand specific confession. More commonly, though, it was the laity who disdained the practice, leaving the clergy little choice but to comply. The parish of Aufkirchen contained one thousand communicants, all Catholic and diligent in worship, yet their priests could not bring them to enumerate sins in penance.[122] In the much smaller parish of Biburg, with its fifty communicants, the visitors found a pastor who: "preaches every Sunday and feast day. He believes thoroughly Catholic positions in all articles excepting the following: his people do not recount their sins in detail. He absolves even after a simple general confession. He explains they do not want to recount their sins in detail."[123] The same was true in Strausdorff, Buech, and Haidhausen, a parish just across the Isar River from Munich.[124] This occasionally happened in the Chiemsee diocese as well.[125] In other parishes and churches the experiences were similar. In Lengrieß, the cleric described his eleven hundred and fifty communicants as Catholics who attended the liturgy and sang Catholic songs, except for one suspicious Our Father. During feast days people were accustomed to drinking brandy, after which some might miss the day's liturgy.[126] There was nothing particularly Protestant about this behavior in early-modern Germany, yet the people here refused confession unless forced by the government, and in any case the priests absolved them without specific enumeration.[127]

Confronted with such resistance, clergymen could have refused forgiveness, but they often appeared more inclined to grant it. In Pruckh, a parish of eight hundred communicants, "all Catholic and not suspected of other religions," the pastor, along with the schoolmaster, affirmed the necessity of specific enumeration, but he admitted to absolving those who did not

---

[121] Ibid., p. 418.

[122] Ibid., p. 695.

[123] Ibid., p. 450.

[124] For Strausdorff, Buech, and Haidhausen, see ibid., pp. 632, 609, 444.

[125] See *Chiemsee*, pp. 213, 236, 243, 294.

[126] Ibid., pp. 477–478. This was standard practice throughout medieval Europe, a practice that both Protestant and Catholic reformers sought to curtail.

[127] "Sagt, er kund sein volckh zur peicht nit erhalten, wann im sein oberkrait nit dartzu helff. Absolviert, etiam sine speciali enumeratione." Ibid., p. 477.

confess each sin.[128] This was the case elsewhere, such as Biburg and Lengrieß. One should not conclude, however, that the clergy were universally willing to accept only partial or general confession. For all the evidence manifesting aversion, the visitation record indicates that specific confession continued to be the norm, and an abundance of examples affirm priests' determination to hear accounts of specific sins, even if their parishioners resisted the idea.[129] Nevertheless, the point remains that even within a solidly Catholic parish, untainted by new beliefs, authorities could not automatically assume specific enumeration for everyone. The congregation might refuse to make detailed confessions, or the pastor might not demand them, and in such cases absolution was still a possibility.

Such violations of the conventional theological requirements demand explanation. Certainly one should not underestimate the influence of Protestantism, and rejecting specific enumeration was a feature of evangelically influenced parishes. A possible reason for refusing to confess specifics was resentment, which of course also fed Protestant fervor. Among the congregations of Bavaria and Salzburg, the peasantry figured prominently among the defiant. A symbolic act requiring submission to clerical and ecclesiastical authority as well as a fee, confession could have a decidedly coercive character.[130] One need only remember those congregations that received the sacrament only in the presence of troops to recognize that, having been forced to confess, they would not willingly reveal intimate, perhaps incriminating details of their lives to the clergy.[131] Averse to the rule of both church and state, the peasantry's distrust of ecclesiastical authority extended to Catholic and Lutheran alike.

In Bavaria, however, the Reformation was not pervasive, and during both the 1520s and the 1550s the Bavarian duchy had undertaken strenu-

---

[128] For the pastor and schoolmaster, see ibid., p. 341.

[129] Ibid., pp. 303, 326, 341, and 422. In *Chiemsee*, see pp. 207, 213, 231, and 241.

[130] The peasantry may have had another concern as well. In Speyer, one peasant revolt in the early sixteenth century was foiled because a peasant had mistakenly trusted his confessor. See Gerald Strauss, ed., "The Articles of the Bundschuh in the Bishopric of Speyer (1502)," in Strauss, ed., *Manifestations of Discontent in Germany on the Eve of the Reformation* (1971), p. 146.

[131] This had parallels among Lutheran pastors in Austria, who complained, "Wenn man den Catechismum hält, halten die Bauern Tantz, Spiel und Kugelplan." See Tomek, *Kirchengeschichte*, vol. 2, p. 360.

ous measures to curtail evangelical activity.[132] More telling is that many of the cases cited involved thoroughly Catholic parishes. It seems impossible, therefore, to explain this refusal solely in terms of the advance of Protestantism.

One must also be cautious about blaming inadequate clerical education. Certainly church officials were scandalized by the low level of clerical competence and understanding. Nonetheless, learned and unlearned clergy alike permitted the practice, and the records indicate at least one priest described as completely unlearned, knowing no words of Latin, who nonetheless understood the requirement of specific confession.[133] The amount of time spent as a priest also made little difference, as the cases involved persons who had been ordained as many as forty-five years before the visitation and as recently as two.[134] Age among the parishioners was not a decisive factor, for in one instance the clergyman remarked that he could not bring the older people to confess specifics,[135] while in another the young people were unwilling to do so.[136]

Another reason for the unwillingness to confess in detail lay in the logistics of confession. The late Lenten confession put a tremendous strain on the clergy, in two ways. First, there was no time to hear confessions completely, and in Lent priests were forced to become assembly lines for absolutions.[137] Second, the crush of people constantly threatened the secrecy of the encounter, in which case specifics could reasonably be omitted.

In 1549 the clergy of Salzburg complained in their own *gravamina* about the laity's unfortunate tendency (perhaps deliberate) of delaying confession until Holy Week itself, when masses of penitents would descend

---

[132] Spindler, *Handbuch der bayerischen Geschichte*, vol. 2, pp. 309–317, 346–351. See also Strauss, "Religious Policy."

[133] *Freising*, p. 314.

[134] Ibid., pp. 341, 609.

[135] "Das allt volckh seiner pfarr will nit gern dran, die peccata in specie zuertzelen." Ibid., p. 432.

[136] Ibid., p. 361. The priest here also claimed that all his parishioners were Catholic, untouched by alien religion.

[137] According to Peter Browe, the size of medieval parishes relative to the number of priests available translated into many penitents and few confessors in the average parish. See "Pflichtbeichte," pp. 362–365. This would be especially true outside the largest and most attractive benefices.

upon their priests demanding absolution and hoping to receive it after a merely perfunctory confession:

> Although the double penance in Lent has long been a praiseworthy custom for many good and necessary reasons, yet disregarding this, many want to confess neither twice nor otherwise at the appropriate time, but crowd in, although in a parish there are over two thousand people or more, and demand that one give them the sacrament on three days, namely on Palm Sunday, Holy Thursday, and Easter Sunday . . . and many say barely two or three words in confession and want then to be absolved.[138]

Given the religious situation in Salzburg, this practice of delay may have had a Protestant cast. Yet there was nothing new about this. Medieval synods deplored lay procrastination and urged timely reception of confession. The visitation records bear out this problem, even in securely Catholic areas. In Freising, one priest claimed, "He often hears on one day some three hundred persons' confession, all of whom he absolves individually."[139] Although it may possibly have been the exaggerated statement of a harried priest, assuming the general correctness of this claim would lead to staggering arithmetic. Even if a confessor used the entire twenty-four hour day, the result would still demand 12.5 confessions per hour, or 1 every 4.8 minutes. Even with twelve hours, a confessor would have to hear twenty-five per hour, or one every 2.4 minutes. If one considers the entire ritual, with the general confession, prayers, and absolution, it is clear that the process had to be perfunctory at best in order to guarantee that an entire parish would be shriven in time to receive Easter communion.

In cases such as these, some priests and parishes adopted *ad hoc* strategies for fulfilling their obligations. In the Bavarian Chiemsee, a priest vis-

---

[138] "Und wiewoll das zwier peichten in der vasten aus vill beweglichen gueten und notdurftigen ursachen von alter her in loblichem gebrauch gewesen, doch solches unangesehen, so wellen ir vill weder zwier noch sonst zu gelegner zeit beichten, sonder dringen dahin, obschon in ainer pharr uber 2 oder mer tausent menschen seyen, dass man sy an den dreyen tagen, nemblich am palmtag, antlastag und ostertag mit dem sacrament versehen soll . . . und sagen ir vill in der beicht kaum zway oder drey wort und wellen, dass man sy darauf absolviers." "Gravamina per clerum provinciae Saltzburgensis in proxima synodo provinciali contra seculares oblata concernentia Austriam inferiorem et comitatum Tyrolensem," in Johann Loserth, "Salzburger Provinzialsynode," p. 285.

[139] "der gesellenbriester . . . hert offt ain tag bei 300 personen peicht die er all besonder absolviert." *Freising*, p. 353.

iting a hospital gathered the poor together, asked them whether they "recognized themselves to be sinners, etc., upon which he absolved them generally and together. This happened in haste and because [time] was
short."[140] Perhaps the priest was disingenuous about his reasons, but he
also claimed that he usually heard specific confessions, absolved on that
basis, and imposed satisfactions, all of which marked him as Catholic.[141]
Outside southern Germany, in the Catholic city of Cologne, the 1560 visitation recorded a general absolution of congregations due to the emer-
gency situation of absolving vast numbers of Lenten penitents.[142]

Christians crowded the church to receive the sacrament late in Lent,
and these throngs of people also made preserving secrecy a difficult, perhaps impossible task. Conversely, the desire to maintain secrecy might finally overcome even concern about scandal, and traditional strictures
about hearing the sacrament in a visible and open place gave way to the
need for privacy. Thus, just as ecclesiastical authorities' concern over the
dignity and performance of the sacrament increased, the issue of its setting grew more pressing. In Freising, Chiemsee, and Regensburg, the
most popular setting was the sacristy, which was in fact prohibited, but
priest after priest admitted to hearing confessions in seemingly prohibited
places, such as the rectory,[143] the storehouse, another room in the church,
or sometimes in the priest's own living quarters.[144]

The same practical concerns are apparent throughout the diocese. In one
church the pastor heard confession in the church, but because the parishioners were so "undisciplined" (*unzichtig*), the hired priest was forced to
hear confession in the tiny room in which he lived.[145] In this situation, it is
difficult to infer from the behavior of the parishioners anything other than
violations of privacy either by eavesdropping or by interrupting the

---

[140] *Chiemsee*, p. 372.

[141] Ibid.

[142] Franzen, *Visitationsprotokolle*, p. 330.

[143] *Freising*, pp. 565, 620, 764: "pfarhof in eim stübl."

[144] In the Chiemsee, confessors explained the practice of holding confession in their
own houses by pointing out how far away the church was, or how far people came for
confession during Lent: "Sitz allwegen im pfarrhof zu peicht, dann die kirch sey weit
darvon." *Chiemsee*, p. 295. "Im sagra hor er peicht und in der faßten im hauß vonwegen,
daß das volckh von ferne herzue khome." Ibid, p. 304.

[145] "Pfarrer hert in der kirchen peicht. Und dieweil das volckh so untzichtig, so mues
der gesellenbriester in dem thorstübel, darinn er wont, peichtheren. . ." *Freising*, p. 353.

process, an interpretation confirmed by other incidents. The pastor of the parish of Vörnpach admitted to hearing confession in the sacristy, also due to the "undiscipline" of the parishioners crowding in around the penitent.[146] The same was true in Sielenbach, where the congregation, described as undisciplined, attempted to intrude upon and interfere with the process.[147]

In situations such as these, it is not hard to imagine a penitent's reluctance to confess in detail. Nor, in fact, was it necessary to do so. If a threat to secrecy existed, the late-sixteenth-century Jesuit Nicolaus Cusanus (1574–1636) recommended that the confessant limit his or her account to venial sins, especially if broadcasting some mortal sin would cause someone public shame. The same was true if, because of great noise and outcry in the church, the priest literally could not hear individual confessions. In such cases, "it is enough to say the general confession and to absolve everyone at the same time. Those escaping such danger are obligated to confess all their mortal sins in their next confession."[148] Perhaps coincidentally, this advice echoes an event reported in the diocese of Eichstätt. A visitation of 1565 revealed that one pastor heard the confessions of numerous persons all at once and then absolved them together.[149]

The combined pressures of time and secrecy, set against the changes occasioned by Protestantism, may also account at least in part for some other practices attacked in the late sixteenth century. Felix Ninguarda, in his *Manuale parochorum* for the Archdiocese of Salzburg, detailed procedures that warned priests to hear confessions individually and secretly: "All priests must be warned, not to hear a penitent simultaneously with another confessor, nor if anyone, hearing another, plucks from it what is being confessed, should it be allowed to be given out: but he should command each to come separately from everyone (so that confession not reach the ears of another)."[150] Ninguarda's admonition in Salzburg was rein-

---

[146] "Her im sagra peicht, von wegen der untzucht des volckhs, das sy so seer hintzu tringen." Ibid., p. 262.

[147] "Hert im sagra peicht, deß volckhs untzucht und tringens halber." Ibid., p. 271.

[148] Cusanus, *Christliche Zucht-Schul*, p. 241.

[149] Adam Hirschman, "Bilder aus dem Leben der Geistlichen der Diözese Eichstätt um die Mitte des 16. Jahrhunderts," *Archiv für Kulturgeschichte* 12 (1916): 87.

[150] "Cavere autem debet quicunque Sacerdos, ne simul cum alio Confessario poenitentem audiat; neque, si quis, audiente alio, ipsi confiteri vellet, id fieri patiatur: sed ab universis (ne confessio ad aures perueniat alienas) separatim ad se venire singulos iubeat." Felicianus Ninguarda, *Manuale Parochorum et aliorum curam animarum habentium* (1582), p. 169.

forced in Passau in 1590, where the *Instructions* demanded that pastors be very careful lest "crowds of confessants overwhelm their confessors, as has happened in many places, but they must take care in order that [confessants] modestly approach the confessional chair one after the other."[151] In the next statute, the *Instructions* also expanded a bit of traditional advice about timely confessions: "Because it is impossible in one day, or in a few hours, to hear carefully and absolve great numbers of penitents, parish priests and preachers are to urge their people with the assiduous admonition, not to defer their confessions until the last days of Easter, or until the final hours, but to approach their confessors in timely fashion."[152] A synod in Brixen (1603) reiterated these rules: "Confessants are not to be admitted in groups, and they are to come away from [the other] penitents to such an extent that what is said between them cannot be heard. The population is frequently to be warned to confess in a timely manner, and not to put it off until the last day or hour."[153] Protestantism undoubtedly played some role in these situations, but the new faiths simply exacerbated a long-standing problem. After all, a Brixen synod had made a similar plea before, in 1449, seventy-five years before the outbreak of the Reformation.[154] Indeed, Ninguarda and the synods could have referred specifically to general confession and absolution if that is what they meant. Instead, each was concerned to create a physical distance great enough so that confessions could not be heard by others, even by other priests. For Ninguarda, the problem seems to have been too many confes-

---

[151] "Pastores non patiantur, vt turmatim confitentes confessarios suos obruant, quemadmodum hactenus multis in locis evenit, sed curent, ut a sede confessionali separati unus post alium modeste accedat." "Articuli circa Poenitentiae," *Articuli Reformationis, omnibus Parochis, Vicariis, Provisoribus, Cooperatoribus & Reliquis Sacerdotibus Episcopatui ac Dioecesi Pataviensi* (1590), Article XI.

[152] Ibid., art. XII.

[153] "Confitentes non admittantur catervatim, tantumque a confitente absistant, ut, quae dicuntur utrinque, non audiantur. Moneatur quoque populus saepius, ut tempestive ad confessionem se conferat, nec ad ultimum diem, vel horam differat." Brixen (1603), *CG*, vol. 8, p. 559.

[154] "Quoniam ex eo, quod populus consuevit differre usque in finem quadragesimae confessionem, tunc veniunt catervatim et simul fit, quod presbyteri non possunt, sicut opus esset, cum tanta diligentia et maturitate confitentes expedire; statuimus, quatenus curati studeant, populum sibi subjectum inducere, ut statim instante quadragesimali tempore ad confessionem se praeparent." Brixen (1449), in Bickell, *Synodi Brixinenses*, p. 24. See Chapter 1.

sors in too little space, and he specifically warned against hearing other confessions even by accident.

The Passau and Brixen statutes also forbade admitting people in groups. Once again, Protestant innovation may have been involved, but if time had become a pressing factor, the practice would have been an attempt to service large numbers of penitents at once. In Brixen, the 1449 statute had also warned that at the end of Lent people tended to come in groups and all at once. The synod admonished priests to warn their flocks not to put off their shrivings until the last hour. Records of synods in other territories reveal similar unusual practices that upset the balance between secrecy and visibility. In Metz in 1610, a synod complained about the "intolerable abuse" of hearing children's confessions simultaneously and prohibited this even in the case of children as young as seven years old.[155] Once again, the new churches may have been a source of such practices, but a more probable answer lay in the traditional patterns of confessing. The synod did not mention a true "general confession" or absolution but focused on children's confessions. This may have referred to a practice, excoriated later by the Jesuit Nicolaus Cusanus, of assembling young children of seven years of age, questioning them, listening to their confessions, and then absolving them together.[156] The fact that Cusanus was discussing first confessions indicates that the practice was a popular Catholic custom rather than a heretical one.

Possible compromises in secrecy were not confined to logistics or the setting of the rite, however. Earlier we discussed the possibility that the "seal" of confession was less than hermetic, with possibly serious social ramifications. For a confession to be valid it must be complete, but completeness necessarily entailed recounting intimate details of individual lives, and their publication was a constant danger if the clergy were not trustworthy. Hence a clerical proclivity to participating in village tavern life, as noted earlier, posed immediate danger to the secrets of confession, and in such cases theologians like Martin Eisengrein suggested that the penitent could

---

[155] Metz (1610), CG, vol. 8, p. 955. In Culm, a similar statute appeared, advising that priests hear confessions "with great discretion, and not in crowds, but separately." Culm (1583), CG, vol. 7, p. 977.

[156] Cusanus, *Christliche Zucht-Schul*, p. 266.

refrain from confessing a serious sin.[157] In addition, to reveal one's sins to any parish priest could mean social shame even if the transgressions were never made public. In Eisengrein's *Beichtbuch*, the question arose of what to do when a penitent confessed incest, or if the person with whom he had committed some private sin were related to the priest (his mother, for example). The question was not theological, nor was it even pastoral. It was a practical issue of one individual's standing in the community and the consequences of bringing shame to another. Even if the sin were never publicly revealed, humiliation occurred in front of the priest. Eisengrein proposed finding another priest ignorant of the parties involved.[158] Failing that, he even suggested that the circumstances and details of such a sin might better be left unconfessed.[159]

## Sacramental Confession at Mid-Century

The Protestant Reformation certainly affected the practice of confession in Bavaria and Austria. Its greatest specific changes were in curtailing the confession of specific sins and excising the traditional element of satisfaction. More generally, it may also have emboldened otherwise Catholic congregations to reject unwanted components of the sacrament, particularly the demand to confess sins in detail. In Catholic areas, however, the strength and influence of the Reformation should not be over-estimated. Except in parishes with deep resentment against the old Church or areas affected by the Reformation, sacramental penance continued to be received as prescribed and as was traditional, on a more-or-less annual basis during Lent. In some places the newer custom of *confessio bina* had also taken hold, although not enough to satisfy the Church. Within this framework, however, serious problems existed. First among them was the state of the clergy, espe-

---

[157] The question of priestly behavior was, of course, a grave concern in the sixteenth century, as it has been in every other century. Yet the issue had implications beyond simply moral standing. Catholic authors such as Martin Eisengrein recognized the social importance of priestly discretion and recommended that, if confession might be compromised by the confessor's turpitude (drunkenness, for example), then the penitent was justified in remaining silent. See his *Beichtbuch/ In welchem die ganz Materi von der Beicht/ So bey den Catholischen allzeit gehalten/ durch Fragstuck erclärt und darneben den Büssenden ein gelegne Weiß/ ihre Gewissen zuerforschen/ unnd ihre Sünd Gott unnd dem Priester zubeichten fürgeschriben wirdt* (1579), p. 302.

[158] Ibid., p. 278. In this he followed Gerson's *Opusculum Tripartitum*.

[159] Eisengrein, *Beichtbuch*, pp. 278–279, 282.

cially secular priests, who led lives not much different from their parishioners but whose ordained status made such lives unacceptable. More significantly, the clergy were themselves often ignorant of some of the crucial elements in sacramental penance: which sins were to be confessed; which sins they themselves could forgive and which were reserved to higher authority; why and how to impose a penance; and above all, how to pronounce the correct absolution. From the standpoint of penance as conceived theologically, this last concern was perhaps the most critical flaw, for if the essence of the sacrament was the absolution, if the sacrament was determined above all by the priest's pronouncing the formula of forgiveness, then flaws in that performance rendered the efficacy of the process problematical.

Four changes are especially significant. First, although private confession remained intact, the specific enumeration of sins was less secure. While most priests and parishes continued the traditional practices, enough divergence existed to cause serious concern to authorities and reformers. The inroads of Protestantism were no doubt one source of this anxiety. Even among the orthodox, however, questionable practices had arisen, either from actual refusal to confess individual sins or simply from ignorance and incompetence. Some of these practices may have been customary adaptations to the situation of medieval confessing, but even these had the potential to compromise the sacrament severely.

Second, although confession required absolute secrecy, it could not be guaranteed in the sacrament, and the evidence from mid-century only confirms the situation found in pre-Reformation penance. To some extent the fault lay with the ministers of the rite, who often proved inadequate to the task through incompetence, perceived immorality, or unscrupulousness. The very setting of penance, however, precluded privacy and jeopardized secrecy. The burdens of time and numbers that accompanied Lenten penance, as well as the requirement that every confession be heard individually within a short span of time, made the process difficult to complete without some kind of facilitating device. Logistically, the desire to keep penance public conflicted with the practical need for privacy, and the twin requirements of the medieval sacrament—openness and secrecy—came ever more tensely into conflict. The balance between secret confession and public process would have to be altered for the sacrament to succeed.

The third important fact disclosed by the records is the difficulty of sorting out and identifying orthodox Catholics in the fluid religious situation of the sixteenth century. An unusual formula of absolution, ignorance of reserved cases, neglect of specific enumeration, or even omission of a saint from prayer—each might indicate that new, unorthodox beliefs were operating. At the same time, visitors found each of these deficiencies even among clergymen who were otherwise staunch Catholics. Few options were unambiguously Protestant or Catholic, and the tools available were inadequate to the task of sorting them out and defining them. The proper formula of absolution was unclear, so that one could not necessarily identify the priest as Protestant if he recited a different one. Even where the priest's religious allegiance was clear, however, his ignorance might be more a factor than his heretical opinions. Knowing who belonged to the old Church and who to the new was thus difficult.

Finally, it is clear that the Church had little control over the morals and education of priests and even less over the laity. As for the parish clergy, they were more similar in behavior, education, and identity to their lay "subjects" than was acceptable to the institutional Church. The laity themselves had little regular contact with the official Church outside the annual confession and communion, and other ritual actions such as baptisms and funerals. While one should not underestimate the significance of these ritual acts or their impact in medieval life, they were adequate neither for pastoral care or catechesis, nor for inculcating the discipline necessary to produce devout, obedient Roman Catholics.

In the end, the problems with penance at mid-century lay in the attitude of priests and penitents alike, for many of whom the sacrament appears to have been mostly a nuisance, albeit a necessary one, and concerning which many compromises had to be made in order for confession to work at all. The situation was perhaps best summed up by a "good, simple priest" in the Regensburg diocese, who "cannot [pronounce] the absolution, gives absolution according to his view of the person, happily goes through it cursorily, for the *Beichtgeld* is at times small. When someone gives him a good *Beichtgeld*, he says thanks, and absolves him pretty much as another. [He says] it is not necessary to recount all sins; the shorter, the better."[160]

---

[160] "Waist nit, wo diß sacrament eingesetzt, kan auch absolutionem nit, praucht absolutionem nach ansehung der person, gee gern cursorie hindurch, dann das peichtgellt sey zu zeiten klein, wann im ainer ain guet peichtgellt geb, sag er im danckh, und halt ine bas mit der absolution, als ain andern. Sey nit von netten, alle sind zu ertzelen, je kurtzer, je pesser." *Regensburg*, p. 397.

# II

The
Catholic
Reformation
and Sacramental
Confession

# Prologue:
# The Council of Trent


The decree on penance issued at the fourteenth session of the Council of Trent on November 25, 1551, marked the first comprehensive conciliar treatment of the sacrament, climaxing the long medieval evolution and pointing to future developments.[1] The chapters of the decree contained a compromise for pastoral use, while the attached canons addressed more sharply the thought of the Reformation, giving greater definition to doctrine than the teaching chapters did.[2] Without resolving most of the issues that had bemused and perplexed medieval theologians, the decree nonetheless gave penance a measure of clarity in definition and theology. It did so not through startling originality, but by selectively canonizing contemporary thought, so that the theology expounded at the Council was in fact a miscellany of late-medieval scholastic developments arranged to condemn the Reformers without choosing definitively among the several branches of scholastic theology. As a result, virtually all the moderate medieval positions found some representation in the final document, while the most extreme stances were excluded. Trent also rejected or restricted several traditional possibilities, such as public penance, general absolution, and lay confession, because of their association with the Protestant reformers. What emerged was a doctrine that emphasized the sacrament as a private and individual rite.[3] These

---

[1] "Pénitence," *D. sp.*, p. 980. For the conciliar debate on confession, see Hubert Jedin, *Geschichte des Konzils von Trient* (1970), vol. 3, pp. 315–337; Spykman, *Attrition and Contrition*; Arendt, *Bußsakrament*; Valens Heynck, "Zum Problem der unvollkommenen Reue auf dem Konzil von Trient," in Georg Schreiber, ed., *Das Weltkonzil von Trient* (1951), pp. 231–280.
[2] Arendt, *Bußsakrament*, p. 125. See also Vorgrimler, *Busse und Krankensalbung*, p. 173.
[3] Vorgrimler, *Busse und Krankensalbung*, p. 187.

conciliar definitions could not, however, answer all questions or still all internal debate, as Jansenism and the controversy over grace demonstrated in the seventeenth century.

The Council affirmed the three traditional acts of contrition, confession, and absolution. The emphasis placed on the absolution, "in which its efficacy chiefly consists," demonstrates the Scotist inclinations of the text and its authors.[4] Similarly, the decree claimed special spiritual effects for confession and absolution: "Reconciliation with God which sometimes follows . . . is wont to be followed by peace and serenity of conscience with an exceedingly great consolation of spirit. The holy council . . . at the same time condemns the opinions of those who maintain that faith and the terrors that agitate conscience are parts of penance."[5] To counter the reformers' attacks, Trent stressed consolation as the end result of an integral penitential process that ended in priestly absolution.

The decree then took up the individual parts of the sacrament, beginning with contrition, "which holds the first place among the aforesaid acts of the penitent, is a sorrow of mind and a detestation for sin committed with the purpose of not sinning in the future."[6] In defining contrition, conciliar authors steered carefully between Thomist and Scotist elements but diminished the position that relied on Peter Lombard and upheld contrition alone as that which effected forgiveness.[7]

*Contritio perfecta* was marked by love of God and could work without the actual reception of the sacrament, while *attritio* (used here for the first time in a conciliar document), or *contritio imperfecta* as the Council also called it: "commonly arises either from the consideration of the heinousness of sin or from the fear of hell and of punishment . . . if it renounces the desire to sin and hopes for pardon, it not only does not make one a hypocrite and a greater sinner, but is even a gift of God and an impulse of the Holy Ghost."[8] The text did not define attrition as a disposition nor state what motivation was required from the sinner. It only described those acts

---

[4] Schroeder, *Canons and Decrees*, pp. 90–91. For the interpretation, see Vorgrimler, *Busse und Krankensalbung*, pp. 174–175; Poschman, *Penance*, p. 197; and Spykman, *Attrition and Contrition*, pp. 201–210.

[5] Schroeder, *Canons and Decrees*, p. 91.

[6] Ibid.

[7] Spykman, *Attrition and Contrition*, p. 218.

[8] Schroeder, *Canons and Decrees*, p. 92.

that had to be present to find forgiveness.[9] *Attritio* could not lead the sinner to forgiveness without the sacrament but disposed him or her to receive it. The Tridentine doctrine excluded a purely passive regret for sin and stressed a process in which sinners not only contemplated their transgressions with distaste but moved away from them and toward God and righteousness.[10]

To summarize Trent's position on sorrow, it is clear that a strong attritionist understanding prevailed at the Council. The problem of what kind of sorrow sufficed for forgiveness, posed early in the century and especially important to Luther, found modest, ephemeral resolution in the description of a minimum, but positive, act.[11] Responding to the Protestant Reformers, the fathers at Trent emphasized the value of attrition, in the process diminishing the contritionism that had caused Luther's anguish but certifying the theology that had provoked his anger. At Trent, though, motive was finally secondary to the sinner's willingness to renounce sin and turn to God in a new life. In reforming Catholic penance in the late sixteenth and seventeenth centuries, this fact would become central to practice and a source of new controversy.

Controversy over the act of confession itself dominated the conciliar debate, due to the ferocity and extensiveness of the Reformation attack. The Council had to find ways to explain the disciplinary function of the sacrament without undermining the consolation it was supposed to provide. For the Reformers, to require (even if only annually) the confession of sins secretly to a priest amounted to tyrannical usurpation of divine prerogatives and outright rejection of Scripture.

Confronted by withering criticism, the Roman Church sought to bolster individual confession in a number of ways, deliberately excluding the positions of Reformers while avoiding intramural theological controversy.[12] To affirm the necessity and possibility of confessing individually all mortal sins of which one was conscious, the Council turned to the idea that the priest was a judge and the absolution a judicial pro-

---

[9] Ibid.

[10] "the desire to perform the other things that are required to receive this sacrament in the proper manner." Ibid. p. 91. Fear was implied in the phrase, "the loss of eternal happiness and the incurring of eternal damnation." Ibid, p. 92.

[11] Jedin, *Geschichte*, III, p. 334.

[12] Schroeder, *Canons and Decrees*, p. 103.

nouncement.[13] Christ had left behind priests as "rulers and judges" who "could not have exercised this judgment" without knowing the details and circumstances of the crimes.[14] The very juridical nature of the sacrament as defined by Trent entailed specific confession, whether or not Christ had divinely instituted this form.[15]

The necessity of annual, complete confession of mortal sins followed logically from the conception of confession and absolution as a juridical affair. With this argument, the Council could refute the Protestant charge that sinners would understand specific recounting of sins as a form of "works-righteousness" and argue that they merited forgiveness. According to the decree, the significance of a complete confession lay not in the penitent's effort but in the priestly judgment based on an accurate assessment of the acts disclosed.[16]

In addition to this juridical defense, the decree explained that a complete recounting was in fact more sure and consoling than a lesser confession: "While therefore the faithful of Christ strive to confess all sins that come to their memory, they no doubt lay all of them before the divine mercy for forgiveness; while those who do otherwise and knowingly conceal certain ones, lay nothing before the divine mercy for forgiveness."[17] The very attempt, or even desire, to confess fully was tantamount to a full confession, for the penitent implicitly gave him- or herself to the judgment of Christ through His vicars and thus fully repented. In the post-Tridentine age, this "formal integrity" frequently held more importance than the "material integrity" of the confession, strengthening a tendency already common before the Council.[18]

Aware of Protestant charges that complete confession was an impossible, torturous burden, Trent sought to affirm both the benefits and the possibilities of a full confession:

[13] Vorgrimler, *Busse und Krankensalbung*, p. 182.

[14] Schroeder, *Canons and Decrees*, pp. 92, 93.

[15] Arendt, *Bußsakrament*, pp. 268–269.

[16] Ibid., p. 268. Other relevant literature includes G. Escudé Casals, *La doctrina de la confesión integra desde el IV Concilio de Letrán hasta el Concilio de Trento* (1967), p. 60; J. M. Pérez de los Ríos, "Confesión genérica, especifica y numérica en el Concilio de Trento," *El sacramento de la penitencia*. XXX Semana Española de Teología (Madrid, 14–18 Sept. 1970), (1972), pp. 345–371.

[17] Schroeder, *Canons and Decrees*, p. 93.

[18] Arendt, *Bußsakrament*, p. 276.

It is also malicious to say that confession, commanded to be made in this manner, is impossible, or to call it a torture of consciences; for it is known that in the Church nothing else is required of penitents than that each one, after he has diligently examined himself and searched all the folds and corners of his conscience, confess those sins by which he remembers to have mortally offended his Lord and God; while the other sins of which he has after diligent thought no recollection, are understood to be in a general way included in the same confession.[19]

Tridentine Roman Catholicism responded to the Protestant idea that full confession was in principle impossible by devising a system of practical steps to guarantee completeness with relative ease. These measures defined the practice and psychology of sacramental confession for the next four centuries.

At the same time, any apparent burden or shame caused by demanding a complete confession would be "lightened by so many and so great advantages and consolations, which are most certainly bestowed by absolution upon all who approach this sacrament worthily."[20] Here the decree focused on the end result, presenting all the elements as preparation for absolution, which would bring dawn to the sinner's dark night.[21]

About the contents of this secret confession, Trent was far more specific about what had to be recounted than earlier councils, which had either ignored any distinction between "venial" or "mortal" sins or had made no provisions for the failure of a sinner's memory. The authors of the Tridentine decree demanded confession only of mortal sins remembered after a diligent examination of conscience, "even though they are most secret and have been committed only against the two last precepts of the Decalogue; which sins sometimes injure the soul more grievously and are more dangerous than those that are committed openly." These sins of "desire" or "covetousness" had come under special fire from Luther.

---

[19] Schroeder, *Canons and Decrees*, pp. 94–95.

[20] Ibid., p. 94.

[21] One is reminded here of Luther's conception of penance as Law and Gospel—the conscience tormented by the demands of the Law (confession) and then relieved by the sweet solace of the Gospel (absolution). In responding to Trent on this point, Calvin did not reemphasize the process as burdensome in practice, but argued that no putative consolation can overcome the fact that Christ had not commanded confession, which by itself made the mandated sacrament a torture. "Antidote to the Council of Trent," *John Calvin*, ed. John Dillenberger (1975), p. 186.

Venial sins, on the contrary, "may, nevertheless, be omitted without guilt and can be expiated by many other remedies." The chapter noted that venial sins did not exclude one from grace, while mortal transgressions, "even those of thought, make men children of wrath and enemies of God."[22] The text did not, however, answer Luther's objection that distinguishing between mortal and venial sins was impossible. Indeed, medieval papal and conciliar documents had never clearly divided the two.[23] Even those theologians who presented a clear exposition (Aquinas and Gerson among them) declined to delineate specific acts as mortally or venially sinful.[24] Whatever sophisticated advice scholastics gave, in practice, lists outlining the Seven Deadly Sins and, increasingly, the Ten Commandments prevailed. These simple and much criticized lists provided what more complex thinkers failed to give, a functional guide to acceptable Christian behavior in everyday life, separating the serious from the incidental.[25]

One more element of Trent's treatment of penance remains to be discussed. The Council rejected the argument that satisfaction was merely faith in the restitution already made by Christ. Recognizing the vulnerability of Catholic theology on this point, the fathers at Trent stressed that all human satisfactions worked exclusively through the merits of Christ, without which they were useless. This applied to indulgences as well, which were considered to work out of the overflowing treasury of Christ's merit applied by the Church through the power of the keys.

The Council strongly defended the idea of supererogatory works, especially for pastoral reasons. Quite separate from the theological definition, the disciplinary element, with its clear hint of social and self control, should not go unnoticed. Satisfactions "check as it were with a bit, and make penitents more cautious and vigilant in the future; they also remove remnants of sin, and by acts of the opposite virtues destroy habits ac-

---

[22] Schroeder, *Canons and Decrees*, pp. 92–93.

[23] Arendt, *Bußsakrament*, p. 267.

[24] Tentler, *Sin and Confession*, pp. 144–148. See also A. M. Meier, *Das peccatum mortale ex toto genere suo* (1966).

[25] Vorgrimler, *Busse und Krankensalbung*, p. 129, laments the absence of personal moral decision in sin catalogues and handbooks, but the question of serious sin was not easily decided by theologians, and if confession were to be a moral teaching device, then instruction about specific acts must necessarily be included.

quired by evil living," said one decree.[26] The fathers of Trent had no intention of giving up the disciplinary value they clearly believed inherent in the sacrament. More positively, this discipline included making penitents "conformable" to Jesus Christ.[27]

Whatever theological ambiguities remained unresolved, the Council of Trent gave a measure of coherence and uniformity to the miscellany of scholastic theology of penance. Most decisively, it reaffirmed the obligation to confess specific misdeeds to an authorized priest. Concentration on the necessity and meaning of complete, specific confession was the central achievement of the Tridentine decree on penance. Pastors and catechists would preoccupy themselves more and more with finding a means of completeness that would enable the priest to fulfill his judicial function and allow the penitent to leave the sacrament with conscience scoured, prepared again to avoid not only sin but all its near occasions.

[26] Schroeder, *Canons and Decrees*, p. 97.
[27] Even here, the authors of the decree were determined to link this satisfaction to the merits of Christ. Ibid., pp. 97–98.

# 3

## "Festivals of Souls":
## Reforming the Rite
## and Structure of Confession

> Princes or republics that wish to maintain themselves
> without corruption must, above all else, maintain free
> of corruption the ceremonies of the religion and must
> hold them constantly in veneration; for there is no
> greater indication of the ruin of a country than to see
> its religious worship not respected.
>
> —Machiavelli, *Discourses*

Confusion characterized German Catholicism in the second half of the sixteenth century, a state of affairs that applied as well to private sacramental confession. Part of the blame for disarray fell on the Reformation, but
that was only part of the story. A rich tapestry of customs and rites that
varied from diocese to diocese comprised late-medieval Christianity, but
in the crisis forced by the Protestant Reformation, such diversity bred uncertainty. As visitation records show, many parishes could not easily be
called Catholic or Lutheran, nor could it be claimed that changes had occurred through deliberate conversion to a new faith.[1] It cannot even be
stated with certainty that aberrant practices were heretical innovations
rather than long-standing customs uncorrected by sporadic ecclesiastical
oversight. Regardless of the Church's commands, congregations were
quite capable of rejecting unwanted practices. When lay people refused to

---

[1] Even in some Protestant regions, however, confusion reigned, as people proved dis-
respectful of confessional boundaries. Parts of Inner Austria were claimed by the Augsburg Confession in the 1570s (see Tomek, *Kirchengeschichte*, vol. 2), but authorities had
trouble ending the peasantry's devotion to images or bell-ringing.

recount sins specifically, troops could be employed to coerce confessions, but the clergy might also simply accept the refusal, however reluctantly. In the absence of any threat to its sovereignty, the pre-Reformation Church had shown less interest in policing clergy or laity, and now in some cases it had few disciplinary options aside from brute force.

In the minds of Catholic reformers, religious upheaval had threatened not only the Church but the souls of its subjects, which had made administration of the sacrament extremely difficult. The old Church had now to find ways of defining the correct performance of penance and guaranteeing that Catholics receive the sacrament in the proper way at the proper time. Along with this external compliance, however, spiritual care required internal discipline, to make Christians willing to reveal intimate details to a priest and to act on his suggestions. Medieval practices were unsuited to individual counsel and spiritual development among lay people. Hence, Catholic Reformers had not only to enforce ecclesiastical discipline and guarantee orthodoxy, but also to create a system to care for the spiritual lives of vast numbers of people.

The present chapter examines the changes that took place in the ritual, setting, and circumstances of confession during the late sixteenth and early seventeenth centuries. The official documents of synods and the manuals and *Agendae* they produced reveal significant changes over the course of the century. Reformers backed by secular authority and even military power sought to guarantee obedience to the laws of the Roman Catholic Church. This meant making sure that all subjects within Catholic territories fulfilled the annual obligation of confession and communion. Visible signs of invisible graces, the sacraments also became visible testimony of submissiveness, both to the Church and to the princes who supported it. This meant, however, that the setting, the performance, and the content of the ritual had to be identifiably Roman Catholic.

In this reworking of penance, ecclesiastics sought uniformity in ritual, replacing the patchwork of local customs with specific diocesan formulae and ultimately with the *Rituale Romanum*. Sacramental ritual came to reflect the newly clarified doctrinal and theological requirements of the Roman Catholic Church and decisively rejected possible Protestant options. This trend is apparent in attempts to impose a single Latin formula of absolution while rejecting the validity of others, even nonheretical versions.

# The Catholic Reformation and Sacramental Confession

Catholic Reformers also introduced changes in setting, to emphasize the formal and juridical character of penance. Concerned about the rejection of penance as a sacrament and the idea of the confessor as judge, the Church undertook to ensure that the dignity of confession would be preserved (or established) and that penitents would recognize that they were in fact participating in a tribunal deciding the fate of their souls. The elements of ritual and setting became more central not only because of spreading Protestantism, but also because of the shocking pervasiveness of lay and clerical ignorance disclosed in ecclesiastical reports and visitations.

Changes in ritual and setting were supported by an attack on the public dimension of penance. Confession was private only during the actual enumeration of sins, but ecclesiastical visitations showed that the rule proved negotiable in practice. In the second half of the sixteenth century, penitential rituals were carefully circumscribed to preclude any hint of general, public, or lay absolution. Coupled with this change was a new determination to separate confessor and penitent from the congregation's potential intrusiveness, demonstrated in a new concern for privacy during confession.

But before the Church could introduce new rules, it first had to ensure compliance with the old ones. While Bavarian visitation records of the 1560s reveal that most lay people there complied with the precept of annual confession, this was not true everywhere. Institutionally, then, the first task of authorities after mid-century was to enforce the regulation of *saltem semel per anno* for laity and clergy alike. The Church sought universal compliance, in part through traditional measures such as posting the Lateran decrees or having priests admonish Catholics from the pulpit. New means of enforcement also came into use. After the Council of Trent, diocesan and provincial synods began to order pastors to keep records of parish events such as births, deaths, and baptisms, and of those who fulfilled their Easter obligations.

## Ensuring Compliance: Church and State

Spiritual reforms would have been futile without solid and muscular backing by worldly force. Fortunately for Catholic reformers, the goal of a uniform Catholic practice conformed to the interests of secular princes as well, particularly in Bavaria, where suppressing Protestantism made secular dissent in the Bavarian estates less likely.[2] Unity of belief and practice contributed to and displayed the harmony of an entire territory beneath a single God, a single religion, and—not coincidentally—a single state binding the whole and guaranteeing its purity. The genius of the Bavarian (and Austrian) Catholic Reformation lay in the blending of particular provincial cultures with the Church's claims to universality and the power of the state.

Wittelsbach (and later Austrian Habsburg) policy was not merely a bludgeon to crush Protestantism, however. From Albrecht V (1550–1579) to Wilhelm V (1579-1598) and especially Duke Maximilian I (1598–1651), the Wittelsbachs sought to fashion a *Bavaria Sancta*, a Holy Bavaria in which Roman orthodoxy and ducal absolutism interacted to build a uniform, authoritarian, pious, and disciplined state.[3] Central to this project was the development of a *pietas Bavarica*, a Bavarian piety inculcating devotion, discipline, and obedience by employing local religious traditions in the service of a larger Roman Catholic orthodoxy overseen by secular institutions.[4] The Habsburgs, too, incorporated Roman Catholic practice into the Holy Roman Empire, using the Catholic Reformation as a tool for binding together state, people, and Church, and for prying traditional lands from their opponents.[5] The goals of this policy are evident in the "Monita Paterna" [Paternal Admonition] that Maximilian I addressed to his son Ferdinand Maria in 1639.[6] Maximilian advised that Ferdinand carefully watch out for "corrupt evil morals" in his subjects and especially "to lead the common person to decorum and civil

[2] Spindler, *Handbuch der bayerischen Geschichte*, vol. 2, pp. 340–346.

[3] On this issue see especially Karl-Ludwig Ay, *Land und Fürst im alten Bayern* (1988). See also Walter Brandmüller, ed., *Handbuch der bayerischen Kirchengeschichte*, vol. 2, *Von der Glaubensspaltung bis zur Säkularisation* (1993). For the Diocese of Freising, see *Geschichte des Erzbistums*, vol. 1, pp. 290–312.

[4] Benno Hubensteiner has examined the piety of Baroque Bavaria in *Vom Geist des Barock: Kultur und Frömmigkeit im alten Bayern* (1967). Philip Soergel treats the concept of a *Bavaria Sancta* in *Wondrous in His Saints: Counter-Reformation Propaganda in Bavaria* (1993), pp. 15–43.

[5] Anna Coreth, *Pietas Austriaca: Ursprung und Entwicklung barocker Frömmigkeit in Österreich* (1959). On the Imperial Habsburg policy in Austria and the Empire, see R. J. W. Evans, *The Making of the Habsburg Monarchy, 1550–1700* (1979), pp. 157–195, 275–308.

[6] "Monita paterna Maximiliani, Utriusque Bavariae Ducis, S. R. J. Electoris et Archidapiferi, ad Ferdinandum, Utriusque Bavariae Ducem, Filium adhuc trimulum," in Friedrich Schmidt, ed., *Geschichte der Erziehung der Bayerischen Wittelsbacher von den frühesten Zeiten bis 1750*, Monumenta Germaniae Paedagogica, vol. 14 (1892), pp. 105–142.

peace."[7] In other words, the ducal policy sought not only to enforce moral and religious laws, but ultimately to bring the subject to order his or her life according to norms established by the dukes.[8]

To achieve this, the Wittelsbach dukes employed visible symbols and public rituals backed by a system designed to enforce their celebration among the Bavarian population. The sacraments exemplified this. Communion and confession lay entirely in clerical hands, and although the clergy had not proved entirely reliable, they were far more easily controlled and regulated than the lay population as a whole. By expanding the use of the sacraments, secular authorities also extended the clergy's control of religious life in Bavaria. The Roman Church itself believed strongly in the use of confession for social discipline. The *Roman Catechism* issued under the direction of Pope Pius V explicitly lauded this element of sacramental penance, arguing, "Another advantage of confession, which should not be overlooked, is that it contributes powerfully to the preservation of social order. Abolish sacramental confession, and that moment you deluge society with all sorts of secret and heinous crimes—crimes too, and others of still greater enormity, which men, once that they have been depraved by vicious habits, will not dread to commit in open day. The salutary shame that attends confession restrains licentiousness, bridles desire and checks wickedness."[9]

Even without the possibilities for moral instruction this presented, the sacramental rituals allowed authorities to command public religious life. Focusing lay piety on the sacraments and official liturgy, to which access was carefully guarded, made the official Church the center of both official and popular religion, as local customs were appropriated to official needs. Combined with a coercive policy of state-enforced orthodoxy, the Bavarian Church, especially, became a bulwark of Roman Catholic religion and politics in German-speaking lands.

The integration of state goals and religious policy which made Bavaria a model of counter-reforming activity began in earnest in the late 1550s.

---

[7] "Monita Paterna," c. 3, pp. 138–139.

[8] Karl-Ludwig Ay describes the process of "Polizey" teaching subjects to live and work according to norms established by the government. Ay, *Land und Fürst*, p. 185.

[9] *Catechism of the Council of Trent for Parish Priests*, trans. John A. McHugh and Charles J. Callan (1947), p. 283.

Duke Albrecht V, once sympathetic to Protestant interests, became increasingly antagonistic to them. Seeing Lutheran nobility as a threat, he became ever more determined to impose spiritual uniformity to enhance his secular authority. Albrecht preempted a potential rebellion of recalcitrant nobles by seizing the Lutheran Count of Ortenburg and suppressing his followers. Numerous other measures were employed to squelch religious dissent: censorship, heavy fines, and finally exile.[10]

Spearheading the ducal policy that upheld Roman Catholic orthodoxy while usurping the actual direction of religious affairs from the episcopacy was the Bavarian *Geistliche Rat* [Ecclesiastical Council]. Established in 1558 and backed at times by the even more formidable *Geheime Rat* [Privy Council], the Ecclesiastical Council supervised clerical reform, lay education, and discipline by conducting visitations and formulating regulations. The Council was to employ secular force to guarantee that lay people honor the Easter season with confession and for 'preventing all superstition, heresy, and shameful error,' as its mandate stated.[11] Communion and confession, the two sacraments demanded annually and controlled by the clergy, were used from an early date to indicate orthodox practice.

For parishioners who refused confession, especially in the countryside, force provided the best answer. Ducal or imperial troops were fundamental to reestablishing and re-enforcing Catholic power. Pastors in Freising noted that in some parishes rejecting the sacrament, only action by the worldly government had brought them to the annual confession.[12] This occurred elsewhere: in Passau in 1558, authorities in Geisenhausen were directed to threaten prison for those refusing to confess,[13] and in 1564, Jesuits investigating religious conditions in lower Bavaria imprisoned priests who could not pronounce the proper form of absolution.[14]

The policies of the *Geistliche Rat* were not limited to parish inspections, however, but demonstrated a concerted effort to compel compliance at all

[10] Spindler, *Handbuch der bayerischen Geschichte*, vol. 2, pp. 342–344.

[11] Annelie Hopfenmüller, *Der geistliche Rat unter den Kurfürsten Ferdinand Maria und Max Emanuel von Bayern (1651–1726)*, Miscellanea Bavarica Monacensia, vol. 85 (1985), p. 178. On the *Geistliche Rat* generally, see also Reinhard Heydenreuter, *Der landesherrliche Hofrat unter Herzog und Kurfürst Maximilian I. von Bayern (1598–1651)* (1981).

[12] See Chapter 4.

[13] Alois Knöpfler, *Die Kelchbewegung in Bayern unter Herzog Albrecht V* (1891), p. 66.

[14] Brodrick, *St. Peter Canisius*, pp. 607–609.

levels. Thus, by 1569, Bavarian School Regulations demanded that school-masters inform pastors about which students did not receive communion and confession. Day students were to obtain a certificate (*Beichtzettel*) from their own pastors and present it to the priest at school. In the absence of this testimonial, the priest had to report noncompliance to the local ducal authority, subject to punitive action.[15] In time, this policy applied to Bavarians in a variety of situations. Students, merchants, and others whose duties took them to non-Catholic territories or cities were required to return home to be certified as having confessed or communicated. Otherwise, they must obtain *Beichtzettel* from Bavarian religious agents, especially in mixed but heavily non-Catholic cities such as Augsburg and Regensburg. Failure to do so brought the risk of being excluded from Bavaria entirely.[16]

The process of enforced compliance in Bavaria was neither capricious nor short-term and indicates the depth and determination of the alliance between church and state. The records indicate that the *Geistliche Rat* continued to seek out and punish the recalcitrant throughout the seventeenth century, keeping lists of the "disobedient." In the sixteenth century, the main issue was reception of both bread and wine in communion, to authorities a sure sign of Protestant tendencies.[17] By the mid-seventeenth century, Protestantism had receded in the duchy itself, but the *Geistliche Rat* still noted that some subjects "wantonly abstained" from Easter confession and communion, which authorities sought to discover and punish by encouraging neighbors to keep watch and report deviance.[18] In addition, authorities continued to require oversight of Bavarian subjects in dangerous "foreign" territories such as Augsburg and Regensburg.

Reforms in Austria lagged somewhat behind Bavaria, due to the force of the Reformation there and the protection afforded it by Maximilian II until his death in 1576. In 1569, a synod at Salzburg produced specific pro-

[15] Ay, *Land und Fürst*, p. 201.
[16] Bayerisches Haupstaatsarchiv [BHStA], Geistliche Rat Protokoll, 1655. For other examples, see BHStA, Blech Kasten 34. See also Hopfenmüller, *Geistliche Rat*, pp. 178–179.
[17] The records of *Geistliche Policey* in the Bayerisches Hauptstaatsarchiv include lists from 1580–1646, naming those who had either communicated under both species or had not done so at all. See BHStA, Blech Kasten 34: Geistliche Policey.
[18] See the decree of 9 May 1641, in BHStA, Blech Kasten 34: Geistliche Policey, fol. 65. See also evidence from the Ratsprotokolle of the 1650s in Hopfenmüller, *Geistliche Rat*, p. 269.

grams designed to defend and renew Catholicism there. Of fundamental importance to this was the promulgation of a new *Agenda* detailing rites and practices for the Archdiocese and the adoption of a manual for parish priests, the *Manuale parochorum*, written by Salzburg's papal nuncio, Felix Ninguarda.[19]

In Passau, decisive reform measures began in 1590 when Bishop Urban von Trench published a set of pastoral instructions, the *Articuli Reformationis* (Articles of Reformation) for all parishes and priests in the diocese.[20] Among its important demands, stemming from the Tridentine reforms, the instruction required all pastors to know their parishioners by name and to record the names of those who fulfilled their Easter duties.[21] Addressing the issues already raised in synods (e.g., Salzburg, 1549) and later visitations, the *Articles of Reformation* for Passau provide a guide to the nature of late-sixteenth-century structural reforms. They embellished traditional admonitions, adding new instructions to meet the challenge of Protestantism and the deficiencies revealed by visitors. The twelve articles on penance affirmed the three parts of confession, the individual recounting of sins in detail, and the secrecy of the process, yet called for greater frequency of reception.[22]

Use of force was more critical in Salzburg and the Habsburg territories of Austria than in Bavaria, especially in the rebellious region of Styria, where political and religious disaffection from Catholicism was intense and where the Reformation had proved strong. Rudolf II's accession to the imperial throne and more importantly the active zeal of Ferdinand II, Archduke of Styria from 1598 and emperor from 1619, enabled Catholic Reformers to come to the fore and help the Habsburgs crush Protestant estates throughout the empire, depriving some recalcitrant nobles of their lands altogether.[23] Catholic princes counted exile among the tools employed to counter Protestantism. Together, the government and the Church formed

[19] On reform measures in Salzburg, see Ortner, *Reformation*, pp. 89–102. On Felix Ninguarda, see Schellhass, *Dominikaner Felician Ninguarda*.

[20] On the importance of this document see Eder, *Glaubensspaltung*, pp. 224–228.

[21] "Articuli circa observationem Parochianorum," *Articuli Reformationis*, arts. I and VIII.

[22] "Articuli circa Poenitentiae Sacramentum," *Articuli Reformationis*. These articles will be discussed below.

[23] For a brief discussion, see Geoffrey Parker, *Europe in Crisis, 1598–1648* (1979), pp. 86–94; Eder, *Glaubensspaltung*, pp. 15–172, 315–460.

# The Catholic Reformation and Sacramental Confession

"territorial commissions" which visited areas, sometimes accompanied by troops, to bring the populace into Roman (and imperial) obedience. A missionary priest of sure orthodoxy (often a Jesuit) sometimes replaced the local pastor and undertook religious instruction. In time, the territorial commission returned to survey the results. Where "peaceful" efforts failed, punitive ones followed. In 1612, the general vicar of Salzburg for Styria introduced a territorial decree requiring annual confession and communion at Easter time. Those who refused, the "Unchristian," were to have their names sent to the territorial government, not the bishop, for action.[24]

Of what such action consisted is shown by earlier processes in Styria. On 2 April 1604, the territorial reform commission of Styria directed the magistracy of Laibach to go from house to house demanding *Beichtzettel* of the population and exacting a ten-ducat fine from subjects who did not have them. To guarantee that the magistracy carried out these orders, the commission threatened physical punishment. As a result, a preacher, Christoph Spindler, was instructed that, because he still showed himself polluted by the Lutheran heresy and had not reconciled with the church by the previous Christmas, he must now either confess to an orthodox priest by Easter or quit the territory altogether. A woman, Wandula Stettnerin, also had until Easter to demonstrate her conversion by confession and communion or else she too must pay a fine and leave Styria.[25]

These forced confessions in Austria (and Bavaria as well) are interesting because they show reception of the sacraments to have been not merely religious acts, but visible signs of allegiance to the old Church. Obviously, they were meant to be public, not private, and their content would be no secret—everyone would know that heresy was the sin confessed. Confession to a Catholic priest symbolized obedience to church and state. Catholics themselves had every reason to want their own confessions to be as public as possible, to show their obedience and forestall punitive actions. Annual penance now explicitly signified something that had formerly been presumed—identification with the Roman Church.

[24] Johannes Loserth, *Acten und Correspondenzen zur Geschichte der Gegenreformation in Innerosterreich unter Karl II und Ferdinand II*, 2 vols. (1898–1907), vol. 1, no. 1951, pp. 616–617. This process is also discussed in Robert Bireley, *Religion and Politics in the Age of the Counterreformation: Emperor Ferdinand II, William Lamormaini, S.J., and the Formation of Imperial Policy* (1981), p. 37.

[25] Loserth, *Acten und Correspondenen*, nos. 1567–1569, pp. 342–343.

Curiously, despite all the discussion of motivation in confession, sincerity seems not to have been an issue here. The judicial machinery of state and church demanded obedience rather than contrition, and less thought was given to purity of intent and disposition than to affirming and displaying the spiritual authority of the Church. From the perspective of long-term Catholic reform, even forced confessions served a purpose. Obedience was an important part of the spiritual program, and authorities believed that forced confessions would ultimately become voluntary as subjects gradually became accustomed to the process. Present coercion prepared for later compliance.[26]

## Establishing a Uniform Ritual

While the Council of Trent sought to articulate a useful and unified doctrine of penance for the Roman Church at large, efforts were also under way to define and to clarify Catholic practice itself. Visiting authorities were often shocked at the diversity of penitential customs practiced in Catholic territories. The formulation and publication of uniform rituals throughout Roman Catholicism added another, visible element to the development of early modern Catholicism and helped to focus worship and authority on Roman models—a process aided by the printing press. The centerpiece of this program was the publication of the *Rituale Romanum* in 1584. (The *Rituale* went through subsequent editions, in, for example, 1614). The *Rituale* included large sections of doctrinal material in conjunction with each sacrament, and, as far as confession was concerned, followed Trent in defining the formula *Ego te absolvo* as the matter of penance.[27] The Roman process was recapitulated at the local level, with dioceses publishing their own definitive collections of rites, giving definite shape and character to religious forms in individual territories. Known as *Agendae* or *Rituale*, these local collections at first diverged quite dramatically from the *Rituale Romanum*, slowing its progress. After much effort, the general conformity of local to Roman rituals was finally assured in 1650.

Standing in the way of harmonious ritual was the lack of clerical education and discipline. This especially hindered adoption of the formula of

[26] Birely, *Religion and Politics*, p. 38.
[27] Gy, "Histoire liturgique," pp. 18–19.

absolution so critical to guaranteeing sacramental validity. Much of the blame lay in the clergy's own ignorance, of both the proper formula and the language in which to pronounce it. Still, the personal failings of the clergy were not the only culprits in the disorganization of German Catholicism. Structural problems also plagued reform. So unclear was the penitential rite itself that differences existed in the wording of the formula of absolution, and even clergymen attempting to follow precisely could not be sure of their own correctness. Even presuming a consistent rite, the lack of guides and handbooks prevented confessors from knowing the correct formula and induced them to use alternate, invalid, or perhaps even heterodox versions.

Compliance with a prescribed ritual demonstrated tangibly and in the face of many opponents that the Church was one. It also clearly and visibly separated Catholic from Protestant. For authorities in Mainz (1551), tolerating discord and dissension in divine observances made it difficult to sustain the Church.[28] The preface to the Trier *Agenda* of 1574 noted the variety of different ritual formulae currently in use; authorities there were specific about the danger of diversity, for out of dissimilitude, impudent persons might have the temerity to add and interpolate elements that existed in no other *Agenda*.[29] In the *Agenda* of Bamberg, to ensure that all the spiritual powers were subject to the episcopal see, even the use of rituals from other dioceses was prohibited. Here the immediate cause of concern is evident in the preface, which mentioned that many in the diocese wanted to receive communion under two species, a sign of Protestant leanings.[30] Consensus in ceremonial matters would preserve the discipline of the faith.

The wish to distinguish Catholic from Protestants (especially Lutherans) was particularly strong in dioceses where the new faiths had won legal rights. The Lutheran *Agenda*, produced in 1571 for adherents of the Augsburg Confession in Austrian lands, made it imperative that the Catholic Church specify and impose an alternative. The reforms instituted by the embattled Roman Church in the province of Salzburg after the important Synod of 1569 testify to this. The archdiocese published an *Agenda*

[28] *Agenda ecclesiae moguntinensis* (1551).
[29] *Agenda ecclesiae trevirensis.*
[30] *Agenda Bambergensiis* (1587).

to bring together the disparate rites of its churches, but still more was needed to provide commonality: hence, Felix Ninguarda's *Manuale parochorum*.[31] The seriousness of the issue is evident from the bishop's stricture enjoining, "all parishes and priests, especially those having the care of souls . . . that in administering the sacraments they conform to the laws and the norms of this book and do nothing that is not contained in these instructions."[32]

Anxiety over Protestantism was not the only issue. Unity in faith, ritual, and authority constituted one of the essential characteristics of renascent Roman Catholicism and sprang from the desire to bring all the pious into one body and under one head. The *Agenda Trevirensis* affirmed that ritual uniformity was no less important than doctrine, and that just as there should be one *Breviary* and one *Missal*, so too should there be one collection of appropriate rituals—one *Agenda*.[33] The Bamberg *Agenda* suggested that harmony in the religious "family" would come from unity in administering the sacraments, that a single practice would lead to uniform discipline and belief.[34] Ninguarda believed that diversity and inconsistency in the administration of the sacraments, especially of penance, brought dire religious hardships (in part because of varied, sometimes excessively harsh penances).[35]

Another important factor in seeking uniform practice was concern over the validity of sacramental absolutions being handed out in parishes and churches. Here the importance of a regular, identifiably Catholic ritual of penance cannot be overemphasized. In a sacramental system in which validity depended on the proper performance of the ritual itself, *ex opere operato*, defects in pronouncing the sacramental word had profound effects. In the case of confession, which theologians and the Council had increas-

---

[31] Episcopal *Mandatum ad Parochos aliosque animarum curam habentes*, in Ninguarda, *Manuale parochorum*.

[32] "Praecipimus itaque omnibus et singulis Provinciae nostrae Parochis, ac Sacerdotibus, praesertim curam animarum habentibus, sub poena indignationis nostrae, et Ordinariorum, et aliis poenis nobis pro arbitrio reseruatis, vt in administrandis Sacramentis, ac caeteris Ecclesiasticis muneribus obeundis, se ad legem et normam huius libri conforment, nihilque faciant, quod non sit huic instructionis consentaneum." Ibid.

[33] *Agenda ecclesiae trevirensis*, "Prefatio," Catholic reformers in Mainz, under the authority of Michael Helding, concurred. See *Agenda ecclesiae moguntinensis*.

[34] *Agenda Bambergensiis*.

[35] *Mandatum ad Parochos*, in Ninguarda, *Manuale parochorum*.

ingly defined as depending entirely on the absolution, variations in this formula could invalidate the sacrament and therefore the act of forgiveness. Hence, sixteenth-century synods demanded the use of one, proper form of the rite of penance. This was made explicit at Culm in 1583, when it was stipulated that the proper formula be learned, remembered, and always pronounced clearly and distinctly.[36] Similarly, the decrees and constitutions issued at Regensburg in 1589 enjoined strict observance of the proper rite of absolution.[37] In Passau the *Articles of Reformation* commanded pastors to employ one formula of absolution, that to be published in the *Agenda* of Passau, to the exclusion of all others.[38]

What the proper rite of absolution was, however, only gradually became clear. The Catholic formula as defined by the Council of Florence (1439) required the declaration "Ego te absolvo," ("I absolve you"), which indicated that forgiveness came from the priest, and intentionally.[39] The *Rituale Romanum* finally fixed the wording as follows: "Deinde ego te absolvo ab omnibus peccatis tuis, in nomine Patris, et Filii, et Spiritus sancti."[40]

Throughout the sixteenth century and later, however, variations continued to exist among Catholic reformers and catechists. Juan Polanco's influential tract on confession conformed to the simple formula in Latin, rendered into High German for pastors.[41] The same cannot be said of the absolution in Johann Leisentritt's 1578 *Catholisch Pfarbuch* (1578): "Et ego authoritate Domini nostri Iesu Christi, qua fungor in hac parte, te absolvo ab omnibus sententiis excommunicationis minoris et maioris, ab homine vel a Canone in te latis, et ab omnibus peccatis tuis, Deo et mihi confessis, contritis et oblitis, et restituo te in gremium sanctae Matris Ecclesiae, et

---

[36] Culm (1583), *CG*, vol. 7, p. 977.

[37] "Constitutions and Decrees for the clergy of Regensburg" (1589), *CG*, vol. 7, p. 1067.

[38] "Articuli circa Poenitentiae Sacramentum," *Articuli Reformationis*, art. III.

[39] Vorgrimler, *Busse und Krankensalburg*, pp. 152–153, notes that the description of the sacrament used in the "Decretum pro Armenis" was taken almost verbatim from Thomas Aquinas. The history of the formula is lucidly discussed in Jungmann, *Lateinischen Bußriten*, pp. 223–234.

[40] *Rituale sacramentorum Romanum Gregorii papae XIII Pont. Max.* (1584), p. 288. Cited in Jungmann, *Lateinischen Bußriten*, p. 234.

[41] "Ego te absolvo, vel (quod idem est) te absolvo, etc." A High German text for the pastor was equally simple: "Ich absolvier dich/ inn dem namen deß Vatters/ und des Sons und des H. Geists/ Amen." Juan Polanco, *Breve Directorium ad confessarii* (1560), p. 24.

participatione Sacramentorum."[42] This convoluted formula not only added to the confusion, but the phrase "confessis, contritis et oblitis" also added a potentially disturbing qualifier—were all sins forgiven or not? This theologically correct formula complicated the process and made the absolution itself potentially less secure. The same was true of Felix Ninguarda's *Manuale parochorum*, attempting to clarify penance for the Archdiocese of Salzburg, in which the precision of the formula itself resulted in potential uncertainty: "Et ego autoritate ipsius, qua fungor, absolvo te ab omnibus peccatis tuis, quae mihi modo confessus, vel confessa es, et ab omnibus aliis, quorum memoriam non habes, ut sis absolutus, vel absoluta hic, et ante tribunal eiusdem Domini nostri Iesu Christi, habeasque vitam aeternam, et vivas in secula seculorum."[43] The author was attempting to conform closely to the dogmatic decisions of the Council of Trent, stressing that the priest would forgive even unconfessed sins, so long as the omission was not deliberate. Given the demonstrated inability of many of the clergy to pronounce the minimum absolution, such precision might simply have confused confessors in his jurisdiction. Ninguarda's work actually contradicted the tendency of post-Tridentine *Agendae*, which sought clarity in simplicity. An easy, authoritative formula of absolution was not universally available in Salzburg and Bavaria until the seventeenth century, when local rites were accommodated to the *Rituale Romanum*.

A second problem had to do with the boundaries of the formula of absolution. By the sixteenth century it was customary to include two petitions known as the *Misereatur* and the *Indulgentiam*.[44] They were almost always included in *Agendae*, which often did not mark the absolution off from such prayers.[45] This seemingly minor problem caused major confusion, evident in the visitations of 1558–60 and the reports of other observers. Often the invalid formulae cited were mangled versions of the

---

[42] Johann Leisentritt, *Catholisch Pfarbuch* (1578), p. 58. This had been used earlier, in the Münster *Agenda* of 1410. See Jungmann, *Lateinische Bußriten*, pp. 230–231.

[43] Ninguarda, *Manuale parochorum*, p. 196.

[44] "Misereatur tui omnipotens Deus, et dimissis omnibus peccatis tuis, perducat te ad vitam aeternam. Indulgentiam, absolutionem & remissionem omnium peccatorum tuorum, tribuat tibi omnipotens, et misericors Dominus." Ibid., p. 195.

[45] See, for example, the Trier Agenda of 1574, in which there is no indication of where the formula of absolution actually begins or ends (*Agenda ecclesiae trevirensis*). The same was true of Leisentritt's *Pfarrbuch* and Ninguarda's *Manuale parochorum*.

texts of ritual handbooks. One priest omitted the formula "ego te absolvo," but used these words instead: "Misereatur omnipotens dimitat tibi peccata si contritus et confessis liberabitur pater et filius et spiritus sanctus. Noli amplius peccare."[46] The first part is a corruption of the *Misereatur*, while the "noli amplius peccare" was a common feature of the dismissal of the penitent, taken from the fifth chapter of the Gospel of John. Another quoted version read, "Ego misereatur Deus omnipotens absolvo ex divino autoritatet et dimittatur in nomine patris." Once again the source was the *Misereatur*, this time conflated with the official *Ego te absolvo*. Other versions included some corruptions of the *Ego te absolvo* itself.[47] Paradoxically, visitors criticized some clergy for pronouncing only the *Ego te absolvo*,[48] but this had in fact been cited by Johannes Polanco and Johann Leisentritt as the minimum correct formulation. Clear and consistent direction was lacking in the pastoral handbooks of the sixteenth century.

This problem existed in Bavaria despite earlier attempts to apply a uniform standard. In the fifteenth century, synods in Freising had printed instructions for absolution, using the correct formula.[49] Unfortunately, it was omitted from the Freising *Rituale* of 1484.[50] The bishop's decision in 1480 to have the statutes printed for the clergy may have placed the formula in individual hands, and indeed visitors nearly a century later remarked on priests reading the formula from a tablet or sheet, but the ephemeral quality of such printings made them only a partial solution to the problem, and many simply recited some other prayer.[51] The same formula, prescribed for the Salzburg province as a whole in 1490, was included in the Salzburg *Agenda* of 1496.[52] Yet copies of this *Agenda* were not in all the dioceses of the province, and the other defective *Rituale* had a se-

---

[46] Knöpfler, *Kelchbewegung*, p. 59.

[47] "Ego absolvete dimitatur et liberatur in nomine p. et f. et sp. S. Vade in pace." "Ego te absolvo peccata tua manu propria. Vade in pace." Ibid.

[48] See the observations at the beginning of Chapter 2.

[49] Freising (1480), CG, vol. 5, p. 513. This repeated the statute of 1440 (CG, vol. 5, p. 178). See Mattes, *Spendung der Sakramente*, p. 199.

[50] Mattes, *Spendung der Skaramente*, p. 200.

[51] "Plurimi sunt qui ex libro absolvunt, sed si illum non haben, recitant aliquem orationem ad placitum pro absolutione." This statement is cited by Knöpfler, *Kelchbewegung*, p. 59.

[52] Salzburg (1490), CG, vol. 5, pp. 572–597. Mattes, *Spendung der Sakramente*, p. 200.

rious impact. As a result, it appears that many priests who had no book out of which to read the proper absolution simply substituted other prayers.

The course of reform was to clarify and to simplify the formula of absolution, guaranteeing that it would be easily understood and performed. This is seen in the *Agenda* of Mainz, printed in 1551, which included a set of *Instructiones pro simplicibus sacerdotibus* [Instructions for simple priests]. Here the authors very clearly spelled out the absolution, taking care to mark it off from attendant prayers. The confessor was simply to: "place his hands on the penitent's head or make the sign of the cross with the intention of absolving, as simply as possible and without any additional clauses, enunciate this form: Et ego te absolvo a peccatis tuis, in nomine Patris, et Filii, et spiritus Sancti."[53] Adhering strictly to this form would leave no doubt that the absolution had been properly performed.

The clear delineation evident in the Mainz formula was only partially reflected elsewhere. In the Bamberg *Agenda* of 1587, a timely laying-on of hands also demarcated the moment of forgiveness. Yet the absolution itself was formulated in a more complex fashion.[54] The situation in Bavaria and the Salzburg province before the Reformation was equally confusing. As noted earlier, the Freising *Agenda* of the late fifteenth century omitted the ritual for penance, and no new *Rituale* was produced until 1612. Until that time, the diocese had to make do with reprintings of the faulty 1484 version. The 1496 Salzburg *Agenda* included the ritual for penance and specifically stated that in absolving sins it was sufficient simply to pronounce "Ego te absolvo."[55] For general purposes, however, a longer formulation was recommended.[56] Once again, the rubrics did not demarcate the *Misereatur* and *Indulgentiam* from the formula of absolution; this was duplicated in the *Agenda* of 1557.

[53] "Et sic tandem manu super caput Confitentis posita, aut facta super ipsum cruce cum intentione absoluendi, simplicissime et sine aliis adiectis clausulis, enunciet hanc formam: Et ego te absoluo a peccatis tuis, in nomine Patris, et Filii, et spiritus sancti." "Instructio pro simplicibus Sacerdotibus," *Agenda ecclesiae moguntinensis.*

[54] The laying-on of hands was to occur immediately after the *Indulgentiam*, to be removed directly after the absolution. See the *Agenda Bambergensiis*, p. 185.

[55] Mattes, *Spendung der Sakramente*, p. 201.

[56] Ibid., pp. 200–201.

# The Catholic Reformation and Sacramental Confession

Even official attempts at reform could complicate matters. In attempting to reform the Salzburg *Rituale* in the late sixteenth century, officials actually made the penitential process more complex. In both the *Agenda* of 1575 and the *Manuale parochorum* completed in 1577 but published in 1582, the rite was made even more cumbersome.[57] Neither the rubrics nor the wording clearly distinguished the absolution from preceding or following prayers. The *Pastorale ad usum Romanum accomodatum* authorized for Passau in 1608 and for Freising in 1612, however, continued the trend visible earlier in Mainz, Bamberg, and Trier. Most noticeable was the propensity to employ the simplest formula of absolution possible and to distinguish this from other prayers. Thus, the new books included the entire absolution from excommunication and sin: "Dominus noster IESVS Christus te absolvat, et ego auctoritate ipsius, mihi licet indigno concessa, absolvo te inprimis ab omni vinculo excommunicationis, in quatum possum, et indiges: Deinde ego te absolvo ab omnibus peccatis tuis, in nomine Patris, et Filii, et Spiritus sancti."[58] This formula also loosed the chains of excommunication at virtually the same time as the absolution, which was a discrete sentence, clearly understandable, even separable if necessary. In addition, the instructions clearly marked off the absolution from both preceding and following prayers.[59]

The instructions in the *Pastorale* also underscored the need for simplicity and clarity in word and gesture: "It is fitting to the form of the sacraments to be most simple, nor to contain anything superfluous."[60] They therefore cautioned confessors not to use superfluous language, and for reasons of simplicity specifically excluded the formula, "Absolvo te a confessis, contritis, et oblitis," advocated elsewhere by Leisentritt. As the instruction argued, these words were not necessary to the formula of absolution.[61]

---

[57] Mattes, *Spendung der Sakramente*, p. 42.

[58] *Pastorale ad usum Romanum accommodatum in Dioecesi Passaviensi* (1608), p. 53. This is almost identical to the Freising ritual published in Ingolstadt four years later: *Pastorale ad usum Romanum accommodatum in Dioecesi Frisingensi* (1612), p. 53.

[59] After the *Misereatur* and the *Indulgentiam*, the *Pastorale* instructed, "postea pro absolutione dicat." Following the absolution, the instruction read, "postea subiungat." *Pastorale Passaviensi*, p. 53.

[60] "convenit Sacramentorum formas esse simplicissimas, nec continere aliquid superfluum." Ibid., p. 54.

[61] Ibid., pp. 53–54.

A second point involved the physical gesture. Imprecision in the rite of laying on hands could cause confusion in understanding the actual sacramental form. The gesture made too early or too comprehensively could lead one to believe that extraneous prayers were also part of the absolution. To prevent this, the *Pastorale* specified that the time when hands could be imposed was limited to the absolution of the penitent.[62] As the imposition of hands itself fell into disuse as the gestural indicator of absolution, more and more emphasis fell on pronouncing the absolution properly. The theologically correct version offered the advantage of an easily recognizable incantation in a world where most penitents did not understand the Latin words pronounced over them and in which the traditional gesture of absolution, the imposition of hands, was being abandoned.

Adopting the Roman model in Bavarian territories brought order to the sacramental process by creating a specific ritual immediately recognizable as Catholic; ignorance or Protestantism could be easily and clearly discerned. At the same time, the clergy and laity, too would have no doubt as to what constituted the sacrament or the priest's decision to absolve. Finally, the question of valid or invalid absolutions, so important to pastoral theologians and observers, was settled by imposing a simple, recognizable form for all. Once the absolution was learned, or perhaps read from a handbook distributed throughout the diocese, the clergy would have a convenient tool for performing their pastoral duties.

### Changes in Setting and Privacy

In addition to fixing precisely the rite of penance, the later sixteenth century produced other changes, most significantly in the setting of the sacrament. One searches in vain among medieval practices for a single, universal way of performing confession, of positioning priest and penitent to define their relationship precisely. During the Counter-Reformation, however, ecclesiastical authorities hoped to eliminate confusion and impress upon congregations and clergy alike the formal, juridical nature of the process. As the post-Tridentine Synod of Augsburg (1567) pointed out, the sacred and solemn nature of the sacrament necessitated inviolable

---

[62] Ibid., p. 54.

rituals.[63] Where tradition did not provide such trappings, ecclesiastics were quite willing to invent them.

Two changes are evident in the Freising and Passau *Pastorale* of 1608 and 1612. First, authorities commanded priests to wear vestments—surplice and stole—for the sacrament. Since traditional depictions of sacramental administration showed the confessor in liturgical garb and the *Rituale Romanum* demanded such vesting, no innovation was involved. Yet the very fact that time and again *Rituale* and *Agendae* specified that confessors wear surplices and stoles when administering the rite emphasizes the measures taken to enhance the dignity of the sacrament. Such measures stressed the formality and gravity of the event and emphasized the fact that in the Catholic world at least, penance was as much a sacrament as the Eucharist and baptism.[64]

The second and more far-reaching change involved the setting itself. The *Articles of Reformation* in Passau were quite traditional: penance must not take place in some obscure corner or space, but in a public place where both confessant and confessor could be seen.[65] The later Passau and Freising *Pastorale* reiterated this but also instructed the confessor to be seated, "as a judge."[66] This directive expressed the Tridentine idea that penance was a tribunal with the priest judging the confessant. It was prominent in the mid-sixteenth century, with synods and *Agendae* advocating various measures to emphasize it. The Augsburg synod mentioned above referred to the priest as a spiritual judge,[67] and the Bamberg *Agenda* of 1587 advised confessors to carry themselves with appropriate gravity.[68]

In his *Manuale Parochorum* for Salzburg, Felix Ninguarda also gave the very traditional advice that one should avoid suspect areas and place the confessor's chair in the church, especially for hearing the confessions of women. Ninguarda explained that he meant by "suspicious places . . . bedrooms or angles accommodated to hiding someone."[69] Beyond scandal, Ninguarda saw another interesting reason for requiring public visi-

---

[63] Augsburg (1567), *CG*, vol. 7, p. 174.
[64] *Pastorale Frisingensi*, p. 53.
[65] "Articuli circa Poenitentiae Sacramentum," *Articuli Reformationis*, art. III.
[66] *Pastorale Frisingensi*, p. 53.
[67] Augsburg (1567), *CG*, vol. 7, p. 174.
[68] *Agenda Bambergensiis*, p. 185. Similar instructions were given in the Trier *Agenda* of 1573.
[69] "qualia essent cubiculum, vel angulus aliquis ad delitescendum accommodatus." Ninguarda, *Manuale parochorum*, p. 169.

bility and a strong sense of decorum: "There the sacraments, which are kinds of festivals for souls, are exhibited: not in houses, or whatever other place is advocated, and at whatever time one wants to celebrate, but preserving all honorable custom and the dignity of the sacraments."[70] As a "festival for the soul," penance should have an appropriately public and dignified setting. Ninguarda's *Manuale* was clear on the subject: the confessor, having already prepared himself, should draw away to a dignified place, and occupy it in seemly fashion, there observing the tribunal in the manner of a Vicar of Christ and a judge of souls.[71]

Despite these instructions, there was little mention of a *fixed* place for this celebration. That too would change, with the birth of the confessional booth in late-sixteenth-century Italy and its gradual introduction north of the Alps. But at this point in time, confession still occurred as it had during the Middle Ages: publicly, hurriedly, and under—at times—physically difficult conditions. All of these factors affected the quality and even the possibility of a complete confession.

The ad hoc medieval approach not only diminished confession's prominence in lay piety, but also permitted potentially dangerous variations to arise. When the setting of the rite was left to priest and parish, the variety of results, however ingenious, had disturbing consequences. The warnings voiced by Ninguarda and diocesan synods are revealing: priests were warned not to hear confessions along with other priests, not to admit penitents in groups, and always to draw away to a separate place where confessions could not be overheard.[72] The Passau *Instructions* expressed similar concern over modesty, individual penance, irregularity, intrusion, scandal, and heresy.

The confessional helped to change this, becoming a distinctive feature of Roman Catholic churches and a permanent reminder both of God's mercy and of ecclesiastical discipline. The confessional physically structured the ideal spiritual relationship between confessor and confessant, as it insulated them from the crowd to allow undisturbed consultation. The

---

[70] "ibi enim Sacramenta, quasi quaedam animarum epulae, exhibentur: nisi domum quis, aut quocunque alio advocatus fuerit, secusque fieri tempora postulent: salua tamem semper morum honestate, dignitateque Sacramenti." Ibid.

[71] Ninguarda, *Manuale parochorum*, p. 169.

[72] See Chapter 2, relying on Ninguarda, *Manuale parochorum*, p. 169.

The Catholic Reformation and Sacramental Confession

confessional also forced the sacrament to be given individually, not in groups. In the confessional, the Church could exert exclusive pressure through the mechanism of conscience cultivated within the penitent by catechism, education, and, finally, habit. Whereas medieval penance, though secret, had been a public event, theology and scrupulosity conspired to make early-modern confession both secret and private, although this development was certainly not completed before 1700 and perhaps not fully accomplished until the nineteenth century.

The confessional booth, hinted at in the 1550s, was perfected in Italy after 1565 by Carlo Borromeo for the Archdiocese of Milan and codified in his *Instructiones fabricae et supellectilis ecclesiasticae*, published in 1585.[73] Certainly the possibility of illicit contact between priest and female penitent was an issue, but Borromeo was concerned with more than simply scandal. He sought "to hear confessions in a convenient and proper way,"[74] establishing the solemnity of the sacrament and guaranteeing decorous behavior. Borromeo took great pains to enhance the sacred nature of the sacrament, and his ideas guaranteed the physical prominence of confession in the church building itself. Indeed, the reverence later accorded the sacrament may also have been Borromeo's creation. Furthermore, his design facilitated the long hours of patient listening that Counter-Reformation confession theoretically required.

Borromeo sought to construct out of fine wood a booth raised above the level of the church floor.[75] The confessional was to be enclosed on both sides, at the back, and on top, leaving the front completely open, except in frequently visited churches, where a latticed door with lock and key was to be attached, "to prevent laymen, vagabonds, or dirty people from idly sitting or sleeping therein, to the irreverence of the sacred function which is exercised there."[76] Another measure intended to enhance decorum by policing lay behavior was to advocate two confessionals, "so that the men do not find themselves intermingled or

[73] See Carlo Borromeo, *Instructiones fabricae et supellectilis ecclesiasticae*, in *Trattati d'arte del cinquecento*, ed. Paola Barocchi, vol. 3 (1962). For an English translation, see Charles Borromeo, *Instructiones fabricae et supellectilis ecclesiasticae*, trans. Evelyn Voelker (1977), hereafter referred to as Borromeo, *Instructiones* (English).
[74] Borromeo, *Instructiones* (English), p. 297.
[75] Borromeo, *Instructiones*, p. 65.
[76] Borromeo, *Instructiones* (English), p. 299.

crowded together with the women when large numbers are gathered for holy Confession. (When this happens one can discern irreverence to the sacredness of the place and the sacrament as well as offense to the pious.)"[77] Here Borromeo exemplified a trend evident in late-sixteenth-century pious circles, the attempt to separate the genders in religious and liturgical functions not only to prevent unseemly behavior, but because for many, any intermingling of the sexes was inherently a dangerous occasion of sin.

Perhaps equally important, Borromeo attempted through his design to separate one penitent from another by placing the confessionals, "in such a manner that the confessor be within the enclosure of the railings and the penitent be outside. By this arrangement, the chapel railings should keep off such persons as would rush up without order to the sacred confessional and locate themselves too closely to the person who is making his confession, to the likely disturbance either of the penitent or of the confessor."[78] The penitent and the priest, themselves separated and perhaps even invisible to one another, would be isolated from inquisitive and intrusive congregations, eradicating a situation common in both medieval German lands and in sixteenth-century Bavaria. Not only had the curious and indecorous crowd threatened propriety and secrecy, but the possibilities of communal or public absolution had afflicted Catholic reformers. The confessional precluded both.

Despite the success of the confessional in Italian churches (notably Jesuit) and its potentially universal applicability, Borromeo's idea did not win immediate acceptance north of the Alps and in Germany.[79] It was not even included in the *Rituale Romanum* until 1614. In German lands, where the goal of precluding scandal dominated, churches had already developed to some extent the tradition of a *Beichtstuhl*, with special chairs joined to a prie-dieu for the kneeling penitent. Thus, a 1567 synod at Constance mandated that confession was to be heard only in the church, in a

---

[77] Ibid., pp. 297–298.

[78] Ibid., pp. 303–304.

[79] Borromeo's own writings and work had much less impact in the Holy Roman Empire than elsewhere. See John M. Headley, "Borromean Reform in the Empire? *La Strada Rigorosa* of Giovanni Franceso Bonomi," in *San Carlo Borromeo: Catholic Reform and Ecclesiastical Politics in the Second Half of the Sixteenth Century* ed. John M. Headley and John B. Tomaro (1988), pp. 229, 243–244.

chair with a small table placed between the confessor and the penitent.[80] This otherwise traditional statute contained a mild innovation: the table.

Later, other synods elaborated upon these instructions from Constance. In the Diocese of Regensburg, the "Constitutiones et Decreta pro Clero Dioecesis Ratisbonensis" of 1589 were more detailed:

> in no case should priests hear confessions in a private edifice, unless because of sickness: and not even in the church, unless in an open space visible to the faithful, not however, as a large part of the Diocese of Regensburg is accustomed, in the sacristy, or behind the altars, or other obscure places and angles: but if by chance no place appropriate to it is to be had outside the sacristy, at least there should be a fitting confessional, in which there is a seat for the confessor, for the penitent a stool, on which he can kneel, and a suitable counter between them in the usual fashion, placed accordingly in the sacristy, so that through the open door of the sacristy both the confessor and the penitent can easily be seen by others in the church.[81]

A similar statute was promulgated in Brixen in 1603.[82]

Other voices, however, also began to sound. In 1591, Jacob Müller in his treatise on church decoration, *Kirchengeschmuck* called for a "box . . . enclosed on all sides, namely above, below, and on both sides, but open in front."[83] In the center, a partition was to be erected "as high, deep, and wide as the box itself. In the middle of this partition should be carved a four-cornered window . . . closed shut with iron or beaten tin or even a thin wooden grate full of tiny holes the size of a pea, not shut like a small door, however, but with nails driven in all places so that nothing can pass through."[84] Müller's described confessional, in which all confessions, the

---

[80] Constance (1567), *CG*, vol. 7, p. 493.

[81] "Cum Ecclesia proprius sit Sacramenti ministrandi locus, in privatis aedibus, nisi ob aegritudinem, Sacerdotes audire confessiones nequaquam debent: et ne quidem in Ecclesia, nisi aperto loco et conspectu fidelium, non autem, ut magna pars Ratisbonensis Dioecesis consuevit, in Sacrario, vel post altaria, aut aliis obscuris locis et angulis: Quod si forte in Ecclesia extra Sacristiam commodus ad id locus haberi nequeat, confessionale saltem idoneum, in quo pro Confessario sedile, pro poenitentie vero scabellum, cui genu flexus innitatur, et tabula intermedia rite accommodata sint, in Sacristia ita collocetur, ut aperta Sacristiae janua tam Confessarius, quam poenitens, ab aliis in Ecclesia exspectantibus commode conspici possint." "Constitutions and Decrees for the Clergy of Regensburg" (1589), *CG*, vol. 7, p. 1065.

[82] Brixen (1603), *CG*, vol. 8, p. 557.

[83] "Man mache erstlich gleichsam einen Kasten . . . auff allen Seiten beschlossen/ nemblich oben/ vnden vnd auff beyden Seiten/ vornen aber seye er gantz offen." Jacob Müller, *Kirchengeschmuck* (1591), p. 159.

[84] Ibid.

sick excepted, were to be heard, introduced Borromeo's idea to southern Germany. Completely open at the front, with no door even for the confessor, this version would guarantee the absolute separation of priest from penitent while retaining the visibility of the entire process.

In the north avoiding scandal was the explicit purpose of all these structures, whatever their design.[85] Both the Brixen and the Regensburg decrees specifically forbade using the sacristy for hearing confessions unless no suitable place was available, in which case the confessional must be used and the sacristy door left open. Officials in these dioceses sought to administer the sacrament in open church but admitted reluctantly that this might not be practical. Among German ecclesiastics, therefore, the "confessional" was first intended as compromise measure to fulfill very traditional functions.

No provision in sixteenth-century German synods sought to guarantee privacy through use of the confessional. In fact, however, confessors feeling besieged by curious and "undisciplined" crowds were frequently forced to retreat to the sacristy. Only in the sacristy could some kind of order be maintained. In northern Europe generally, the possibility of isolating priest and penitent from the crowd had become evident early in the seventeenth century. A synod in 1607 decreed: "There should be erected confessionals, which by means of a partition separate the confessor from the penitent, and by another partition separate the penitent from those following."[86] Here the rule was especially intended to separate confessor from women confessants but it also isolated the penitents one from another, thereby enabling confession to occur without public intrusion and guaranteeing that it would be an individual rather than a communal experience.

Although the impact of the confessional would eventually be great, one must not overestimate its early importance, for the development was barely begun by the end of the sixteenth century. The oldest surviving German confessional is the *Beichtstuhl* in Murau, Styria—a chair with a

---

[85] At Constance, the instructions about a chair and partition occurred in a statute about women's confessions. In Brixen, "If anyone presumes to hear the confessions of women differently, then he is immediately suspended from divine service and from the hearing of confessions." Brixen (1603), *CG*, vol. 8, p. 557.

[86] "Ubi erecta necdum sunt confessionalia, quae Confessarium a poenitente asserculo cancellato, ac poenitentem a sequentibus alio asserculo disjungant." Mecheln (in the Habsburg Netherlands) (1607), *CG*, vol. 8, p. 777.

A model confession from the Catholic Reformation. Georg Mayr, S.J., *Petri Canisii Societatis Iesu Theologi Cathechismus Imaginibus expressus* (Augsburg, 1613). Bayerische Staatsbibliothek, Handschriftenabteilung. This is one of the first German portrayals to employ a form of the confessional box. The penitent reads from a book, and it is possible that he is reading sins marked in a catechism or perhaps written down. Bystanders can watch the scene but instead politely avert their eyes.

Confession—a satiric view. Rene Fülop Miller, *Macht und Geheimnis der Jesuiten* (Berlin: T. Knauer, 1929). French woodcut, eighteenth century. In this frankly satirical account, confession is a setting for a highly visible scene that is more a social event than an act of piety. The bystanders are more interested in their neighbors' confessions than their own, as all eyes focus on the confessional, where the priest listens to one penitent while taking money from another.

prie-dieu attached, dated 1607. Jacob Müller's 1591 *Kirchengeschmuck* described the contraption, but actual devices did not appear until after 1600.[87] In the early seventeenth century (1602), a depiction of confession on the baptismal font at the cloister church of the Fraueninsel, an island in the Bavarian Chiemsee, depicted a penitent kneeling in the open before a priest performing the traditional laying-on of hands.

The *Rituale Romanum* of 1614 officially required a grille between confessor and penitent: "He should have in the church a confessional seat positioned conspicuously and in an apt place, and a perforated grate between penitent and priest is commanded."[88] Nonetheless, the *Rituale* of the Dio-

[87] Schlombs, *Entwicklung des Beichtstuhls*, pp. 41–42.
[88] "Habeat in ecclesia sedem confessionalem quae sedes patenta conspicuo et apto ecclesiae loco posita, crate perforata inter poenitentem et sacerdotem sit instructa." *Rituale Romanum* (1614), chapter 2.

cese of Freising did not mention confessionals until the edition of 1673. In 1612 and 1625, they echoed the traditional advice, referring only to a place as public and well-lit as possible.[89] Only in the mid-1600s did the enclosed confessional house described by Borromeo become the norm in German-speaking lands.[90] Even then, German synods made no mention of the confessional's ultimate use as a sacred setting for a private spiritual event.

Traditional goals obtained in devising early confessionals. Whatever secrecy they provided, the requirements of canon law dictated that early confessionals were far more open and public than the curtained and closed devices of the nineteenth and twentieth centuries. The device permitted the sacrament to take place apart from the congregation, enhancing secrecy but keeping penance strictly public and above board. While privacy was becoming more and more valuable, it was also more than ever in the interest of lay people to have the fact, if not the content, of their confessions observed. If obedience was enforced and omission punished by the state, as was the case in Counter-Reformation Bavaria, where people were encouraged to be vigilant about their neighbors' compliance, then a measure of publicity was an advantage, not a deterrent, especially at Eastertide. Only as communal ritual waned and spiritual counsel waxed did complete privacy, defined as total isolation from onlookers and the priest, become critical to receiving the sacrament.[91] Although this shift began in the sixteenth and seventeenth centuries, it was not completed until later. By the nineteenth and twentieth centuries, privacy had become so central to the success of confession that older confessionals were sometimes reconstructed to provide it.[92]

---

[89] "Sacerdos sedeat . . . in aperto templi loco: unde si tenebrae sint, etiam lumen habeat apud se, ad tollendam omnem suspitionem." *Pastorale Frisingensi*, p. 50.

[90] Braun-Troppau and Schmitt, "Beichtstuhl," p. 185. It should be noted that many of these confessionals were technically far more open than Borromeo advised.

[91] Assuming the privacy of the confessional, Jeremy Tambling argues that the confessional paralleled the *Panopticon* so fascinating to Michel Foucault [*Confession: Sexuality, Sin, the Subject* (1990), pp. 68–69]. In addition to its faulty comparison between the confessional and the *Panopticon*, Tambling's statement here is anachronistic. By design early confessionals did not provide isolation and anonymity. That came later and was, I believe, more a product of lay demand than ecclesiastical indoctrination.

[92] Many of the older confessionals in the Jesuit church of Saint Michael in Munich (1597), rebuilt after its destruction in 1944, were brought from the nearby church of Saint Cajetan. These renovated confessionals had wooden walls added to enclose the formerly open sides and doors added in front, blocking the view from outside and providing additional privacy in the front.

Even before real privacy became a reality, however, the confessional served a vital function: it made confession a physically prominent element of Roman Catholicism. Always present to remind the faithful of their obligation, the structure also provided a constant opportunity for the repentant. Because it was situated permanently in the church, the confessional booth gave the sacrament a conspicuousness and dignity it had previously lacked. This is demonstrated not only by the confessionals themselves, but by woodcuts depicting their use. Here privacy in the modern sense is still absent, as the crowds waiting their turn take a great interest in the proceedings. The event, however, appears at least decorous, a highly formal ritual embodying all the solemnity and display of baroque Catholicism. In the late seventeenth century, confessionals became more elaborately carved and decorated, paralleling the Baroque altars designed specifically to house and display the Eucharist, making penance itself a familiar but awesome object of devotion and a manifestation of sacred, Catholic truth.

Confessionals gradually became more numerous, especially in the late seventeenth century, making them a prominent feature of Tridentine Catholicism. Indeed, it was eventually impossible to imagine receiving the sacrament in any other place or any other fashion. Was this a matter of the Church imposing the device on unwilling lay people? The answer to this for early-modern Europe is by no means clear and the evidence hard to find. In France, some pastors abandoned the confessional because penitents refused to use it.[93] A different answer appears in a report from parishes in non-German Habsburg lands, in Apatine on the Danube near Mohács in Hungary where Christian armies had come to grief in 1526. According to the visitors,

> in the church itself there is no suitable place where so many and frequent confessions can be heard; especially where there are many deaf, stammering or otherwise hard-to-hear [people] due to the clanging of bells, the organ, and the people's loud singing, the confessor understands less than do the bystanders. Besides, since neither the confessor nor the poorly clothed penitents are in condition to endure a longer time without damage to their health during Advent, when all come to confess, or at Easter time, if the frost yet remains, so that even frequent

[93] In Sennely-en-Sologne, in the late seventeenth century villagers were unwilling to enter the confessional, because it implied guilt for some grave sin. As a result the local pastor stopped using the confessional. See Briggs, "Sins of the People," p. 323.

confession can become difficult and hateful, and it can therefore happen that out of fear of being heard, serious sins remain unconfessed. Since therefore this place has neither a suitable confessional nor can any such be set up, experience has taught, that if both the confessor and also the penitents are offered a comfortable possibility for confessing, the faithful are more inclined to make a correct confession. Therefore confessions until now were conducted in a separate room, in which the priest in an alb and stole sat in such manner that he could see none of the penitents. The closed door of the room however, has a glass window, through which all in the next room see who among the penitents goes in.[94]

Although this was not Bavaria, the situation was certainly familiar. Physical conditions discouraged long or frequent confessions, which would be trying experiences due to the numerous disruptions. Intimacy and counseling in such circumstances were difficult at best and impossible if the penitents themselves presented physical challenges. More important, the threat to secrecy also inhibited the recounting of serious sins, a fact acknowledged by the ecclesiastical visitors. Parishioners would only participate willingly when privacy was assured, when the penitent could be made invisible to the priest and the entire procedure sequestered from the ears of the congregation. Here were laid out all the problems and inconveniences inherent in the medieval sacrament, ultimately to be resolved by the confessional. To demonstrate how gradual this process of change was in northern Europe, one should note that this Apatine report was not from the sixteenth or even the seventeenth century. It was written in 1762, nearly two centuries after the publication of Borromeo's treatise.

The impact of the confessional in Germany and northern Europe was considerably less than complete throughout the early-modern period. The report from Apatine shows, however, that lay Catholics themselves recognized the potential difficulty of confession and were reluctant to participate unless their deepest secrets were protected. The ultimate success of the confessional and the process it enclosed depended not on the Church's ability to impose it, but on the desire of the Catholic population for privacy and secrecy in their spiritual accountings.

By the end of the sixteenth century, then, decisive changes had occurred in the setting of confession and its relation to Catholic piety. A uniform,

---

[94] Anton Selgrad, ed. and trans., *Kanonische Visitationen der Apatiner Pfarrei im XVIII. und XIX. Jahrhundert*, Apatiner Beiträge, vol. 17 (1979), p. 29.

recognizably Roman Catholic rite replaced the patchwork of local practices. More gradually, a new place was established for administering the sacrament in a fashion conducive to the private counseling of individual sinners, without communal or congregational intrusion. In the redefined sacrament of penance the Church had an instrument suitable for inculcating a morality of its own choosing, one suited to the hierarchical and disciplinary needs of the Catholic Reformation.

These changes can in fact be summarized as the simplification of the sacrament in order to facilitate and to encourage access for believers. Paring down the formula of absolution and making the ritual uniform throughout Catholic lands made the process less confusing, and attempts to guarantee privacy reduced anxiety about possible disclosure. Seeking to make the reception of penance and communion routine events in the lives of all believers, Catholic Reformers advocated frequent reception; the sacrament was continuously present as a regular option for the faithful. Did these efforts also alter the nature of piety itself, transforming the relation of the Church to the world, of the believer to the Church, perhaps even of the believer to his or her own conscience? To answer this question will be the task of the final chapter.

# 4

## "The Precious Jewel":
## Confession in the Everyday World

They say publicly that they are Catholic, but not Jesuit
Catholic, against which I say, also publicly: whoever is
not Jesuit, is also not Catholic.

—Georg Eder, Report on
Conditions in Austria, 1585

Traveling through Bavaria in the first decades of the seventeenth century, Philip Hainhofer, a Lutheran diplomat from Augsburg, described
the religious life of the Bavarian ducal residence in Munich: "They appear to be earnest yet friendly in speech: receive great obedience and
respect, they are quite zealous in their papal religion, confess and communicate often, go diligently to church and to council, and through their
fear of God, sobriety, Christian life and good example, they also make
their officials and councillors pious and diligent."[1] Hainhofer portrayed
the pious world of baroque Bavaria, epitomized in the person of Maximilian I, who reigned for more than fifty years. Sober and devout in affairs of both Church and state, Duke Maximilian served as a model for
his court and his subjects. This nobleman was not an anomaly, for all the
elements of his religiosity had been intensively cultivated among the
faithful from the middle of the sixteenth century onward, and by the beginning of the seventeenth they had become hallmarks of the devout
Roman Catholic.

[1] Christoph Häutle, "Die Reisen des Augsburgers Philipp Hainhofer nach Eichstätt,
München und Regensburg in den Jahren 1611, 1612 und 1613," *Zeitschrift des his-
torischen Vereins für Schwaben und Neuburg* 8 (1881), p. 79, cited in Dieter Breuer, "Ab-
solutistische Staatsreform und neue Frömmigkeitsformen," *Frömmigkeit in der frühen
Neuzeit: Studien zur religiösen Literatur des 17. Jahrhunderts in Deutschland*, ed. Dieter
Breuer (1984), pp. 5–25.

A powerful ingredient of the duke's piety was its frequent, even routine, recourse to the sacraments of communion and confession. Such practices differed markedly from those of even devout Christians a century earlier, and they reveal the extent of the changes wrought after 1560. A uniform, simplified, and increasingly private ritual gradually became pervasive, while officials determinedly sought to bring the population into compliance with Catholic rules. It remains to be seen whether, and how, changes in the inner, spiritual working of the sacrament proceeded from or accompanied these outer developments. This is a complicated task, for the traditional parts of the sacrament—contrition, confession, and satisfaction—remained unaltered, and all the characteristics that would become prominent in the seventeenth century were already present in the fifteenth. As will be seen, however, the relation among these various elements and their significance altered during the sixteenth century. Developments in external practice indicate important changes in the function of sacramental confession. Changes in structure finally allowed the sacrament to fulfill on a wide scale the purposes intended for it by medieval theorists.

## Changes in the Frequency of Confession

The determination of secular rulers and religious reformers guaranteed that at least minimal compliance with Roman rules would be enforced in Bavaria. But to achieve the Church's goals of uniformity and discipline, and of building a Roman Catholic society in German lands, successfully enforcing the precept of annual confession was not enough. Catholic Reformers also sought to increase dramatically the frequency of reception for cleric and layperson alike, a change which, however slowly (it had barely begun by the third quarter of the sixteenth century), significantly altered the sacrament of penance. Regular, frequent confession permitted closer monitoring by the Church of both the secular clergy, held almost universally in disrepute and considered prone to dissolution and heresy and the laity, vulnerable to Protestantism. Indeed, according to Felix Ninguarda, frequent lay confession was as important as clerical confession, since the laity were even less likely to refrain from sin.[2]

---

[2] Ninguarda, *Manuale parochorum*, p. 156.

# The Catholic Reformation and Sacramental Confession

Although an attempt was made to increase the frequency of reception as early as 1500, more intensive efforts became apparent shortly after mid-century in statutes from synods. At the post-Tridentine Synod of Augsburg held in 1567, the traditional rule and custom of Lenten penance was upheld, along with the observation that Lent was the appropriate time for the confession of sins. Later, however, the same synod exhorted the flock to confess not only once or twice or solely during Lent but much more often, at the principal feasts of the Church.[3] In the same year, a synod held at Constance made a similar recommendation; other synods later concurred.[4] Four or even five separate confessions, scattered regularly throughout the year from Passion Sunday to the Octave of Easter, Christmas, Pentecost, the Assumption of the Virgin (August 15), and the Feast of All Saints, along with "other solemn feasts,"[5] became the goal. In Salzburg, Ninguarda's *Manuale parochorum* stipulated that the faithful should confess, not only at Eastertide, but at various other times including Pentecost, Christmas, Epiphany, All Saints, and the Marian Feasts of the Annunciation and Assumption. The clergy were to exhort the faithful to such expanded reception.[6]

Local and individual efforts reflected these official demands, even intensified them, and the proliferation of literature advocating monthly and even weekly reception of confession (and communion) was striking in the late sixteenth century. That Catholic Reformers sought more frequent reception of communion, in addition to more intense attendance at Mass itself, there is little doubt.[7] While it was not completely new for saints or extremely devout persons to receive the sacraments so often, it was quite novel to suggest that this could ever extend to the entire laity as a regular component of religious life.

---

[3] Augsburg (1567), *CG*, vol. 7, p. 173. As noted above in Chapter 1, a movement toward more frequent confession was evident in Spain and Italy during the late fifteenth century, and Jean Gerson's views are well known. In Germany, this occurred much later, perhaps through the international experience of Catholic reformers appearing after mid-century.

[4] Constance (1567), *CG*, vol. 7, p. 490; Regensburg (1589), *CG*, vol. 7, p. 1066; Brixen (1603), *CG*, vol. 8, p. 545; Constance (1609), *CG*, vol. 8, p. 863.

[5] Metz (1610), *CG*, vol. 8, p. 956.

[6] Ninguarda, *Manuale parochorum*, pp. 112–113.

[7] H. Outram Evennett, *The Spirit of the Counter-Reformation* (1970), pp. 37–40.

In south German lands, the innovation found its greatest champion in the newly prominent Society of Jesus.[8] With their affiliation to the Habsburgs and to the ducal house of Wittelsbach in Bavaria, the Jesuits rapidly became both the major and the most controversial Catholic reforming force in Germany. In 1546, before the Society arrived in Bavaria, Peter Canisius wrote to a student in Louvain:

> I think you should concentrate your efforts rather on gaining young men than on winning over theologians and other such important people. . . . You tell me that you do not like the custom of more frequent Communion which has been introduced in many places. You point out the dangers that may arise, quoting what St. Basil says in his treatise on Baptism. But our concern is with young men serving their apprenticeship to learning. Surely they will not serve Christ the worse by more frequent Confessions and Communions? Where, I ask you in all earnestness, is to be found a more certain remedy for sickness of the soul and a better spur to holy living than in Holy Communion? Again, where do studies thrive best, where are the cold and apathetic set on fire most easily, where are men of the world taught with least effort obedience and the fear of God, where, finally, do married people learn best how to conquer and control the desires of the flesh? Is it not in those places where the practice of frequent Communion flourishes?[9]

Canisius displayed in this letter an awareness of the relative novelty of the practice. He also recognized that it was controversial; indeed, the letter was written to a student with strong scruples about the matter. Finally, while he referred to the advantages for students in schools, he clearly also believed that more frequent communion would most benefit the laity, those "men of the world."

Other Jesuit writers also expressed the Society's ardent belief in frequent reception for the laity. One member, the Italian Fulvius Androtius, authored the *Della frequenza della communione*, translated as *Seelen Speiß unnd Communionbüchlein*. As explanation for the book, Androtius wrote:

> Because little used, a beautiful, precious jewel, which, unknown, lies hidden, wrapped in cloth, in a chest, it has seemed good to me in this book to uncover

---

[8] On Jesuit advocacy of frequent reception, see John W. O'Malley, *The First Jesuits* (1993), pp. 136–137, 152–157; A. Lynn Martin, *The Jesuit Mind: The Mentality of an Elite in Early Modern France* (1988), pp. 72–73, 83; and Joseph de Guibert, *The Jesuits: Their Spiritual Doctrine and Practice* (1964), pp. 374–385.

[9] Braunsberger, *Beati Petri Canisii*, vol. I, pp. 207–209, quoted in Brodrick, *St. Peter Canisius*, pp. 77–78.

the precious gem and the rich treasure which every man has, to whom God the Lord has shared the grace of frequent communion, so that, when he sees and recognizes what a great consolation and excellent pearl he receives from the loving mercy of God, he will hold himself in the same love and worthiness, give thanks, and always be careful not to lose it.[10]

As in Canisius's earlier letter, Androtius noted that this "precious" practice was little-used and practically unknown. Instructional books of the period routinely admonished students to more frequent communion. In Münster, the *Underricht für die Seelsorger und Pfarrherrn dess Stiffts Muenster*, written in 1613, directed teachers to instruct students that they ought to receive communion often during the year.[11] In the catechetical section the question was posed, "What will you do specially to honor Jesus Christ your Lord on account of the Redemption?" Among the answers, it sufficed to respond, "I will go often to the Holy Sacrament of the Altar."[12]

It is perhaps in catechisms that the new tendencies are most evident. While the earliest efforts at Catholic instruction did not mention the subject, works dating from the last third of the sixteenth century became quite explicit, so signaling a new standard of lay reception. In Trier, the *Catechismus und Praxis* of 1589 recommended frequent communion and confession as a "common medicine" against all sin.[13] The tract deemed lax those who did no more than fulfill their annual obligation:

How often ought one go to the sacrament?
The negligent are brought to it through the commandment of the church, and therefore [receive] this daily bread annually to their great shame and the destruction of true faith and godliness, as was lamented even before the time of St. Augustine. The devout, where not every day, as ancient Christians did,

---

[10] "Dieweil wenig nutzet ein schön köstlich Kleynot / welliches vnbekannt / in einer truhen in tüchlin eingewicklet verborgen ligt / so hat mich für gut angesehen / in disem Büchlein zuentdecken das köstlich Kleynoth vnd den reichen Schatz / so der jenig Mensch hat / wellichem Gott der Herr die Genad deß offt Communicierens mitthailt / auff daß / wann er sicht vnnd erkennt / wie grosse Wolthat vnd fürtrefflichs Berlein / er / von der liebreichen barmhertzigkeit gottes empfacht / er dasselbig lieb vnnd in Würdigkeit halte / ime auch stets danck darumb sage / vnd sich allwegen deß verlierens besorge." Fulvius Androtius, *Seelen Speiß unnd Communionbüchlein* (1591). On Androtius, see Guibert, *The Jesuits*, p. 378.

[11] *Underricht fur die Seelsorger und Pfarrherrn dess Stiffts Muenster, wie sie den Kindern unnd andern unwissenden den Catechismum nuetzlich furtragen sollen* (1613), p. 43.

[12] Ibid., p. 60.

[13] *Catechismus und Praxis*, (1589), p. 116.

nevertheless go often in the year with great joy and the desire of their hearts.[14]

The "commandment" to which the catechism referred was the precept of annual Easter communion. The author recommended much more frequent reception, but despite the injunction to communicate often and the appeal to the ancient Church, the catechism was probably not advocating daily reception. After all, attending the sacrament and receiving it were distinct acts, not to be confused. This is more evident in the section of the tract advocating daily mass: "In the holy office of the Mass, not only are the body and blood of Christ the Lord offered up to God the Father as a true sacrifice of praise by the priest and by those present with him, but all those present who are worthily prepared are nourished in a spiritual way with the body of the Lord through the mouth of the priest."[15] The worthy were to receive vicariously; only the celebrant himself physically took the sacrament. Although the devout were to receive this spiritual food on a daily basis, they were to receive it in a spiritual way.

Yet another tract provides a guide to what "frequent communion" for the laity actually meant. The *Catechismus, Das ist Christlicher Bericht von wahrer Religion und Gottes dienst*, a Jesuit tract printed in Cologne in 1587, also employed an argument about daily communion from Christian antiquity and discounted annual communion as insufficient. In the author's words: "It is quite good and useful for all Christians to take this sacrament, not once or a few times in the year, as the negligent are accustomed to doing, who only go to the sacrament when forced by the commandment of the Church, but if not every day, as ancient Christians did, one should nevertheless approach it every Sunday or once a month with great joy and desire."[16] Here the author stressed monthly and even weekly communion, not merely for the clergy or for specific groups, but for all Catholics. To this catechist and to the author of the *Catechismus und Praxis*, the medieval standard of frequent communion—3 to 4 times annually—was now unacceptable. Nicolaus Cusanus, S.J., believed that four times

[14] Ibid., pp. 126–127.
[15] Ibid., p. 52.
[16] Petrus Michaelus Brillmacher, S.J., *Catechismus, Das ist Christlicher Bericht von wahrer Religion und Gottes dienst/ Sampt einem andechtigen Bettbuch* (1587), p. 154.

was the minimum, but that it was better to do so every month or even every week.[17]

Seventeenth-century literature continued to advocate weekly communion for the laity. This is most evident in the 1630 tome, *Catechismus in aüsserlesenen Exempeln*, by the Jesuit Georg Vogler. The book consists of Peter Canisius's *Shorter Catechism* amplified with argument and embellished with stories of pious and impious acts. It was designed so that a teacher would never lack a proper illustration for his lesson,[18] and Vogler also supplied a variety of rhymes and songs covering virtually every part of Catholic doctrine and life. He based his advice on the daily communion presumed even for small children among ancient Christians.[19] Vogler refrained from suggesting daily reception to his modern audience but nevertheless wrote, "They are to be praised, who communicate on all High Feasts, or even every week, and thereby earn the monthly indulgence." As testimony, he noted the example of saints who received every week.[20]

Later Vogler continued the theme as he took up the Church's commandment to communicate at Easter time. While noting the rule, Vogler sought to entice young people to frequent reception by setting forth the benefits available:

> What advantage is more frequent communion to those who do it?
> 1. They always receive new grace.
> 2. They earn a special crown and glory in heaven.
> 3. They are more devout and can more easily live without mortal sin.
> 4. They are more certain and sure of eternal holiness.[21]

He also defended the practice, saying once again that it was not new, but went back to the earliest Christians.

---

[17] Cusanus, *Christliche Zucht-Schul*, p. 279.

[18] Georg Vogler, *Catechismus in aüsserlesenen Exempeln, kürzen Fragen, schönen Gesängern, Reymen und Reyen für Kirchen und Schülen von newem fleissig aüsgelegt und gestelt* (1630). For a thematic analysis, see Wolfram Metzger, *Beispielkatechese der Gegenreformation: Georg Voglers "Catechismus in Außerlesenen Exempeln" Würzburg 1625*, Veröffentlichungen zur Volkskunde und Kulturgeschichte, no. 8 (1982).

[19] Vogler, *Catechismus*, p. 202. Vogler himself noted that when children were 10 or 12 years old and could distinguish between the sacrament and common table bread, they should not be held back from communion.

[20] "Sein die zuloben/ welche alle Hohe Fest/ oder auch wol alle acht Tag communicieren/ vnd den Monatlichen Ablaß darbey verdienen." Ibid., p. 202.

[21] Ibid., pp. 900–901.

The foregoing discussion shows that some form of reception more common than the traditional practice was becoming a standard for lay people in the late sixteenth century. This seems universally to have been the case, although there were significant disputes over what the norm should be. The Jesuits clearly sought radical increases in lay reception to the point of advocating weekly communion, although they hinted at the possibility of daily reception, a standard that would not be widespread until the twentieth century.

The Jesuits and others defended this more frequent reception on the grounds that it was actually the ancient tradition of the Church. The evidence also demonstrates, however, that they were aware how new and controversial the custom was in their own age.[22] Canisius, for example, in his Louvain letter defended the practice on spiritually utilitarian grounds. Androtius, too, praised the spiritual usefulness of frequent reception as a neglected treasure. In the *Christliche Zucht-Schul*, Nicolaus Cusanus, S.J., saw the need to defend the practice, asking rhetorically, "Is it a new custom to communicate so often? No, rather a very old one, for in the age of the Apostles all Christians took care to do this every day."[23] Vogler, in his catechism, cited Saint Bonaventure, who through reverence for the sacrament forbade himself such frequent reception but was advised by an angel that he should receive and not separate himself from his Lord.[24]

An early biography of the Jesuit Francisco Borgia, third General of the Society, described Borgia's habit and the controversy it aroused:

> He would attend the most blessed Sacrament of the altar in secret once a week, but publicly at the yearly feasts, in order to set a good example for the citizens. This so diligent practice of receiving communion, however, caused much talk among many, so that one judged in one way and the next in another, and among the common folk as commonly occurs there were as many heads as opinions. For the ancient praiseworthy practice of more frequently communicating was entirely fallen away. Because of this a few not unlearned people could be found of the opinion that it would redound to the greater honor and reverence of the most blessed sacrament when one received such Angelic Food

[22] O'Malley, *First Jesuits*, pp. 136, 153.
[23] Cusanus, *Christliche Zucht-Schul*, pp. 278–279.
[24] Vogler, *Catechismus*, p. 202.

not so often, but very seldom, or once a year according to the commandment of the church.[25]

The practice was so controversial that Borgia practiced it covertly, and the diverse opinions on whether receiving communion honored or dishonored the sacrament included the belief that it should only be taken once a year. Others, however, argued that if received worthily, frequent communion had the power to "warm cold hearts" and help people to avoid sin.[26]

All these writers were careful to include the need for worthy preparation, which meant confession, as a prerequisite for communion. Thus, to receive communion more frequently also meant to confess more frequently. According to Ninguarda in Salzburg, since the laity were more susceptible to sin than the clergy (in defiance of all the evidence, it must be noted) they must confess more often as well.[27] Catechetical literature once again corroborates his thinking. Johannes Nass reluctantly accepted more frequent communion for those worthy of it, but only "after a completed confession and true penance."[28] This contingency was invariably the case. According to Peter Michael Brillmacher's *Catechismus*, worthy reception required steadfast faith. It also meant "putting off the old Adam, that is our sinful life, through contrition, confession, correction of past sins, and the purpose of a new direction and life."[29] The *Catechismus und Praxis* of 1589 included communion "by those who either have not confessed or have not confessed correctly" among the sins committed against the Third Commandment (honoring the Sabbath).[30] A pedagogical tract published in Thierhaupten in 1592 made a similar argument, adding that one should also forgive one's neighbor as a means of preparation.[31] Jacob Scopper, in a series of sermons collected into a catechism, treated penance before he discussed the Eucharist, rather than the opposite, more typical

---

[25] Pedro de Ribadeneira, *Leben Francisci Borgiae, dritten Generals der Societat IESV*. trans. Conrad Vettern (1613), p. 48. Here the international character of Jesuit life and missions is evident, with the work and lives of the order elsewhere in Europe influencing their approach in Germany.

[26] Ibid.

[27] Ninguarda, *Manuale parochorum*, p. 156.

[28] Johannes Nass, *Handbuchlein des klein Christianismi* (1570), p. 30.

[29] Brillmacher, *Catechismus*, p. 154.

[30] *Catechismus und Praxis*, p. 135.

[31] *Catholische Fragstuckh uber den Catechismum* (1592), p. 91.

order, because confession must precede communion in reception. He reasoned that "without prior penance we might not worthily be part of the Lord's table, and this makes us certain of receiving forgiveness."[32]

The traditional connection between communion and confession meant that increasing one automatically meant increasing the other, but the effort to spur regular confession involved more than the Blessed Sacrament. As noted, Peter Canisius was an early and ardent advocate of frequent reception. In his *Beicht unnd Communionbüchlein*, Canisius advocated frequent confession as a means to increased grace. He greatly feared, "that they who confess only once a year, according to the general custom, commit great harm."[33] Preparation was one reason: he lamented that "in general one finds few people, unfortunately, who come to confession correctly and well prepared." Most could not meet the conditions required for proper confession.[34]

Canisius's counsel found lay advocates as well. Adam Walasser, a Bavarian layman who compiled texts designed for lay use, published a *Geistlicher und Weltlicher Zuchtspiegel* (1572) intended to instruct "all estates of men, how to conduct themselves honorably in spiritual and worldly affairs, at home or abroad."[35] A section attributed to Canisius, the "Christian and holy teaching, how a young man should conduct himself in the world," offered the following advice:

> The year is long, the world is evil, youth is wild and inexperienced, while the temptations are many and dangerous, and the flesh is inclined to evil. Therefore you should complain all the less about going to holy confession often during the year, especially however at the beginning of Lent, Easter, Pentecost, Ascension, All Saints Day, and Christmas. I say this to you as certain, although the world

[32] Jacob Scopper, *Catechismus, Das ist/ Christliche Unterweisung und gegründer Bericht/ nach warer Evangelischer und Catholischer lehr* (1562), p. LXIIII.

[33] "Ist ja vast zubesorgen/ daß die mit irer Beicht gar vbel bestehen/ welliche im gantzen Jar nur einmal/ nach gemainem brauch/ beichten." Peter Canisius, *Beicht unnd Communionbüchlein* (1579), p. 52.

[34] "Ja in gemain zureden/ findet man der leut wenig/ laider/ welche jetzundt recht vnnd wolgeschickt zu der beicht kommen." Ibid., p. 51.

[35] Adam Walasser, comp., *Geistlicher und Weltlicher Zuchtspiegel. Schöne Christliche Lehr und Regeln/ wie sich allerlay Standts Menschen/ inn Geistlichen und Weltlichen sachen/ im hauß und darauß erbarlichen halten sollen* (1572). On lay defenders of Catholicism during the sixteenth century, see Karl von Reinhardstöttner, "Volksschriftsteller der Gegenreformation in Altbayern," in *Forschungen zur Kulture- und Literaturgeschichte Bayerns*, ed. Karl von Reinhardstöttner (1894), pp. 46–139, especially pp. 58–60.

and the Old Adam might be against it, from more frequent confession you will receive God's special grace, illumination of your understanding, peace of heart, increase of devotion, avoidance of sin, bettering of life, and all happiness.[36]

While this text advocated six times for confessing, another Canisian tract in Walasser's collection, the "Christian house-rules for masters and married people," advised monthly confession.[37]

The author of the "Christian teaching for young people" explicitly pointed out the dangers inherent in limiting penance to one time per year. Other writings by Canisius supported the idea that annual confession was spiritually dangerous. The same idea concerning annual confession echoes throughout the catechetical literature. In the *Catechismus und Praxis*, the author excoriated those who "during the entire year sin gravely from day to day, and who confess in Holy Week more out of custom and so they will not be seen as Unchristian than out of love of God, hatred for sin, or resolve to a better life. They are singing a little song and never improve themselves, indeed have not done any work to improve."[38]

Instead, one should confess much more often, whether or not one was to go to communion. The *Catechismus und Praxis* recommended confession, along with communion, as a general preventive medicine against sins.[39] This included even small children. According to Nicolaus Cusanus, children at seven years of age were to undergo their first confession, even though they were not allowed to receive communion for several years

---

[36] "Das Jar ist lang/ die welt ist böß/ die jugent ist wild unnd unerfaren/ die anfechtungen aber seind vilfeltig und gefährlich/ so ist das flaisch zu dem bösen auch vast genaigt/ desto weniger solt du dich beschweren/ offt im Jar zur heiligen Beycht zugehen/ besonder aber im anfang der Fasten/ zu Ostern/ zu Pfingsten/ am tag der Himmelfart Marie/ an aller Heiligen tag/ und zu Weyhenächten. Ich sag dir für gewiß/ ob schon die Welt unnd der alt Adam möcht darwider sein/ so wirstu doch bey offter Beycht empfinden sonderliche genad Gottes/ erleüchtung des verstands/ friden deß hertzens/ mehrung der andacht/ vermeydung der sünd/ besserung deß lebens/ und alle glücksäligkait." Peter Canisius (att.), "Christliche vnnd Gottsälige Lehr/ wie sich ein junger Knab gegen Gott vnd der Welt halten soll," in Walasser, *Geistlicher und Weltlicher Zuchtspiegel*.

[37] Canisius, "Christliche Haußordnung für die Herrschafft und Ehleut," ibid.

[38] "Das gantz Jar durch/ von tag zu tag schwerlich sündigen/ vnnd in der Karwochen mehr auß gebrauch/ vnd daß sie nicht für Vnchristen angesehen worden/ als auß liebe Gottes/ haß der Sünden/ vnnd fürnemen eines besseren Lebens beichten/ singen allzeit ein Liedlin/ bessern sich nimmer/ auch besserung halben keine arbeit anwenden." *Catechismus und Praxis*, p. 135.

[39] Ibid., p. 116.

thereafter.[40] He went on to pose the question, "Is it good for small children to confess often during the year? Of course, for 1. They receive each time new grace and holiness. 2. They create great hatred and disgust for sin. 3. They therefore learn how to confess."[41] Brillmacher in his catechism argued that the rule of annual confession "is for those who desire to avoid the sacrament out of negligence or other reasons."[42] In Muenster, the *Underricht für die Seelsorger und Pfarrherrn dess Stiffts Muenster* of 1613 introduced a darker theme as a reason for more frequent confession. Instructors were to warn students about the dangers of delay in doing penance: "One should not put off bettering his life from day to day or year to year, but think at all times, whether this year, day, or hour will be the last of life, or whether God will give me at the time an opportunity to do penance for my sins."[43]

The catechism of Georg Vogler demonstrates most fully the catechetical approach to frequent confession. In his opinion, children must confess either every week or every other week.[44] This was a dramatic change from late-medieval catechisms, in which three to four times per year was considered adequate.[45] In the section discussing the commandments of the Church, Vogler made it clear that, although required, annual confession was by no means sufficient. To the catechetical question, "Why should one not put off penance for an entire year?" Vogler answered first from Scripture that one should not postpone penance from day to day. He used an example: when an ox or ass falls in a stream, one does not wait a whole year to pull it out—why then permit one's precious soul to linger in God's disfavor? Through a different but equally graphic image, Vogler attempted to tap the penitent's love of God, arguing that every sin crucifies Christ anew: "Do you want him to hang [on the cross] for an entire year,

---

[40] Cusanus, *Christliche Zucht-Schul*, p. 265. This was quite traditional, as noted by the anonymous chronicler of Biberach cited in chapter one. Hermann Weinsberg of Cologne also confessed well before he received his first communion.

[41] "Ists gut / daß kleine Kinder offt im Jahr beichten? Freylich: dann 1. Sie verdienen allemahl newe Gnad / und Seligkeit. 2. Sie schöpffen grössern Haß und Abschewen von den Sünden. 3. Sie lernen also wol beichten." Ibid.

[42] Brillmacher, *Catechismus*, p. 169.

[43] *Underricht fur die Seelsorger*, p. 42. The proximity of death was a common theme in the Jesuit catechesis of the city. See Hsia, *Society and Religion in Münster*, pp. 197–198.

[44] Vogler, *Catechismus*, p. 245.

[45] See Chapter 2 above.

not removing him through penance?" Finally, a Christian should not rob him- or herself of grace and its benefits for such a long period of time.

Vogler also included three "spurs" (*Bußsporen*) to penance: when one's dog or pig becomes dirty, one takes it to the brook to clean it rather than wait. Similarly, sin is in the conscience as a louse is in clothing, a swine in a beautiful garden, or a splinter in the eye; why not remove it immediately? Lastly, moving from the mundane to the spiritual, one should remember that God so hated sin that He gave His beloved Son to death—why then is one so bold as to house it for an entire year?[46] Vogler summarized these reasons in a "Chorus" given at the end of that section of his catechism:

> Neben der Jahr beicht / öffter beicht
> Wilstu haben dein Gwissen leicht:
> Thu Buß so balds dir werden mag /
> Schieb sie nit auff von Tag zu Tag
> Damit dich Gottes Zorn mit Schall
> Uhrblitzlichen nicht uberfall.
> So bald dein Ochß in Bronnen falt /
> So bald dein Schwein wird ungestalt /
> So bald dein Kleyd unsauber ist
> Ehe Ungezieffer gantz ein nist
> Suches thu alle Hülff und Raht:
> Und dein Seel steckt ein Jahr im Kaht.
> Das Christus an dem Creutze hang
> Ein gantzes Jahr / ist gar zulang.[47]

---

[46] Vogler, *Catechismus*, pp. 895–896.

[47] Ibid., pp. 897–898. I have left it in the original to preserve the sense of the rhyme and loosely translated as follows for the same reason:

> Beside annual confession, confess more often,
> your conscience will be lighter then:
> Do penance just as soon as you may,
> Don't put it off from day to day
> So that by the lightning strike of God's anger
> you won't be put in any danger.
> As soon as your ox into the well falls,
> As soon as some deformity your pig befalls,
> As soon as you soil your Sunday best,
> Before the vermin build a nest,
> You seek advice and someone's help:
> While all the year your soul is mired in filth.
> That Christ upon the cross should hang
> an entire year is far too long.

The last verse appealed not to practical concerns about the state of the soul, but to the feeling of love for God that should exist in the penitent: "That Christ upon the Cross should hang / an entire year is far too long." Through such means Vogler and others coaxed young Catholics into the practice of frequent confession.

Frequent confession granted Catholics a certain degree of spiritual security, but its advocates went beyond the mere forgiveness of sins. Instead, the practice could be a tool valuable for eradicating sin and occasions of sin altogether. Rather than react to sins, penitents could attack them with confession as a weapon. This was the consistent goal of catechists throughout the seventeenth century. A handbook for lay people (especially students) from the late seventeenth century posed a now "common complaint" among penitents: "My God, what does it help me to confess so often? I confess every week or even more often and never better myself? I come again to the confessional every time with my old sins and offenses."[48] The penitent's goal was to go beyond forgiveness to actual improvement, to which the author responded, "The devil can suffer nothing less than the more frequent use of sacramental confession. . . . Why do you want to believe this liar and deceiver?"[49] And then (a bit Jesuitically), "A noble fruit of penance and a great part of improving is that although one does not get better and more pious, one does not however become more evil and worse." The author also explained, "Frequent confession maintains devotion, preserves innocence, purifies the conscience, takes away venial sin, reduces temporal punishment, increases divine grace, etc."[50] The primary goal of perfection now rendered absolution almost secondary, but until such improvement occurred, the practice still proved useful by restoring and preserving grace.

---

[48] "Mein Gott / was hilfft es mich / so offt beichten? Ich beicht fast alle acht Tag / oder noch öffter / und bessere mich doch niemalen: Komm allezeit mit meinen alten Sünden und Gebrechen widerum in den Beichtstul / etc." *Kurzer Unterricht Recht und wohl zu beichten. Von Einem der Societat JESU Priestern beschrieben* (1677), p. 82.

[49] "Der Teuffel kan nichts weniger leiden / als den öffteren Gebrauch der Sacramentalischen Beicht / daher gibt er dir solche Gedancken in en Sinn / und solche Wort in das Maul; warumb wilst du disem Lügner und Betrüger glauben?" Ibid.

[50] "Ein edle Frucht der Buß / und ein grosser Theil der Besserung ist es / wo nicht besser und frömmer / doch nit böser und ärger werden. Das offt beichten erhaltet die Andacht / bewaret die Unschuld / reiniget das Gewissen / nimpt hinweg die tägliche Schulden / minderet die zeitliche straff / mehret die Göttliche gnad / etc." Ibid., pp. 82–83.

## The Catholic Reformation and Sacramental Confession

According to this author's own experience, frequent confession meant something else as well. Those who "so frequently confess are generally much more devout, more moderate, and more innocent, than others who so seldom confess."[51] Frequent reception had now become both a measure of piety and a way of disciplining the self. For all these spiritual writers and catechists, reverence for the sacraments did not mean shrinking from reception, but just the opposite. Christians now dishonored the sacrament by not taking advantage of it.[52] The position of Catholic Reformers on this subject marks a passage from medieval to early-modern Catholicism: the traditional practice of annual communion and confession, generally adhered to in Catholic territories until the mid-sixteenth century, now implied indifference or even hostility to 'true' religion. The standard had changed, however slowly actual practice might follow. In Bavaria, the Catholic rulers set the tone publicly by their own devotions. One should also note the clear message that those who made only a Lenten confession lacked zeal and perhaps wanted simply to avoid being characterized as "Unchristian." Protestants living in Catholic territories made only a perfunctory attempt to fulfill Church law, or actually had to be forced to comply. The extent and intensity of one's devotion to the sacraments, now symbolized by the frequency of reception, became a matter of religious self-definition. Catholics must receive, willingly and frequently, for to do otherwise might incur suspicion of unorthodoxy.

### Frequent Reception and Confraternities

While ecclesiastical and catechetical efforts along with private devotion increasingly encouraged frequent confession and communion, one institution promoted it with special zeal: the Marian Congregation, the pious sodality begun in 1563 in Rome, spread throughout Europe by the Society of Jesus, and established in Cologne by Francis Coster in 1575.[53] Ac-

---

[51] "die Erfahrnuß bringt es / daß die / so öffter / beichten / gemeiniglich vil andächtiger / eingezogner / und unschuldiger seynd / als andere / so selten beichten." Ibid.

[52] Cusanus, *Christliche Zucht-Schul*, p. 276.

[53] Louis Châtellier, *The Europe of the Devout: the Catholic Reformation and the Formation of a New Society* (1989), p. 4. Confraternities have received much attention as central institutions of medieval and early-modern piety. Gabriel Le Bras discussed them in his *Introduction à l'histoire de la pratique religieuse en France* (1942–1945), vol. 1. Recent studies for Germany are lacking, and the field is rich with potential. On the Marian Congrega-

cording to the handbook Coster produced for the confraternity, members were not only to receive communion monthly as well as on the feasts of Christ and of the Virgin, they were also to confess every week.[54] This demand was not found in traditional pastoral care, in Church law or synodal statute, or in most other confraternities.[55] Unprecedented frequency and regularity in confession were central to the confraternity's function.

Introducing frequent confession through the Marian Congregations was a significant event, for it meant that the practice would become a norm for devout Catholics throughout Germany and Europe. Because the sodalities themselves were quite successful with lay elites during the Catholic Reformation, their religious customs acquired substantial force and visibility. In areas dominated by the Roman Church, Marianists included the most powerful, wealthy, and influential members of society. In the Holy Roman Empire, for example, the imperial family was represented, and in Bavaria the ruling family "went so far as to set an example and become head of the movement."[56] The nobility were not the only participants, for the movement involved the bourgeoisie from the beginning.[57]

In addition to lay elites and the nobility, however, the founders of the Marian Congregations hoped to extend the sodality's influence throughout society: "The whole of society was envisaged from the start; it was this which must be transformed, from top to bottom, even if the stated objective, confined to the spiritual formation of certain good pupils, appeared modest, even negligible."[58] Although this ambitious goal was articulated only during the late sixteenth century, its progress after that

---

tions in Germany, see J. B. Kettenmeyer, *Die Anfänge der marianischen Sodalität in Köln 1576–1586*, Katholisches Leben und Kämpfen im Zeitalter der Glaubensspaltung, no. 2 (1928); Otto Leisner, "Zum 400-Jahr-Jubiläum der marianischen Kongregationen im deutschen Sprachgebiet," *Freibürger Stimmen* 44 (1974): 142–150. On one of the early founders of these congregations, see Johann Feuerstein, *Lebensbild des heiligmäßigen P. Jakob Rem S.J. (1546–1618)* (1931).

[54] Francis Coster, *Schatzbüchlein Gottsäliger und Catholischer underweisungen/ der Christlichen jugent* (1579).

[55] Châtellier, *Europe of the Devout*, pp. 4–5. Even the Oratory of Divine Love did not require such a practice.

[56] Ibid., p. 27.

[57] Ibid., p. 20.

[58] Ibid., p. 16.

time was quite considerable, with congregations founded at Cologne, Dillingen, Augsburg, Ingolstadt, Speyer, Fulda, Heiligenstadt, Trier, Würzburg, and Munich.[59] Extending the confraternity to all sectors of society meant that frequent confession and communion went well beyond the nobility or small isolated groups and became an organized practice for all Catholics. By the mid-seventeenth century, the sodality was visible at every level of urban society in Catholic Germany and attracted large numbers of members.[60]

Frequent reception of both confession and communion were prominent features of the confraternity's programme. Indeed, the handbook included an entire chapter entitled, "Common Argument by Which Frequent Penance is Praised, through Analogies,"[61] in order to win members to the practice. These fifteen arguments display plainly the reasoning on which the call to frequent lay penance was based. First among them was security against untimely death: "Whoever neglects to confess his sin places himself in great danger of the quite heavy burden which he would have to suffer after death if he should die unexpectedly and soon, as often happens. One who confesses often, however, is free from such danger."[62] The Christian who seldom confessed also demonstrated that he had more respect for men than for God, whose anger he did not fear.[63]

Interestingly, while terror of hellish suffering was the first reason given, it did not dominate the discussion. The author placed greater stress on prudence than fear: "the sinner would act negligently and foolishly in this life where he does not run to Christ and obtain the certificate of forgiveness through the sacrament of penance."[64] The exemplum only reinforced

[59] Ibid., pp. 30–32.

[60] The numbers were impressive: 2000 at Cologne, 3000 at Ingolstadt, and 2000 in Fribourg (out of a total population of 5000), and in some places every family was represented. Ibid., p. 51.

[61] "Gemaine Argument/ mit welchen die offtgehaltene Beicht/ durch gleichnussen gerhümet wirdt." Coster, *Schatzbüchlein*, pp. 31–39. In the Würzburg handbook a virtually identical section was included within the "Beichtform" in the format of questions and answers. *Handbüchlein der Bruderschafft unser lieber Frawen* (1610), pp. 135–145. It was also published separately by Adam Walasser as a tract, "Warumb es gut sey, offt zu beychten."

[62] Coster, *Schatzbüchlein*, p. 31.

[63] Ibid., p. 33.

[64] "Also wurde auch der Sünder in disem leben vnfürsichtigklich vnnd närrisch handlen/ wo er nit/ durch das Sacrament der Buß/ zu Christo laufft/ die Handschrift/

this idea: a king, owed a great sum by his subjects, appeared in his lands to pronounce that so long as he stayed there he would forgive the debts of all who came to the court and received a certificate, but upon the royal departure all remaining debts must be paid to the last. The moral was obvious: "I hold that there would be no one who would not rush to receive such a certificate, especially because of the uncertainty of the king's departure, and whoever was burdened with the greatest debt would hasten the most."[65]

Emphasis on prudence over fear discloses that the author was teaching a kind of spiritual management rather than inculcating anxiety in his readers.[66] Frequent confession was to be the index of this cautious management and not the result of fear-mongering. Coster stressed preparation, ordering the conscience in such a way that even death could cause no rude interruption in the spiritual life. The other exempla demonstrated this in striking fashion. Frequent confession was like sweeping one's room on a regular basis, cleaning a costly shirt, or washing one's hands before dinner. Not only was the conscience cleansed, but its purity was more easily preserved, and just as a perpetually dirty room could not be swept clean with only one try, neither could a soul that neglected confession easily clear away sin. More graphically, hair that was not combed regularly became more and more entangled. In the same way, the unconfessed, unclean soul gave rise to the worm of conscience and worse at the hour of death.[67] In contrast, regular use of the sacrament made sin easier to recognize. Like a clean towel on which even the smallest patch of dirt was apparent, so too the frequently scrubbed soul revealed even the tiniest smudge.[68]

---

vergebung der Sünden/ zu erlangen/" Ibid., p. 32. R. Po-Chia Hsia makes a similar point, arguing that a heightened concern over mortality during the Catholic Reformation did not produce macabre horrors and fears. Instead, Christians were preoccupied by the idea of an "untimely" death (*Society and Religion in Münster*, pp. 197–198).

[65] "Halte ich darfür/ es wurde kainer sein/ welcher solche Handtschrifft vmb sonst zu erhalten/ nit eylen wurde/ insonderhait/ weil deß Königs Abzu vngewiß wäre/ vnd wurde der am hefftigsten ime zu eylen/ welcher mit der grösten schuld beladen ist." Coster, *Schatzbüchlein*, p. 32.

[66] This attitude runs counter to that described by Jean Delumeau, who argues that Catholic preachers and pastors sought to impress their subjects with the "tortures of the afterlife." Jean Delumeau, *Sin and Fear*, esp. pp. 373–400.

[67] Coster, *Schatzbüchlein*, pp. 38–39.

[68] Ibid., p. 35.

Frequent confession, then, was for Coster and the Marian sodalists a kind of spiritual "housekeeping." Just as a child might maintain a room, or as a family head would cautiously manage a household, so too ought one to prepare and regulate the moral life. By so doing, the serious obligation of caring for the soul could become a quite routine matter, a task undertaken in the normal course of the week. Self examination and absolution were neither special nor extraordinary but could become part of the everyday religiosity of the active layperson. Indeed, the more frequently it was done, the easier it was to do. The more difficult and anxious chore fell to those who had not regularly confessed and were confronted with the necessity of doing so.[69]

## The Complete Confession

Theologically, contrition was the central problem in confession (see Chapter 1), but the complex issues involved in defining and distinguishing contrition and attrition rarely made their way into handbooks and manuals for the pastoral clergy or the laity. This literature simplified the matter by proposing observable acts and tangible dispositions to demonstrate a sorrow adequate to clerical absolution. The Council of Trent had provided a partial (and temporary) solution to the issue of disposition by affirming attrition as sufficient for the sacrament, so that the literature now spoke of true regret for sin and a firm purpose of amendment as basic to absolution. Some authors even went so far as to provide rules for knowing if grace resides in the soul. Others believed firmly that contrition was not that difficult to awaken, that the proper consideration of divine love and mercy could spur the properly trained soul to true love of God. It was an intra-Catholic debate, Jansenism, that actually brought the question of contrition once again to the fore.

In everyday religious life, however, completeness of confession proved the more significant issue, particularly since, by the middle of the sixteenth century, the central distinction between Catholic and Protestant (especially Lutherans) had become the requirement to confess specific sins in detail. Especially in the Salzburg ecclesiastical province that consisted of Bavaria, Salzburg, and numerous Habsburg lands, where the Augsburg Confession

[69] Ibid., p. 39.

had become (temporarily) the official Protestant religion, visitors and ecclesiastics did not ask about contrition; they asked whether the priest demanded specific confession and whether the parish was willing to accept it. Thus, in the process of separating the various practices into new churches (whether Protestant or Catholic), the Lutherans held onto an individual but general confession followed by individual absolution, while the Catholics were determined to require the revelation of specific misdeeds.

This determination on the part of Catholics raised a number of questions. How comprehensive must a confession be, and how were penitent and priest to judge its completeness? The complex casuistry of the fifteenth century had failed to reach the common Christian of the early sixteenth. Pre-Reformation handbooks sometimes neglected even to distinguish between mortal and venial sins, much less to discuss the necessity of revealing the one rather than the other.

Protestant Reformers had attacked the very idea of complete confessions, arguing that no human being could uncover all his or her evils and that attempting to do so could only lead to despair of God's mercy. In the Catholic Reformation, authors confronted with these Protestant assaults found it necessary to qualify the meaning of "complete confession." Catechists recognized that some balance must be struck between the demands for completeness and the frailty of individual penitents. As a matter of conviction and doctrine they emphasized the general point that Catholic confession had to be particular and complete, but the tendency of pastoral care was to make great allowances for weakness.

Requiring a complete confession was a commonplace of medieval penitential advice, and most handbooks placed strong emphasis on it. The counsel given in an Augsburg *Beichtbüchlein* of 1504 is typical:

> You are required to confess all mortal sins which are known to you after diligent examination of conscience, and not only those which you have committed in your own person, but also those which other men have committed and of which you are the source through advice, help, arousal, request, giving anger, permission, or which you ought to have punished, so that you are at least guilty of half, out of duty or brotherly love and you have not done it.

The sins themselves were only part of the sinner's responsibility:

> Not only are you required to confess mortal sins, but also the circumstances of the sins, which are seven. Person: whether you have sinned with consecrated or

ecclesiastical persons, whether you have treated them wickedly with word or deed. Place: whether you have wickedly entered, burned or destroyed a consecrated place, whether you have sinned in a consecrated place, church or churchyard. Time: whether you have sinned on Sunday or on a holy day. Number: how often you have committed a sin, and how long you lay and were hardened in a sinful will and intention, and how often you have fallen again into the sin. Cause or motive: whether you have sinned out of custom, out of your own evil, willingly or forcedly, out of ignorance or out of stupidity and great temptation. Damage: what evil has resulted. Manner: whether you sinned publicly . . . whether in your actions you have not held to the correct order of nature.[70]

This schema arose from the juridical side of medieval penance as part of the ecclesiastical legal system, and the potential difficulties of so involved a treatment of sin proved an easy target for Reformation polemicists. Although it has already been noted that the Lenten context aided the penitent through its meditations and sermons, and while there is no evidence of large numbers of tormented consciences, especially in the parish rituals, such a standard of completeness could bring anxiety to some sober souls. Among those serious Christians who sought out learned mendicants as confessors, moreover, it is plausible that a demand for thoroughness was particularly difficult to fulfill.

One should mention, however, that completeness was particularly demanding in the context of an annual or almost annual penance, which meant considering the sins of an entire year. It would be unsurprising if, over the course of a year, many penitents simply forgot some of their actions. It is thus equally unsurprising that the lists of sins were long, or that individuals might become ensnared in their own tangled memories, or that confessors' interrogations (when they occurred) might prove difficult (indeed, the confessor's interrogation was perhaps the most sensible means of recalling sins to penitents, especially those less able to read). Medieval sacramental confession, with its seasonal and ritual setting inherited from an earlier time, was not suited to the disciplinary demand for full disclosure increasingly characteristic of Roman Catholicism. The development of a complex judicial and pastoral ideal, which required precise enumeration to work properly, necessitated far more extensive contact not only between confessor and confessant but between the penitent and his or her own conscience as well.

[70] *Drei Beichtbüchlein,* p. 85.

Furthermore, although the process made allowances for sins which had been overlooked, and compensated for them through a general confession, the manuals for confessors and penitents did not emphasize the fact. In the *Beichtbüchlein* written by Johannes Wolff, only the section for children making their first confessions contained a prayer covering forgotten sins. The other sections demanded the confession of all mortal sins and made no concession to frail memories.[71] The Augsburg *Beichtbüchlein* of 1504 similarly mentioned the forgiveness of forgotten sins only briefly, in the closing prayer.[72] The text warned about forgetting: "And therefore it is dangerous, through neglect and sloth, to forget the mortal sins one has committed."[73]

The effects of Reformation polemic changed this considerably, as did growing Catholic awareness that large numbers of people did not confess specific sins. The Church's task was to inculcate at the parish level a system of precise recounting of sins while preventing the development of overly scrupulous consciences. Thus, Catholic literature became far more strident in assuring the faithful that it was indeed possible to recount all one's important sins. At the same time, authors became more precise in defining complete confession, reassuring penitents that, Protestant claims notwithstanding, limits existed to the demand for completeness.

Early in the conflict, Johann Dietenberger produced a catechism in which he described Catholic confession: "To confess, however, is not a short conversation between two, as some supposedly would like to say, but is according to the opinion of St. James, to confess with the mouth, and to an ordained priest, to say secretly, all and each of the ways, in particular knowingly, he himself has committed mortal sins, piece by piece, whether they be secret or open, and from the priest himself desire and receive absolution."[74] It could be said to be part of the definition of a Catholic that he or she confess, neither generally nor to God alone, but with specific recounting of all mortal sins.

---

[71] Ibid., pp. 6–75.

[72] Ibid., p. 95.

[73] "Und darumb ist es sorglich, durch versümnisz und tragheit die todtsünden, so ein mensch begangen hat, vergessen." Ibid., p. 126.

[74] Johann Dietenberger, *Catechismus. Evangelischer Bericht und Christliche unnterweisung der fürnemlichsten stück des waren heyligen Christlichen glaubens*, in *Katholische Katechismen*, p. 91.

## The Catholic Reformation and Sacramental Confession

Dietenberger was firm on the subject of complete confession but other early defenders of Catholic confession were milder. Another work, written in 1549 by Michael Helding, the suffragan bishop of Mainz, was more moderate on the subject: "Now ought to be recounted those sins which come to the penitent's consciousness when he ponders and diligently examines himself. Those which do not come to mind after diligent consideration, as they are taken up by the general confession, will be no less remitted than the named [sins]."[75] A third Catholic author, Johannes Fabri, went even further, answering the Reformation's attack on the psychological consequences of demanding complete confession by arguing that in fact medieval doctrine was not nearly so stringent on the matter: "That, however, each person should specifically confess all his sins, has not the meaning and also is in no person possible, that he could or might recount all his evil thoughts, words, and works, and what good deeds he has omitted, for as David says, 'Who recognizes all his sins?' Therefore it is enough, that one recount, confess and say conscious sins, which struggle against the conscience and trouble it."[76] In each of these cases, the author was careful to mention prominently that complete confession did not mean that every sin must be detailed, but that the failures of the sincere penitent would be accepted.

While Catholic Reformation catechists stressed the specific and complete confession of sins, as had their forebears, they were also careful to point out that this did not and could not mean each and every sin, remembered or not. Peter Canisius emphasized "complete" confession, but he did not go so far as to include for his young readers all the seven conditions stipulated in late-medieval manuals, for example, in the pre-Reformation Augsburg handbook of 1504. Canisius's *Beichtbuch* included the following qualification:

> Is one then responsible for confessing everything he has done, small and large?
> No, for it would be impossible for a man to know all and each of his sinful thoughts, words, and deeds and to recount them specifically, from piece to piece. It is however quite possible to a contrite sinner, without difficulty, that he,

[75] Michael Helding, *Catechesis Das ist, kurtze Erklerung unsers h. Christlichen Glaubens* (1555), in *Katholische Katechismen*, p. 403.
[76] Johannes Fabri, *Ein Nuetzlich Beychtbuechlein wie der mensch sich seiner sünd erinnern unnd die bekennen soll.* Augsburg, n.d.

in secret before God's representative, confess and recount the conscious mortal sins, and those with which his conscience is afflicted and burdened.[77]

Canisius here sought to console his readers (as had Fabri in Augsburg) by admitting human frailty, but he also wanted to reassure them that, for the most part, what the Church demanded was also possible for human beings.

Thus, answering Reformation attacks by stressing the leniency of Catholic doctrine was one solution to the catechetical and polemical problem. Another was to guarantee completeness. Some Catholic Reformers countered Protestant polemic by arguing that complete confessions were not only possible, they were less difficult to achieve than they seemed. This approach is evident in a work by Georg Lautherius, published in Munich in 1572. Lautherius began: "It has never been taught that one is responsible to confess sins that he neither knows nor understands, but only those which come to his senses and knowledge after diligent, busy examination of his conscience." He then went on to scorn the claim of impossibility: "If one investigates his conscience a little with earnestness, he soon finds something, of which his own heart gives witness, that is sin before God and the world."[78] The same belief was apparent in the *Beichtbuch* of the reconverted apostate Martin Eisengrein, a true advocate of sacramental confession. At the beginning of his "Certain Way to Examine the Conscience," the author addressed the problem of completeness, stating:

> So that no one might, with the sectarians of our time, flee confession for the reason that recounting each and every sin is impossible, and delude himself with such vain folly: See, so our Lord and savior Jesus Christ, according to his inexpressible good . . . has given his believers the ten commandments so that we can

[77] "Nein / dann es wäre dem menschen vnmöglich / alle vnd jedliche seine sündige gedancken / wort vnd werck zuwissen / vnnd dieselben vnderschidlich von stuck / zu stuck zuerzelen. Das ist aber wol möglich / ja einem rewigen Sünder auch vnbeschwerlich / daß er vor Gottes Stathalter in gehaim bekenne vnd erzele die wissentliche todsünden / vnd mit welchen sein gewissen sunst behafft vnd beschweret ist." Canisius, *Beicht und Communionbüchlein*, p. 12 v.

[78] "Man hat niemals gelehret / daß einer die sünden / so er nit waist noch versteht / zu beichten schuldig sey / sonder allein die / die ihme nach fleissiger / empsiger erforschen seines gewissens / in sinn vnd gedechtnüß kommen. Wenn einer sein gewissen ein wenig mit ernst ersuchet / er findet bald etwas / daruon ime sein aigen hertz zeugknüß gibt / es sey sünd vor GOTT vnnd der welt." Georg Lautherius, *Drey christlich . . . Predigten . . . wie Buss zu wircken* (1572), p. 124.

have them as a mirror, always before our eyes, to see, and through that to recognize, how much we have, through newness of life, progressed and increased
in received and accepted faith, or from the instruction of the Spirit, perhaps
been sanctified, or whether we have offended and grieved the Spirit of the
Lord, or have held the same white robe of innocence unsullied overall. Further,
if we do not hold our vow after Baptism, we then in the mirror of the ten commandments expressly view and recognize our blemishes, with which we have
carelessly soiled and stained the beauty of the robe we have put on.[79]

For Eisengrein and for other Catholic reformers, Protestant claims provided a challenge. While they were careful to argue that limits existed to
the demand for completeness,[80] they were determined to demonstrate that
Christians could, with the proper training and method, recall their misdeeds, mortal or even venial. This claim was in fact necessary, for the goal
of the Counter-Reformation was not merely to beg forgiveness for human
weaknesses. It was to extirpate sin altogether, as much as that was possible, and to encourage the Catholic flock to lead sinless lives.

### General Confession of an Entire Life

Catholic reformers, especially the Jesuits, believed that a complete confession became more possible as it occurred more regularly and frequently. Such practices offered spiritual security to the conscience but
even more importantly enabled Catholics to combat sin effectively. Satan
waged war on the battlefield of the conscience, and now it was possible to
defend oneself against the snares of the devil. This was not all, however,
for new and powerful weapons allowed Christians to go on the offensive
against sin and damnation. Nowhere was this tendency in Catholic Reformation practice more visible than in the "General Confession of One's Entire Life," a practice of obscure origins which began to appear in German
catechetical tracts and handbooks for confession shortly after the mid-sixteenth century. It became increasingly popular in the later sixteenth and
seventeenth centuries, once again through the influence of the Society of
Jesus and the *Spiritual Exercises* of Ignatius Loyola.[81] This General Confes-

---

[79] Eisengrein, *Beichtbuch*, pp. 616–617.

[80] Ibid, p. 618.

[81] John O'Malley does not credit Ignatius with its invention, but with the extension of
the practice in devout circles. See O'Malley, *First Jesuits*, p. 137–139. According to Jean
Delumeau, the general confession was already recommended by Jean Gerson. *Sin and
Fear*, p. 202. It only became a widespread practice in the late sixteenth century.

sion was quite distinct from that recited during mass or at the beginning of confession itself. Seemingly daunting in conception, one handbook designed to prepare for it defined the general confession of an entire life as: "a general, secret recounting before the priest of all sins which we have committed in our entire life and must of necessity be confessed: or of sins from different special previous confessions: so that we, through the power of the proper absolution, experience forgiveness of sins."[82] That such a task might seem daunting the author understood, and he recommended that it be undertaken only under the care of a spiritual counselor.[83]

The General Confession was popularized by the Society of Jesus and applied especially to them and to other priests.[84] They and others recommended it to lay people as well. The handbook of the Marian Congregation also considered the preparation for General Confession useful at other times as well. Another book directed at lay people, written by a Capuchin and printed in Munich in 1635, advised General Confession for: "a perennial sinner, whose misdeeds hang over his head, [who] finally becomes just and wants to flee, through the sacrament of penance, the eternal punishment which is certainly and unmistakably prepared for him."[85] The author of this text also suggested that those who became more deeply attached to Catholicism could undergo the process, perhaps as an accompaniment to spiritual rebirth.[86]

---

[82] "Ein general oder gemeine Beicht ist/ ein allgemeine heimliche erzehlung vor dem Priester aller Sünden/ so wir in vnserm gantzen leben gethan haben/ vnd müssen nothwendig gebeichtet werden: Oder aber der Sünden/ von verscheiden besondern vorgehenden Beichten: damit wir durch die krafft der rechtmeßigen aufflösung/ vergebung der sünden erlangen." *Geistlicher und heilsamer Unterricht/ ein general oder gemeine Beicht anzustellen. Gezogen auß den Lustgarten der Geistlichen ubungen* (1610).

[83] *Geistlicher und heilsamer Unterricht*, p. 5.

[84] O'Malley, *First Jesuits*, pp. 138–139.

[85] "Wann ein viljähriger Sünder/ dessen Missethaten ihm sein vber sein Haupt gangen endlich durch das Sacrament der Buß/ gerechtfertiget werden/ vnd der ewigen Straff/ so ihm gewiß vnd vnfehlbar berait/ entfliehen will/ so ist vonnöthen/ daß er dise vier nachfolgende Puncten durchgründe vnd erforsche/." *Newer Beichtform. Das ist, Geistliche Underrichtung/ wie mennigklich leicht und ohne grosse Mühe/ ja ohn ainiges Schreiben/ in wenig Stunden/ sich von vilen verflossenen Jahren her/ zu einer vollkommen General, wie auch nicht weniger zur Ordinari-beicht/ so er zu Zeiten im Jahr/ als zur Oesterlichen Zeit/ und ander Festtagen zu thun pflegt/ sicherlich beraiten/ unnd solche mit Frucht verrichten könne* (1635).

[86] This is certainly the force of the "fruits" of such a confession, bringing clearer recognition of God's great love and mercy and especially awakening a true and selfless love for God.

## The Catholic Reformation and Sacramental Confession

The General Confession served not only as a regular spiritual tool but as a kind of "reconversion experience" quite useful in the late sixteenth and early seventeenth centuries. It marked the moment when a religiously indifferent person decided to recommit his or her life. In lands marked by heresy and Protestantism, the General Confession marked the moment when apostates reembraced Roman Catholicism. The Jesuits themselves attached such importance to it that in the *Litterae Annuae* tabulating the activities of provinces, the number of General Confessions was a separate category, along with number of communions and students in the colleges.[87] New members of the Marian Congregations were also required to make the General Confession upon entrance to the confraternity, and it thereafter served to anchor their weekly or monthly efforts.[88]

In particular, undertaking a general confession of one's entire life offered numerous benefits, three of which stand out. First, in Coster's words, the act "diminishe[d] entirely the pain and agony of Purgatory, which we must suffer after this life because of our sins."[89] Again according to Coster, Purgatory could, in effect, be experienced during life by reawakening the pain and shame over each sin and thereby, through the merits of Christ, either eliminating or reducing the deserved punishment. At the same time, repetition of all one's sins awakened in the sinner the love of God, as the same source described it, for, "when he ponders all his sins, he marvels at the goodness of God, who has for so long tolerated such disgracefulness and lawlessness of sin." It was considered more moving to confront all one's sins simultaneously than partially and at different times.[90] Second, General Confession "corrects all the defects which we have committed in other confessions and increases the certainty of our holiness." Third, "it makes us richer in virtue, stronger in the struggle against sin, more valiant in all healthy exercises, and brings us to truer and stronger peace of conscience and hope for our salvation."[91]

These three results addressed potential sources of anxiety among Catholics. For those concerned about the sufferings of Purgatory, the Gen-

---

[87] For listings, see BHStA, Jesuiten 101–131.
[88] BHStA, Jesuiten 89.
[89] Coster, *Schatzbüchlein*, pp. 99–100.
[90] Ibid., pp. 97–98.
[91] Ibid., pp. 6–7.

eral Confession offered surcease of sorrow. The other two benefits guaranteed salvation to the extent possible within the Catholic system. By correcting the defects of past confessions, the General Confession helped to ensure the certainty of the absolution, while the examination and recounting of past sins enhanced the probability that one had confessed completely, or at least to the extent of which the conscience was capable. If so, then one could also be sure that forgotten sins were truly remitted. Thus, while the Council of Trent precluded certitude of salvation in the Lutheran sense, this devout use of the sacraments gave the believer hope that his or her redemption was being accomplished.

As practiced by the early Jesuits, the General Confession was a spiritual exercise rather than simply a "fail-safe" compensation for past mistakes.[92] Once it appeared, however, the practice was irresistible to spiritual authors and catechists. It is not hard to understand why. Anyone who doubted the validity of a past confession could rectify it through such an exercise. The pastor in Tegernsee, south of Munich, recommended it for everyone, citing its numerous benefits—forgiveness of many venial and mortal sins while bringing yet others to light.[93] The author of the Cologne guide considered it advisable for all Christians to undertake the general confession at least once.[94] General Confession would also serve to help in the following specific cases:

1. Those who have never confessed.

2. Those who have been silent about some mortal sin through shame or contempt.

3. Those who have confessed only out of custom and without sorrow or purpose of amendment.

4. Those who have deliberately confessed to priests who did not understand their sins or who were not permitted to hear or absolve them.

5. Those who have confessed while under the ban [of excommunication].[95]

---

[92] Ibid.

[93] Georgius Mayer, trans., *Gemaine Beichtform. Wie der Sünder leychtlich zu erkantnuß seiner Sünden kommen/ und dieselben ordenlich Beichten kan* (1577), p. 1.

[94] *Geistlicher und heilsamer Unterricht*, p. 5.

[95] Ibid., pp. 4–5.

In other words, the practice allowed the penitent to compensate for any defective past confession, conscious or unconscious, whether arising through the penitent or the confessor. Given the situation of penance, even in Catholic territories, the General Confession held great possibility.

According to a later text, the *Kurtzer Unterricht Recht und wohl zu beichten* of 1677, the General Confession was to be combined with the regular recounting of sins. Thus, at the beginning, the penitent (Albrecht, in this case) would announce a desire to undertake a General Confession of sins dating from a specific date, perhaps to cover the previous year. The confessant would then proceed to list his participation in all sins according to a specific format (e. g. the Ten Commandments or Seven Deadly Sins), announcing at the end, "These are my committed sins and misdeeds, which I have been able to remember since the last general confession." The wording was important, because it cited specifically what the penitent could remember, not all his sins. Following this, "Albrecht" would then proceed to recount "sins which I have committed since the last ordinary confession, which took place one week ago."[96]

Even for those Catholics whose devotion had not translated into a regular program of confessing, the techniques used to recapitulate an entire life were useful. The *Newer Beichtform* of 1635 mentioned this possibility in the title, recommending it for "ordinary confession, which one is required to do during the year, as at Easter time or other feast days."[97] In the case of "Albrecht" in the *Kurtzer Unterricht*, the General Confession served as a periodic check, both to mark spiritual progress and to relieve the conscience of undue anxiety over the past. The use of such a technique helped reduce the possibility of a scrupulous or overly fussy conscience. A system of checks and balances permitted the Counter-Reformation conscience both progress and spiritual security while demanding rigorous attention to sinful acts.

### The Examination of Conscience

Each of the practices discussed above was intended to make confession a routine event in religious life. Frequent confession for the laity represented a systematic effort to integrate the sacrament into the lay world as

[96] *Kurtzer Unterricht Recht*, p. 244.
[97] *Newer Beichtform*, pp. 5–6.

one element in a well-managed spiritual household. The "General Confession of an Entire Life" mitigated any difficulties arising from reception. Both practices were designed not only to guarantee complete confessions but to make the act of confessing easier, more certain, and less anxious.

A third crucial element in this routinization was the examination of conscience, and this staple of late-medieval pastoral literature therefore took on a new significance in the Catholic Reformation. The key to complete confession lay in examining past behavior and remembering all the misdeeds that required confession—mortal sins, in other words. Having done so, one could then rest assured that everything required for forgiveness had been done. Preparation was essential, especially for those who sinned often and confessed seldom. It was a great error to confess only once or twice a year, and "nonetheless run up to the confessional with no or far too little preparation and examination of conscience, and there recount with lukewarm, impenitent hearts what more or less comes to mind on the surface; and therefore out of highly culpable negligence conceal more mortal sins than they say and confess to the confessor."[98]

The examination itself was naturally dominated by sins—distinguishing, categorizing, and tallying them. The methods for doing so reveal the Catholic Reformers' approach to the question of evil and sinfulness. In his 1537 *Katechismus*, Johannes Dietenberger advised Catholics: "See above, the trespasses against the ten commandments are written there, and whoever finds and knows himself guilty of trespass of the commandments, he confesses it clearly from piece to piece and withholds no mortal sin knowingly, for whoever withholds one knowingly, remains in God's anger and guilty of all the other sins."[99] A fuller description appeared in a *Beichtspiegel* printed by the lay author and publisher Adam Walasser:

[98] "Es irren die jenige sehr weit / welche / obwohlen sie vilfältige schwäre Sünden begangen / und die Buß ein halb oder gantzes Jahr auffgeschoben / nichts destoweniger mit keiner / oder mit garzugeringer Vorbereitung / und Gewissens-Erforschung / dem Beicht-Stuhl zulauffen / und allda / was ihnen gähling / oder ungefä einfällt / nur obenhin / und mit lauem unbußfertigen Hertzen erzehlen; und also auß höchststräfflicher Nachlässigkeit mehrere Todtsünden verschweigen / als sie dem Beicht-Vatter ansagen und bekennen." *Guldener Himmels-Schlussel: Das ist: hochnothwendige Unterrichtung / recht und volkommenlich zubeichten* (1692), p. 12.

[99] Dietenberger, *Catechismus*, p. 144, reprinted in *Katholische Katechismen*, p. 91.

> Because, however, there are many who either out of great simplicity, coarse negligence, or also from many worldly preoccupations, neither can nor want to ponder their sins for a long time, the following table is set forth for the necessary yet swift recognition of greater and more serious sins, in which [table] they might espy themselves and learn which of these sins they have committed, and know to recount in confession the committed [sins] alone, yet all of them, where possible.[100]

By reading the enclosed tables, the penitent could recall the sins committed over the past months or year, then submit them to the confessor. The extensiveness of the list made the probability of completeness greater.

Handbooks dedicated to preparing for the general confession of an entire life used the same approach. Most of the *Geistlicher und heilsamer Unterricht* was taken up with a list of sins according to the Ten Commandments. The penitent was not, however, simply to ponder them and pray for God's mercy. Instead, the process was systematic and involved four specific parts. First, the sinner must consider all those places in which he or she lived, the persons with whom he or she kept company, the officials he or she served, and the things done or desired against these. Second, the penitent must consider well the following (fifty-page) list of sins which demonstrates plainly how one sinned against each of God's commandments. Third, he or she must bring together in writing everything that had been done against each commandment in every place, office, and time. Finally, the sinner must choose a wise and well-trained confessor and explain to him all evil inclinations.[101]

At its most basic, examining the conscience involved a systematic attempt to recall both sins and the circumstances under which they were committed as a prerequisite for confessing them.[102] Some used the "Gen-

---

[100] "Dieweil aber deren vil / so eintweder auß grosser Einfalt / grober Nachlässigkeit / oder auch von vile weltlicher Geschäfft / nicht können oder wöllen lang ihren begangnen Sünden nachdencken / wirdt ihnen zu notwendiger / doch geschwinder Erkandtnuß der grössern vnnd schwerern Sünd / folgender massen ein Tafel fürgestellt / auff daß sie sich darinn erspiegeln vnnd lernen / welche auß dise allen sie begangen haben / vnd die begangnen allein / doch alle / wo möglich / in der Beycht / wissen ordentlich zuerzählen." *Beichtspiegel / Kurzer und nothwendiger Bericht / wie ein Christenmensch sich zu dem Sacrament der Buß schicken / seine Sünde erkennen / bereuen / beychten und büssen soll*, printed with Adam Walasser, "Warumb es qut sey," pp. 100–101.

[101] *Geistlicher und heilsamer Unterricht*, pp. 9–10.

[102] The *Guldener Himmels-Schlussel* focused on specific sins, and recommended the penitent consider the time of commission, the people (male and female), their estate, office, and business. *Guldener Himmels-Schlussel*, p. 12.

eral Confession" for exactly this purpose, as did Georg Mayer of the Tegernsee.[103] Writing down one's sins (a medieval technique) helped keep track of them, especially if one had difficulty remembering them when confessing. This was particularly true of the annual General Confession.[104] No matter how long the lists of sins, limits existed to the difficulty of the examination of conscience. In each of the cases presented, the examination consisted mainly of noting specific misdeeds in a catalogue. Indeed, the very thoroughness of such lists alleviated the burden of searching the conscience, for the devout Catholic preparing to confess could be reasonably certain of having also exhausted the possible sins. In this way, sixteenth-century polemicists deflected the Protestant Reformation's argument about the inherent sinfulness of human nature, which made complete confession not only impossible, but absurd. Seventeenth-century Catholic catechists also concentrated on specific sins and the best ways to eradicate them, rather than dwelling on the more general theme of human iniquity. Here two essential images held Catholics in good stead: sins were either ecclesiastical crimes to be weighed by a churchly judge, or individual infirmities to be healed by the sharp compassion of the confessor's art. In either case, the Catholic response to sin was neither existential nor vague, but technical and specific. It remained only to find the proper, sure mechanism for remembering and retelling.

### Routines of Conscience

To be effective to the Catholic population at large, religious discipline had to be workable in the lay world, where constant spiritual oversight was impossible. Exposed in the secular world to the wiles of Satan, lay Catholics did not live according to a monastic rule, with days and hours dedicated to religious life and sanctification. Taken together, the examination of conscience working through frequent confession and regular General Confessions provided a system of spiritual development applicable to lay people, employing a degree of self-regulation as a substitute for ecclesiastical discipline. Through the examination of conscience lay people policed themselves, guided by the Church through frequent regular confession and an occasional General Confession. The Counter-

[103] Mayer, *Gemaine Beichtform*, p. 1.
[104] *Kurzer Unterricht Recht*, p. 2.

Reformation sacrament was thus a matter not only of social control, but of self-control.

This is apparent in the relationship between confession and examination of conscience. The proliferation of handbooks and lists of sins was useful, not only because these publications provided clear guidance, but because they placed the investigation and recognition of sins in the hands of the penitent. Rather than passively awaiting a priest's questions, the penitent had already completed the process, awakened contrition, remembered and repented of sins, before approaching the confessional. For the person who confessed regularly rather than annually, the handbooks and lists of sins could replace the external and congregational rituals of Lent with private and individual devotions repeated throughout the year. In other words, Lent became portable and permanent. Indeed, the final move might be to dispense with even written material. According to the *Kurzer Unterricht Recht und wohl zu beichten*, "Those who frequently confess have no need for a 'mirror of confession' or a book in which sins are written or printed following the order of the Ten Commandments or some other manner: for without this they will easily be able to bring their sins to mind."[105] For these people, the entire process had been internalized, and they had their sins always before them. Far more than in medieval religion, the emphasis in confession now fell on the penitent's orderly preparation rather than on the confessor's skill.

Handbooks for lay people graphically demonstrate the ways in which examinations of conscience were used in the Catholic Reformation to systematize and intensify an element already present in medieval Christianity. The Jesuits, however, employed the examination of conscience most extensively and scientifically, with profound results. Marian Congregations offered indulgences not only for confessing frequently or undertaking a general confession, but for making a nightly examination of conscience.[106] Indeed, some Jesuit writers treated the examination as one of the basic parts of the sacrament, equal in importance to contrition, confession, and

---

[105] "Welche oft beichten/ haben keines Beichtspiegels/ oder Buechs vonnöthen/ darinn die Sünden nach der Ordnung der zehen Gebott/ oder auff ein andere weiß geschriben oder getruckt seynd: Dann ohne disem werden sie leichtlich ihre Sünden können in die Gedächtnuß bringen." Ibid., p. 2.

[106] Thus, in Cologne. See *Handbüchlein*, p. 19. One should also see the approbation in Coster's *Schatzbüchlein* of 1576.

satisfaction. The first part of Francis Coster's handbook of 1579 dealt with penance, to be performed by sodalists once a week. According to Coster, "The carefulness and the diligence of those who oft and many times confess consists of four things: 1. Examination or investigation of the conscience. 2. Pain and sorrow over sins committed. 3. The confession itself. 4. Purpose and means of improvement."[107] For Coster, remembering and codifying sins was as significant to the process as the theological elements, serving as the basis for all that followed. In fact, as will become evident, in practice the examination was the most important part of the sacrament.

In the examination itself, the tendency to concentrate on individual misdeeds is again striking. Coster spent no time discussing the idea of sinfulness or guilt. Rather, he focused from the beginning on specific sins and advised a systematic compilation of them. The Catholic ought to differentiate the sins and mark in writing those things of which he found himself guilty.[108] Preferably, this would be done every evening, and if so, no great examination had to be performed at the exact time of confession. Instead, the penitent need only bring to mind those faults which had been marked[109] and review them on a monthly basis so as to clarify and to remember his faults.[110] Those, however, who had not been quite so diligent and sought to confess should "go into themselves and peruse the following examination, and bring together in the memory in writing or otherwise what applies to him."[111] The list of sins consisted of nine pages divided into offenses against God, neighbor, and self.

Yet another congregation, the Confraternity of the Three Kings in Cologne, expanded this procedure to include five points: 1) thanksgiving

---

[107] "Die sorg vnd der fleiß dessen / der offt vnnd vilmal beichtet / stehet beynahe in vier dingen: Als in 1. Examinierung oder erforschung des Gewissens. 2. Schmertzen vnd Rhew der begangenen Sünden halber. 3. Der Beicht selbs. 4. Vornemen vnnd mittel der besserung." Coster, *Schatzbüchlein*, p. 11. One might also note that the satisfaction emphasizes rehabilitation rather than punishment.

[108] Ibid., p. 13. As with many other elements of the spiritual program outlined here, the direct inspiration was Ignatius Loyola's "Spiritual Exercises." See Ignatius of Loyola, "Spiritual Exercises," in *Ignatius Loyola: Spiritual Exercises and Selected Works*, ed. George Ganss (1991), pp. 131–132.

[109] Ibid., pp. 13–14.

[110] "Welcher aber solche feine ordnung nitgehalten hat / vnd zur Beicht sich beraiten wil / der soll in sich selbs gehen / vnnd die nachfolgende erforschung durchsehen / vnd was in angehet / Schrifftlich / oder sonst in die Memory verfassen." Ibid.

[111] *Handbüchlein*, pp. 142–144.

for God's goodness, 2) petition for a true recognition and hatred of all sin, 3) the examination itself, 4) a prayer for forgiveness, and 5) a firm intention to better one's life and confess the day's sins.[112] Those who had not confessed in some time were to spend longer conducting this investigation and were urged where possible to read a book listing sins according to the Ten Commandments. The Three Kings examination, which occupied four pages of the text, did not simply list the offenses. It asked how the individual had spent the day from morning till evening: "Did I awaken at the proper time or did I sleep too long?" "Was I diligent or undiligent, true or untrue in work?"[113] "How have I conducted myself in the household? Have I supervised my wife and children correctly?"[114] To rectify the most common sins, the sinner ought to assign himself a special penance, or give so much in alms, "because through this the habit of sin will be bettered."[115] In this way, the examination went beyond noting sins; it was also a tool for inculcating proper behavior and attitude in the devout.

Going beyond the range of the confraternities, Nicolaus Cusanus, in his *Christliche Zucht-Schul*, also employed the examination to root out sins altogether, one after another, beginning with the most besetting and moving systematically to the next. Every morning should begin with a resolve to defeat one particular sin, begging help from God, the Virgin Mary, one's guardian angel, and one's patron saint.[116] During the day the sinner should be attentive and on guard against that particular sin. In the evening, he or she should consider whether and how often the sin had occurred, comparing each day to the previous one for signs of improvement, and resolving to do better the next day. This should continue "until this sin has been overcome: and after this continue in the same manner against another sin, one after the other."[117] For Cusanus, then, the process of examining the conscience not only permitted the sinner to know, recognize,

---

[112] Ibid., pp. 160–161.

[113] Ibid., pp. 144–146.

[114] Ibid., p. 150.

[115] Cusanus, *Christliche Zucht-Schul*, p. 258.

[116] Ibid. Here Cusanus, like other Jesuits, was following the recommendations of the first week of the *Spiritual Exercises*.

[117] "Diese Mittel soll man so lang brauchen / biß diese Sünd überwunden ist: und darnach wider andere Sünden/ eine nach der ander dieselbe Weiß halten." Ibid.

and confess misdeeds on a routine basis, but had an active function as well—enabling the penitent to eliminate sins systematically, one by one.

The idea was to make confession so regular that although it was a matter of grave importance, it also became routine. Contrition and complete confession would become easier and be followed by sure absolution. Forgiveness, however, was only part of the goal. As a regular technique, the examination of conscience combined with confession became a means to extinguish sin altogether. Even for less zealous Catholics, however, the examination of conscience and General Confession greatly simplified the sacrament. The *Newer Beichtform* printed in Munich in 1635 claimed to show how one "might come to a perfect general, or even ordinary, confession, covering many past years, easily and without great difficulty, indeed without any kind of writing, in a few hours."[118] As described by the author (identified only as a Capuchin), the process was astonishingly simple. It began with prayers to the Virgin, to the Holy Spirit, and to one's guardian angel. Then the penitent was to kneel in God's presence for at least a quarter of an hour, pondering the time since the last confession, his or her estate, kind of work or office, places lived since youth, and the people with whom he or she lived or most often associated.[119]

Having done this, the penitent was then to consult the table of sins provided. This list marked off individual faults by horizontal lines, with the edges of each cut so that it could be lifted out separately. A vertical strip was then glued to the edge of the page, providing a slot into which the individual lines were then inserted: "You will find diligently marked in all the lines almost all the sorts of sins with which people act against the commandments of God. Thus, you should look through and examine in this tablet line by line whether you find yourself guilty of this or that vice, which your conscience and the material will give you lightly to recognize."[120] When this was done: "If, however, you find something of which

---

[118] *Newer Beichtform.*

[119] Ibid.

[120] "So stehe darnach auff/ setze dich zu Tisch/ unnd stelle dir die Täflein für Augen/ welche hernach sollen gesetzt werden/ in welchen du in allen zeilen schier allerhandt Sünden/ mit welchen die Menschen wider die Gebott Gottes handlen/ fleissig auffgezaichnet finden wirst. Derhalben soltu dann in disem Täflein alle zeilen nach einander durchsehen vnd erforschen/ ob du dich in disem oder jenem Laster schuldig befindest? welches dir dein Gewissen/ vnd die *Materia* leichtlich zu erkennen geben wird." Ibid.

your conscience accuses you, then you should, with a pen-knife or needle which you have at hand, pull out or lift the cut-out note and place it on the glued white side [this process left cut-ins projecting a little way into the right-hand margin, while inapplicable sins remained tucked into their slots]."[121] The penitent must mark those sins which he or she knew had been committed. The list was therefore not the basis for examining the conscience, but the sum of it.

Having consulted the tablet, marking sins along the way, the confession was simple: "Then go with this tablet to the priest and lift up the first commandment and read one after another what you yourself have pulled out and confess the sins which you find marked in the pulled-out notes. It is even unnecessary to change anything, only, when you have continued for awhile, that you occasionally repeat the following words, namely: Further I confess that I, etc."[122] After the confession one should tuck the notes back into their slots, ready for the next use. As the author remarked, "What is easier? What is quicker?"[123]

This rather astonishing set of instructions exhibits the effort to provide an easier, surer means of remembering sins for the general confession of an entire life, which represented an extreme within the system. As the author noted, however, this manual could be used for regular confession as well. He also explicitly cautioned those undergoing the process not to feel anxiety over it; although the more complete the examination of conscience was, the more perfect it became, still, "too great and immodest anxiety hinders progress." To allay this one should only attempt the exercise after choosing a good confessor.[124]

---

[121] "So du aber etwas findest/ in welchem dich dein Gewissen anklagt/ alßdann soltu mit einem federmesser oder Nadel/ welche du bey handen haben wirst/ daß auffgeschnittene Brieflein deroselben zeilen herauß ziehen oder auffheben/ also daß dasselbige auff der angeklebten weissen seyten außgezogen sey." Ibid.

[122] "Alßdann gehe mit disem Täflein hin zum Priester/ und heb an von dem ersten Gebott/ vnd liß nacheinander/ was du daselbst herauß gezogen hast/ und beichte die Sünden/ welche du in dem/ von dir/ auß gezognem Brieflein/ gezeichnet findest. Es ist auch unnötig etwas zu ändern/ nur allein/ wann du ein zeitlang fortgefahren bist/ daß du vnderweilen dise nachfolgende Wort widerholest/ nemblich: Weiter bekenne ich/ daß ich/ etc." Ibid.

[123] "Nach vollendter Beicht aber/ so begib dich widerumb in ein Gemach/ oder absonderlich Ort/ nimb das Federmesserlein oder Nadel/ und schiebe ein jegkliches Brieflein wider an sein Ort. Sihe/ da hastu die *Practicam*. Was ist leichters? Wast hurtigers?" Ibid.

[124] Ibid., p. 81.

Not unexpectedly, the 1635 text went to great lengths to reassure the penitent. If, in perusing the list, "you find nothing, and nothing comes to you after you have thought a little, then go on without any care and scruple, and be anxious no longer, for you have done what is possible for you."[125] This was not designed to be the anguished process of guilty consciences; it was rather a systematic way of checking specific deeds. Later in the book, the author became milder yet: "For it is not really possible that one can mark all in the smallest and the least. Confess therefore what you can and what you know, and what comes to you, therewith you do enough, and you are not bound or obligated further."[126] In this book, then, as in the others, the author went far to mitigate the potential burdens of "full, complete confession." More important, the *Newer Beichtform* sought to remove anxiety from confession entirely. More important was recognizing and remembering sins, which in this book was more a technical matter than a drawn-out process of introspection. To the Catholic for whom penance was infrequent or who wanted to make a general confession, the examination was simply a question of following the proper method. To the Catholic for whom confession was an integral, frequent component of spiritual life, the entire process was familiar. No book was necessary, for the mechanism was already well-established in the memory. For such people, the habit of conscience became routine.

### Manners and Morals

Control of the inner self and regulation of the conscience were mirrored in the outer behavior of the penitent. As noted in an earlier chapter, the act of confessing often occurred amidst the hurly-burly of Lenten activities and other people. For Catholic reformers, however, the disposition before, during, and after confession was a measure of the penitent's own sincerity. This behavior would also contribute to making the church a suitable forum for penance. Men coming to confession should

[125] "Findestu aber nichts/ und kompt dir auch nichts für/ nach dem du dich ein wenig bedacht hast/ so fahre alßdann ohn ainige sorg vnnd scrupel fort/ und sey nicht mehr sorgfeltig/ dann du gethan hast/ was dir müglich gewesen ist." Ibid.

[126] "Dann es ist nicht wol müglich/ daß man alles bey dem geringsten vnd mindesten mercken könne. Beichte derohalben was du kanst/ und was du waist/ und dir einfält/ damit thust genueg/ und weiter bist nit obligirt oder verbunden." Ibid.

lay aside their weapons beforehand and not bring them into the confessional.[127] Women were to take care in dressing for penance. Those coming with vain clothing, reeking bouquets of flowers, and bare necks clearly demonstrated that they were more interested in showing off their decoration and "vain gestures" than in a true and repentant confession.[128]

In church, the penitent should spend some time in preparation before coming to the confessional. Those who simply rushed in were likely to have spent little time examining their consciences. Even more, one should not then vehemently push one's way through those who have already been waiting, for this shameless behavior might keep others from completing a confession already begun. Privacy was an issue here as well, for confessants might worry that their sins would be overheard by people standing or kneeling too close to the confessional.[129] While recounting sins, he or she should keep the face averted from the confessor and speak in a measured voice, loud enough for the priest, but too soft for others, to hear.[130] The confession itself was to be made clearly, and two conditions were to be avoided. It was not seemly for the penitent to speak in a piteous or half-crying voice, especially if this was not from the heart. Similarly, the confessant must not treat sins boastfully, as though they were knightly deeds rather than the acts of a now-repentant sinner.[131] Furthermore, the confession must be to the point, and not waste time.[132] Finally, in speaking to the confessor, the penitent should use clear but proper language, even while describing vices. This was out of deference to the confessor, whom the penitent was to revere.[133]

---

[127] *Kurzer Unterricht Recht*, p. 63.

[128] *Guldener Himmels-Schlussel*, p. 67.

[129] "Vilweniger durch andere/ welche allbereit ein Zeitlang allda gewartet haben/ mit grober Ungestümmigkeit hindurch tringen; welche unverschambte Frechheit der Beicht-Kinder zum öfftern verursachet/ daß andere ihre angefangene Beicht unvollkommenlich verrichten; in dem sie besorgen / es möchten ihre Sünden von denen/ so gar zunahe am Beicht-Stuhl stehen oder knyen/ angehört/ und vermerckt werden." Ibid., pp. 65–66.

[130] *Kurzer Unterricht Recht*, p. 63.

[131] Ibid., pp. 63–64.

[132] *Guldener Himmels-Schlussel*, p. 68.

[133] *Kurzer Unterricht Recht*, pp. 63–64.

Through rules such as these, catechists sought to create behaviors that would encourage and mirror the sobriety of the penitent's own conscience. This etiquette had another goal as well. To Catholic reformers, the boisterous and crowded setting of confession so prominent earlier not only made a mockery of this event and the quiet reflection appropriate to it, but also threatened the secrecy vital to the process. The Church had sought to control this through the use of the confessional, but something more was needed. Catholics themselves had to learn to understand the seriousness of penance and respect the needs of other penitents. The potential influence of bystanders had to be eliminated for penance to serve both the Church and the individual soul.

The specificity of this seventeenth-century literature indicates the function and significance of confession in forming the Counter-Reformation conscience. It is entirely possible that the systematic process of focusing on sins might lead, perhaps unintentionally, beyond specific acts and toward a kind of rigorous introspection. By exhaustively investigating actions and sins, the techniques of examining the conscience and confessing could also focus the Catholic's attention on his or her motives and nature. Routine self-analysis, examination, and prayer helped to re-form the conscience on orthodox lines. The discipline of self-examination according to prescribed norms helped to shape the conscience in a way that emphasized always the goal of pure love of God, in other words, of contrition. As a result, the introspective Catholic would seek at all times a high degree of authenticity in understanding the self. One must recognize and acknowledge one's authentic motives and desires as a prelude to reconstructing the conscience on truly Catholic lines. Routine examination and confession thus helped not only to reveal the authentic self but to convert it.

As the handbooks themselves suggest, however, the "examination of conscience" was not intended to be a journey of introspective self-discovery. It was designed to reveal particular acts or vices to be absolved and ultimately extirpated. The sacrament was therefore neither necessarily, nor even primarily, an investigation into the deepest of human motives or desires. Instead, it focused the spiritual life of the layperson on distinct actions, ever more preoccupied with knowing, avoiding, remembering, and excusing sins. Adam Walasser intended his sixteenth-century *Beichtspiegel* for people who did not live in monasteries but in the secular realm and who as a result were either theologically naive or too preoccupied with worldly concerns to undertake a rigorous religious regime. The author of the *Newer Beichtform* of 1635 also understood this well.

# Conclusion:
# "Careful, Not Fearful"

"Yes," he said, "I caught him, with an unseen hook
and an invisible line which is long enough to let him
wander to the ends of the world, and still to bring him
back with a twitch upon the thread."
   —G. K. Chesterton, "The Queer Feet"

In the city of Munich today, on any Saturday afternoon following the fren-
zied shopping that ends with the early closing of the great stores, the
baroque church of Saint Michael provides a respite from the relentless
consumerism of modern Germany. Amidst the gawking of visitors from
many lands, discerning eyes will recognize the vestiges of the native population, kneeling or sitting in pews or perhaps standing in line by one of
the side altars. There a green light often flashes on, a door opens, and a
person silently emerges from a cloistered booth, his or her place (more
often *her* place) immediately occupied by another. What occurs inside is
invisible to the bystander, nor can the passerby overhear the event. Even
if one could hear, a tacit agreement keeps the waiting crowd at a distance.
Despite the flash of cameras and the voices of guides, at the confessionals
a preternatural quiet prevails. Though the confessionals are new, that still-
ness constitutes perhaps the most enduring legacy of the Catholic Reformation.

Such quiet came later than the sixteenth century, and it did not come
easily. Slowly, the official and pastoral changes wrought during the
late sixteenth and early seventeenth centuries altered the religious
landscape of German Roman Catholicism. The "Copernican revolution
in pastoral care" was no overnight upheaval but centuries in the mak-

# Conclusion

ing.[1] During the course of a century, both official and pastoral approaches to sacramental confession changed markedly. To bring order and security to the celebration of the sacrament, the Church in Germany simplified ritual and language while simultaneously making penance uniformly and distinctively Catholic, impossible to confuse with Protestant practices. Reformers attempted to create a sense of the sacrament's significance and dignity by surrounding its performance with solemnity, from specifying the confessor's vestments to controlling the behavior of bystanders.

To limit the noise and disruption produced by crowding and curiosity, Catholic reformers in Germany very gradually adopted the Borromean confessional. This imposing space enhanced the solemnity of sacramental penance, ingeniously maintaining its public visibility while precluding even the hint of scandal. Physically separating confessor from penitent and isolating both from the congregation created a quasi-private setting in which the confessor could comfortably provide individual counsel and advice to large numbers of lay people, whose revelations could now occur with less fear of interference or eavesdropping.

Even with the adoption of the confessional, however, a more reverent, discreet attitude toward the sacrament required changes in etiquette. The early confessional was relatively open, not designed for privacy. Catechists therefore emphasized good manners for confessants, regulating individual behavior, appearance, and even dress. The etiquette of waiting also demanded circumspect behavior, especially in maintaining the secrecy and solemnity of other confessions. Taming the madding crowd was necessary to allow the sacrament to work. Individual sacramental confession could then be both intimate and public. Eventually, but certainly not before the eighteenth century, the public and communal dimension disappeared entirely behind the curtains or doors of confessionals. Sacramental penance became the truly private and voluntary affair it remains to this day. Coincidentally, but even more gradually, the Catholic religion itself lost the power to enforce moral laws and had to

[1] On the general changes that the Catholic Reformation brought, see Bossy, "Counter-Reformation," pp. 51-70; idem, *Christianity in the West, 1400-1700* (1985); Evennett, *Spirit of the Counter-Reformation;* Châtellier, *Europe of the Devout.*

rely on its own ability to persuade and the voluntary compliance of individual Christians.

Within this newly ordered physical and social space, the medieval rule of annual shriving no longer sufficed either for piety or discipline. Mere compliance with Church law now implied religious indifference or worse. By 1600 frequent confession and communion, once limited to the clergy and the most rigorously pious lay people, now marked the true Catholic, to the point that confraternities certified their members' devotion by referring to it. Even the definition of "frequent" had changed. Quarterly reception was now the miminum standard, and the truly devout went weekly or monthly to penance. Catechisms derided annual reception as negligent and even suspicious, lauding instead those who routinely employed the sacraments.

Still, the question remains: having altered the structure, setting, and timing of confession, did Catholic reformers in Bavaria also succeed in changing the population's practices and attitudes? Behavioral patterns suggest important but uneven developments. Inner transformation is by definition harder to substantiate. Some priests were themselves aware of profound developments in sacramental practice. In his long defense of chastity, the Jesuit Jeremias Drexel encouraged the habit of frequent confession and surveyed the changes of the past century. "I think, not without heartfelt sighs," he wrote, "how it was in the world a hundred years ago in Luther's time. Oh unworthy age! Then one could distinguish Catholic from heretic only with difficulty. A person made his confession only once a year and quite reluctantly, without any zeal, or performed such confession only as an outward ceremony and old custom. For commonly, the more seldom we undertake such things, the more negligently and evilly we perform them." Drexel's assessment of the late-medieval church is surprisingly negative, but he exulted in the present situation: "Now, however, through the kind watchfulness of God, the times have changed, so that I may truthfully say that whoever in our time makes only one confession in the entire year, gives himself away to everyone and demonstrates to everyone that they should not consider him to be anything other than a completely cold, half-hearted Christian, who, were he not held to it by the commandment [of the Church], would not even once purify his conscience through confession, but would remain jolly with his sins and

# Conclusion

vices."[2] His account is marked by his confidence about the new standards in place and their pervasiveness throughout Bavaria.

Drexel's confidence is confirmed by other evidence of Bavarian sacramental practice. Overall, lay reception of both confession and communion clearly increased over the course of the seventeenth century. By the 1700s, bishops and visitors could rely upon lay confession and communion approximately five times per year, marking an expanded number of large liturgical feasts: Easter, Christmas, All Saints (1 November), Portiuncula (2 August), and the feast of the parish's or parish confraternity's own patron.[3] Such an arrangement guaranteed that regular receptions were evenly distributed throughout the year, living up to the hopes of late-medieval catechists like Kolde and even Jean Gerson. To this regular cycle, of course, would be added the traditional times of illness, death, or marriage.

While more frequent sacramental reception obtained everywhere in Bavaria, in rural dioceses like Regensburg (except for the Protestant city of Regensburg itself) and in towns like Passau at the edge of the territory, more traditional practices could also be found. In Regensburg, despite the pleasing increase in frequency, the bishop complained that many lay people still came to confessions ill-prepared and unrepentant. Eighteenth-century visitations in the diocese revealed that the old issues of crowding and decorum were still significant, with two or more people trying to

---

[2] "Allda fällt mir ein/ und bedencke nit ohne hertzliches seufftzen/ wie es vor hundert jahren/ zu Luthers zeiten/ in der Welt zugangen seye. O unguldine zeiten! Damals möchte man die Catholische schwerlich von den Ketzern erkennen. Man verrichtete järlich die Beicht nur einmal/ und zwar liderlich/ ohne ainichen eyfer/ oder geschah solches beichten nur als ein purlautere Ceremoni und alter brauch. Denn gemainklich/ je seltener wir dergleichen ding in dz werck richten/ je hinlässiger und ubler wir selbige vollziehen . . . Es haben sich nun aber die zeiten durch die gütige fürsichtigkeit gottes/ jetzt also verendert/ daß ich mit warheit sagen darff/ wer zu diser unser zeit im gantzen Jahr nur ein Beicht verrichtet/ der gibt von ihme selber jederman dise anweisung/ daß sie ihne für anderst nit halten sollen / als für einen gantz kalten lawen Christen/ welcher/ da er nit durch das gebott darzu gehlaten wurde/ auch das gantze Jahr sein gewissen nicht einmal durch die beicht rainigte/ sondern mit seinen Sünd unnd Lastern wol vergnügt blibe." Jeremias Drexel, S.J., *Nicetas, das ist Ritterlicher Kampf und Sig wider alle unrainigkeit, und fleischlichen wollust,* trans. Christopher Agricola (1625), pp. 338–340.

[3] Karl Hausberger, *Geschichte des Bistums Regensburg,* vol. 2, *Vom Barock bis zur Gegenwart* (1989), p. 46; idem, *Gottfried Langwerth von Simmern (1669-1741), bistumsadministrator und Weihbischof zu Regensburg,* ed. Georg Schwaiger, Beiträge zur Geschichte des bistums Regensburg, vol. 7 (1973), pp. 207–221. For Passau, see Konrad Baumgartner, *Die Seelsorge im Bistum Passau zwischen Barocker Tradition, Aufklärung und Restauration,* Münchener theologische Studien, vol. 19 (1975), pp. 414–415.

squeeze into the confessional at once. The age-old struggle between regular and secular clergy continued, as pastors still tried to keep their flocks from going to the regular clergy for confessions, as had been the case since 1215.[4] For many, greater frequency did not curtail the traditional custom of delaying confession until the last minute. Allowing for these continuities, however, the new practice of regular confession throughout the year had become a reality, and, for the Catholic Church, an opportunity.

Other evidence reinforces the conclusion that a more intensely pious, highly visible alternative to traditional practice had taken hold among a significant segment of the Catholic population in seventeenth-century Bavaria. Members of the Society of Jesus, required to report annually on their pastoral and educational activities, took great care to quantify sacramental reception as an index of their own catechetical success. In Bavarian cities during the seventeenth century, we know that the number of communions skyrocketed. Munich demonstrates this change: in a city of approximately 16,000 in 1615, the Jesuits alone reported having distributed 89,000 communions that year, or five for every inhabitant of the city.[5] In 1690, just before the figures from Munich and Freising were merged (skewing the numbers), the Society administered 147,247 hosts, although the city's population had still not reached 20,000, a ratio of more than seven to one.[6] By 1770, Munich had about 37,000 inhabitants, and the Society's churches claimed 230,000 recipients of communion.[7]

Clerical reception no doubt accounted for some of this increase. The Jesuits' figures would of course also include male sodality members (about 5000 men) and their families, who constituted a significant part of the urban population in Catholic Germany.[8] Other recipients might include

---

[4] According to an episcopal mandate of 15 February 1724, pastors were to advise their penitents to kneel and prepare themselves before confession. Further, confessors were to take care that two or three people did not try to squeeze into the confessional at once. See Hausberger, *Gottfried Langwerth von Simmern*, p. 222. This was also a continuing problem in France. See Briggs, "Sins of the People," pp. 324–325.

[5] BHStA, Jesuiten 102. For the population of Munich, see Hans Mauersberg, *Wirtschafts- und Sozialgeschichte zentraleuropäischen Städte in neuerer Zeit* (1960), pp. 61–74.

[6] BHStA, Jesuiten 115.

[7] BHStA, Jesuiten 131.

[8] In Munich (1770) the various Jesuit confraternities totalled some 5000 males, meaning that nearly half the city's families were somehow involved. Châtellier, *Europe of the Devout*, pp. 196–197.

visitors to the city or non-confraternity members accustomed to attending the Jesuit Church of Saint Michael or perhaps, after 1710, the nearby Bür-gersaal Kirche. It is also possible that people from the countryside utilized Jesuit spiritual facilities, raising the further possibility that they brought a new kind of piety back with them to village and farm. Obviously, not every inhabitant received communion from the Jesuits, and sodality members and their families, who pledged to receive monthly or weekly, could account for many receptions. Even so, such numbers indicate the prominence of frequent sacramental reception among a significant (and elite) portion of the capital's population.

Other smaller cities with a strong Jesuit presence displayed similar increases in sacramental piety, even without the continued presence of the ducal family. The university city of Ingolstadt, the population of which did not reach 7,000 until 1700,[9] registered 15,000 communions in 1615 and 59,000 communions in 1673, decreasing to 35,500 in 1700, before increasing once again to 72,900 in 1715.[10] Here the Jesuit sodalities were even more prominent, numbering about 3,000 members in the mid-seventeenth century. Jesuits in Straubing, a still smaller city (with fewer than 5000 inhabitants by 1800), nonetheless managed to distribute 11,250 hosts in 1641, a number which climbed to 46,250 in 1690 but diminished to 25,060 in 1700. By the early 1700s, the numbers once again increased to a total of 38,753 in 1715.[11]

Even if the Society of Jesus was an exception or if its members, gauging piety by numbers, inflated the numbers of adherents, one conclusion is inescapable: frequent reception of the sacraments became a common and significant practice for Roman Catholics in seventeenth-century Bavaria. As noted, the evidence refers specifically to communion and not to confession, and some caution is thus in order. Because both the Jesuits and more traditional clergy had already demonstrated their determination to protect the sanctity of communion by insisting on penance first, any increase in the number of communions entailed significant increases in confession as well. Myths about the Jesuits and their success (or treachery) in

[9] For the populations of Ingolstadt and Straubing, see Paul Bairoch, Jean Batou, and Pierre Chèvre, *The Population of European Cities from 800 to 1850* (1988), pp. 4–9.

[10] For figures in 1615, 1700, and 1715, see BHStA, Jesuiten 102, 117, 120.

[11] BHStA, Jesuiten 106, 117, 120.

the confessional therefore had a basis in fact: the order was confessing far more people far more often than any other single religious group in early-modern Bavaria. Equally important, as Louis Châtellier has pointed out, the reach of Jesuit confraternities extended to every level of society and, in the Bavarian cities, almost every family had some representation in the congregations.[12] Their ostentatious displays of piety placed pressure on Roman Catholics at all levels. After all, by 1600, from the dukes on down, frequent sacramental reception both of communion and confession was explicitly an index of devotion. Even if the new practices were limited to sodality members and their circles, these constituted a significant presence in Bavarian towns and cities.

It is safe to conclude that in the midst of the larger Bavarian population, itself now confessing more often, a significant and organized element had adopted an even more intense approach. A new type of Roman Catholic piety, propagated by the Society of Jesus, distinguished itself from the traditional religiosity of the general population.[13] These *dévots* defined Roman Catholic piety from the seventeenth century onward, receiving even greater strength from the participation of the Bavarian ruling families. In sum, the fact that reception increased overall, and that officials were satisfied with the number (as opposed perhaps to the quality) of confessions, indicates that the standards of piety were changing for German-speaking Catholics, particularly in Bavaria. While the majority of Catholics did not match the fervor inspired by the Society of Jesus, most went more frequently to confession. The confessional gradually became a rule in Catholic churches, rather than an exception.

These facts permit a number of general conclusions. What has emerged most clearly in the pages of this book is the change in the orientation and

[12] Châtellier, *Europe of the Devout*, pp. 50–66, 196–197.
[13] R. Po-Chia Hsia has traced the transformation from the civic piety of late-medieval Münster to a more self-assertive religiosity under the auspices of the Jesuits. See *Society and Religion in Münster*, pp. 116–122, 177–198. His work does not deal with the sacraments, however. Marc Forster has cautioned that reform was conditioned by regional factors and by the presence of a strong Catholic secular power. In Speyer, for example, where a Catholic state was lacking, the continued vitality of Catholicism was due to its accomodation to traditional forms of piety rather than their rejection. See *Counter-Reformation in the Villages*, pp. 245–246. In Bavaria, the Counter-Reformation proved capable of adapting old and new kinds of piety. See Philip Soergel, *Wondrous in His Saints*, pp. 229–232, and Hörger, "Organisational Forms," pp. 215–216.

# Conclusion

function of sacramental penance during the tumultuous century and a half that witnessed the Protestant and Catholic Reformations. Despite its official importance, late-medieval confession was curiously tangential to the religious life of most lay Christians. This fact forces us to reconsider not the significance of medieval confession but the nature of that significance. For most medieval men and women, sacramental penance was not primarily a forum for spiritual counsel, no matter how pastoral theologians had come to view it. Instead, confession served ritualistic and juridical ends as a channel for the distribution of grace and divine favor, and it anchored the myriad nonsacramental penitential practices available to medieval Christians. Crowded at the end of Lent, involving large numbers of people attempting to confess at the same time, burdening the secular clergy (who in turn complained about the unruly crowds), confession was too intermittent and too irregular to provide what one Reformation figure called "ghostly counsel and advice."[14] People did not seek out confession as a forum for counsel or for pastoral care, perhaps not even to adjudicate disputes. Instead, they expected to be certified as worthy to participate in the great community celebration of Easter. What the congregation required of the clergy was expertise and effectiveness in performing the rites, not spiritual consolation.

In this pre-Reformation religious world, public and social elements were as important as theological and ecclesiastical ones. After all, one did not undergo confession alone or in private, but beside one's fellow parishioners. Sacramental confession was much more than its theological meaning implied: it was a shared event. One may have confessed secretly, but penance itself was experienced communally in every parish, village, or town. When one revealed one's sins, it was not usually as an anonymous penitent to an impartial but sympathetic judge. The pre-Reformation clergy were not aloof from their congregations but were in fact neighbors who were entwined with their parishioners in the same web of relations, friendships, and conflicts. In any confession, both confessor and confessant had to weigh the social ramifications of individual penance.

During the course of the sixteenth century, Roman Catholic ecclesiastics increasingly deemed this traditional situation intolerable. Not only did

---

[14] John Bossy's characterization of medieval confession (see Introduction, above).

the Reformation launch a successful theological attack on confession, but Catholic reformers themselves undertook to change the practice of sacramental confession to make it conform to the demands of a renewed pastoral ideal. Changes in the timing and setting of the rite thus signaled an important transformation of its function in religious life. With the new emphasis on frequent reception in the sixteenth and seventeenth centuries, confession evolved from a seasonal event employed by most Christians to prepare for Easter communion to a regular, even routine practice in the spiritual life of the pious, and eventually the entire laity. Preparing for and receiving sacramental penance came to be a continuous process that pervaded the lives of Catholics to an unprecedented degree and promoted the self-conscious and self-disciplined layperson idealized by the Counter-Reformation.

The introduction of the confessional at the end of the century diminished the pressure from the congregation, reducing its ability to influence the process of penance. As sacramental penance increasingly became a solitary dialogue between confessor and confessant, the values and thinking of the official church began to take precedence over the mores of the local parish or congregation. For the confessor, too, a more isolated position in the confessional permitted the kind of counseling recommended by the authors of handbooks and *summae*, a process difficult if not impossible to carry out under more traditional, public circumstances.

Once a seasonal ritual tied to the rhythms of Lent, penance became an event independent of season. Catholics, especially the most devout, now repeated the process of confession, absolution, and communion on a regular basis, even weekly or monthly. This meant that traditional ideas about religious time, which ran in annual cycles, also had to change. Lent, in other words, was internalized and became a permanent condition of the conscience. The disciplines of Lent—prayer, fasting, and meditation on death—stretched throughout the year, their austerity pervading all of Catholic piety. The public and seasonal drama of sin and repentance which defined the liturgical year was less important for many than the drama played out privately and regularly in the conscience.[15] As a result,

---

[15] Thus the liturgical year was "ironed out." See Andrew Barnes, "Religious Anxiety and Devotional Change in Sixteenth-Century French Penitential Confraternities," *Sixteenth Century Journal* 19 (1988): p. 402.

preparing for confession also became an essentially individual affair, with communal or public rituals playing a smaller role.[16]

Frequent confession and communion marked a shift in popular attitudes toward the sacraments themselves. Formerly, physical reception of communion had been far more restricted. Revered as an awesome symbol of divine power and presence, the Host was approached with trepidation and only after intense seasonal preparation. Both clergy and laity shared this view. During the sixteenth century, however, that understanding changed, and dramatically. By the seventeenth century, Catholic reformers were encouraging lay people to approach the Blessed Sacrament with a frequency exceeding even that of many priests. Though still held in awe, displayed in altars designed as monstrances and in Eucharistic processions, the Host was no longer a presence that worked on the world from a remote distance. The most sacred element of Roman Catholic religion was now commonly available and generally recommended.

This new attitude toward communion also had an impact on penance. The very idea that lay Catholics, after worthy preparation, should take frequent communion meant that sanctification in the world was considered a real possibility. The lay individual could be made holy even in the midst of a profane world, which of course required a continuous, individual effort at sanctity. Frequent communion demonstrated that sin had been conquered. Frequent confession was the Church's chosen weapon.

The program of regular Catholic confession in a relatively isolated space also provided the Church with a potentially effective means of discipline. One important result of this effort was to enhance the clergy's role in managing lay religious and moral life. The increased accessibility of confession diminished non- or extrasacramental means of grace and forgiveness, and religious practice focused more and more on the clergy's ability regularly to channel grace through the sacraments. Greater frequency of reception also meant commensurately greater individual con-

---

[16] In this sense, John Bossy is quite right about shifting "the emphasis away from the field of objective social relations and into a field of interiorized discipline for the individual." See "Social History of Confession," p. 21. For most people, however, this happened not in the twelfth and thirteenth centuries (p. 22), but during the Catholic Reformation.

tact with a priest as tutor and moral judge, while the development of privacy in confession eliminated pressure from congregation and community. This brought lay people into much closer association with the teaching of the institutional Church, which now had the opportunity to transmit its views on behavior and morality to a large population in an individual, highly personal fashion.

Paradoxically, however, subordinating the individual to the Church also involved greater reliance on the individual. Reciprocally, self-discipline was also more firmly under clerical guidance than had ever been the case in medieval Christianity. By conforming outwardly to the norms of Roman Catholicism, the layperson also appropriated them inwardly, as habits of the conscience. The discipline of the Church led to the discipline of the self, which then submitted voluntarily to clerical tutelage.[17] To this end, the process of penance must go beyond the confines of the confessional; the penitent must come to the sacrament already prepared, already disciplined. The regular examination of conscience permitted this: stressing preparation meant that much of the responsibility for searching and rooting out sin, and for creating and maintaining an orderly conscience, fell on lay people themselves.[18] While the clergy now possessed more control over the terms of morality and the process of discipline, they nonetheless demanded that lay people individually exercise greater self-restraint. A clerically defined morality was not simply to be imposed upon the laity—lay people were to incorporate it and make it their own. Clerical control became self-control.

By emphasizing frequent confession and examination of conscience, Catholic Reformers hoped to strengthen the Roman Church and thwart the advance of Protestantism. Yet this defense of tradition resulted in a Catholicism that differed decisively, if unintentionally, from its medieval

[17] In Habsburg lands, the confessor of Emperor Ferdinand II, William Lamormaini, S.J., believed that orthodoxy must first be reimposed by force, and habit would then lead to internal change, especially among youth. See Bireley, *Religion and Politics*, p. 38. In cases of heresy or disobedience, ecclesiastical discipline was perfectly acceptable to authorities, regardless of individual disposition. As R. J. W. Evans writes, "whereas the bulk of the population observed a code of Church discipline, the elite observed one of self-discipline." (*Making of the Habsburg Monarchy*, p. 311.)

[18] John Bossy has argued for a shift to preparation during the fifteenth century (*Christianity in the West*, p. 127). This could only occur for Roman Catholicism as a whole when the sacrament was received regularly by large numbers of people.

# Conclusion

forebear.[19] The new Roman Catholic did not seek merely to discover and confess sins. Instead, the Catholic was to seek perfection, which meant not only avoiding mortal sin but rooting out the inclination to it and applying that discipline to venial sin as well. Counter-Reformation confession went even further, for the object was to create a conscience aware of the smallest sin or temptation and able to "pursue" sinfulness in an attempt to eliminate it altogether.

Catholics waged their struggle with sins privately, within the individual conscience they then subjected to priestly examination. Their goal was discipline.[20] The mechanism of penance required keeping a watchful eye on the reflection and consent given to one's misdeeds. Essentially stoical in nature, it required a conscience, mediated by the intellect, distinctly separate from and more powerful than the physical and mental entity it oversaw.[21] The point of the examination was to enable the conscience to exert control over both mind and body. A devout Catholic could and should remain wary not only of the world, but of him- or herself. This presumed the ability not only to distinguish among temptations but to be constantly aware of and distinct from them at all times.

Confession provided an external discipline that enabled the Church to monitor individual progress and failure, and to regulate behavior. For the devout, the external ecclesiastical control of bodies and minds must become internal and voluntary. This of course was what Catholic rulers from Duke Maximilian of Bavaria to the Habsburgs of Austria intended—the congruence of secular and ecclesiastical forms and ideas

[19] For a discussion of the "law of unintended consequences" as it applies to the Catholic Reformation, see Wolfgang Reinhard, "Gegenreformation als Modernisierung? Prolegomena zu einer Theorie des konfessionellen Zeitalters," *Archiv für Reformationsgeschichte* 68 (1977): 226–252.

[20] On discipline, see Gerald Strauss, *Luther's House of Learning*, p. 238, which defines discipline (*Zucht*) as "a systematic, habit-shaping regime, part upbringing, instruction, and character formation, part surveillance, control, and punishment, a procedure expected to mold and tone the personality until obedience to established rules became automatic." Strauss concentrates on Lutheran pedagogy, but his description is strikingly similar to Catholic thinking on the subject.

[21] This Catholic Reformation piety reflected the triumph of a neo-stoical tendency in Renaissance Europe, described in William J. Bouwsma, "The Two Faces of Humanism: Stoicism and Augustinianism in Renaissance Thought," *Itinerarium Italicum*, ed. Heiko Oberman and Thomas Brady (1978), pp. 3–60.

mirrored even in individual piety, the order of the world reflected in the conscience.[22]

This penitential system was distinctive in its activist approach to perfection. Rather than waiting for the "shipwreck of sin" from which penance, as the "second plank after baptism," rescued the sinner, the Catholic was now to use the sacrament as a way of knowing temptation and disciplining action. In Ignatius Loyola's metaphor, the soul was a battleground between God, "our supreme Commander and Lord," and Satan, "the mortal enemy of our human nature."[23] Rather than hoping passively for God to rescue sinful, imprisoned humanity, the spirituality of the Counter-Reformation went on the offensive, to attack sin and conquer it, following in this way the standard of Christ as the soul's captain. The examination of conscience enabled the lay Catholic constantly to regulate his or her thinking and behavior so that the slightest deviance or temptation would be instantly apprehensible, the smallest sin immediately evident. Recourse to the sacrament and a skillful confessor then enabled the penitent to clear his or her conscience quickly and with relative ease. At the same time, the Catholic, constantly on guard against sin and temptation, could gradually reduce sinfulness, monitoring his or her progress toward perfection.

Thus could routine and frequent use of confession lead, ideally, to routine sinlessness. Late-medieval Christians were expected to confess *frequens*, but this meant that one should confess as soon as, and whenever, one became aware of a mortal sin. The medieval sinner responded to sins as they (inevitably) occurred. The "modern" approach of the late sixteenth and seventeenth centuries was different and involved a program of weekly or monthly confession in which the confessant was urged to search the conscience ruthlessly and bring sins to light. One actively sought out offenses for the purpose of exposing, revealing, and ultimately eradicating not only the sin but the condition which had caused it.

Confession thus became a forum not only for the revelation of sins to a priest, but for revealing them to the self as well: it became above all a mat-

---

[22] For the political, religious, and social ramifications of discipline, see Gerhard Oestreich, *Neostoicism and the Modern State* (1982). A useful synthesis of the literature is R. Po-Chia Hsia, *Social Discipline in the Reformation: Central Europe, 1550–1750* (1989).
[23] Ignatius of Loyola, "Spiritual Exercises," p. 154.

ter of self-knowledge, which was defined as recalling sins rather than plumbing the depths of one's depravity and desire. One might complain that this made for a superficial religion of exactly the sort that Protestant Reformers often attacked, and that it trivialized human sinfulness. This very "superficiality," however, enabled lay people to manage sin and guilt effectively, and this goes to the heart of the Catholic Reformation as a widespread pastoral reform. Sacramental penance could serve as an effective tool of lay education, discipline, and spiritual life only if it became more than a Lenten ritual. It had to become a common practice, available and convenient at all times for the busy layperson. For this to occur, confession had to become simple, even routine.

It is here that one might talk about "psychologizing" penance and sin.[24] It is true that by design, the sacrament was a matter of examining and testing motive. Because attrition was officially acceptable as a disposition for absolution, however, the problem of motive was not paramount among most Roman Catholics, a fact which greatly disturbed Jansenists.[25] Sin itself remained a highly objective set of acts rather than a quality or condition of the mind. The growing psychological dimension in confession meant appropriating an objective moral code. Penance, more and more, relied on the penitent's ability to govern his or her own actions, an internal discipline which he or she then subjected to priestly regulation. The devout Christian of the Catholic Reformation was marked by prudence, carefully examining the world and his or her conscience and exercising self-restraint in thought, word, and deed. The dukes of Bavaria understood this well. In setting out instructions for their children's religious education, they sought frequent confession and daily examinations of conscience, which not only increased piety and virtue but were "also a very good and useful means to worldly and political prudence and care-

---

[24] "Bossy, "Social History of Confession," p. 27.

[25] The Jansenists criticized the Jesuits for not caring enough about motive, as Blaise Pascal makes clear: "allow me to tell you my view, and point out the excesses to which this doctrine gives rise. When you say that 'attrition motivated solely by fear of punishment' is enough with the sacrament to justify sinners, does it not follow that one could expiate sins in this way all one's life, and so be saved without ever in one's life having loved God?" Pascal concludes, "Thus those who have never loved God all their lives are by you made worthy to enjoy him throughout eternity." Blaise Pascal, *Provincial Letters* (1967), no. 10, pp. 158–159, 162.

fulness."[26] This deliberate wariness allowed lay people, those banished children of Eve still consigned to the vale of tears, to walk cautiously in a dangerous world, avoiding the traps and snares of Satan.

Did preoccupation with sin and conscience produce a culture haunted by guilt and imbued with pessimism about the world and human nature?[27] Certainly the sermons and religious literature of the age, like that of the late-medieval period, were replete with references to the burning fires of hell and even the difficulties of Purgatory. Sin, too, pervaded such writings, presenting the world as worthy only of contempt. Did such thoughts also permeate the consciences of seventeenth-century Europeans? Powerful though this suggestion is, it is nonetheless difficult to accept. While the Church's preaching filled the world with sin, in fact the system to combat it had never been so well organized.

Although the preoccupation with sins may conjure up the image of morbid consciences dwelling on their own guilt, this was not the nature of penitential piety in the Catholic Reformation. Curiously, Catholic focus on specific sins deflected attention from questions about the general corruption of human nature. The early-modern Catholic was in some ways the opposite of introspective, not judging the heart but weighing individual acts and deeds, assessing nature by them, rather than interpreting individual behavior according to a pervasive sense of thorough human sinfulness. Catholics employed the mechanisms of confession to check their deeds and judged themselves accordingly. Describing the goal of confession, one author wrote, "I do not want you to be fearful and anxious, but cautious and careful."[28]

The habitual round of Catholic examination and confession should make us careful about identifying the sacrament with the guilt complex

---

[26] "So soll Er auch auß anlaitung des Beichtvatters, Hoffmaisters und Praeceptors täglich, ehe dann Er schlaffen gehet, sein *examen conscientiae* bey sich machen, weil solches nit allain zue der Gottsforcht, auáreittung der laster und vortpflanzung aller guetten Tugenden hoch vonnötten, sonnder auch zu Weltlicher und Politischer *prudenz* und fürsichtigkheit ein sehr guets und ersprießlichs mittel ist." "Instruktion für den Hormeister und Präceptor des Prinzen Johann Franz Karl," *Geschichte der Erziehung*, vol. 14, p. 95.

[27] This is the general conclusion of Jean Delumeau, *Sin and Fear*, pp. 555–556.

[28] "Ich will nit/ daß du forchtsam und ängstig seyest/ sonder behutsam und sorgfältig." *Kurzer Unterricht Recht*, p. 58.

attributed to this period by some historians.[29] Although intensified emphasis on self-examination and introspection could have had such results, the very routinization of confession entailed instead a system in which sin and guilt were objectified and resolved in a regular program of equally objective absolution and satisfaction. As presented by authors and theologians, frequent confession so routinized forgiveness as to diminish the presence and power of sin. Guilt was always balanced by the renewed sanctity continuously available through the cycle of penance. Even among sensitive consciences, therefore, introspection led not, as Delumeau had it, to a "collective guilt complex," defined as "a pathological anguish before God's judgment, an escalation of doubts, a rumination on sin (original, deadly, and venial), and a fixation on death."[30] What actually resulted was instead a chronic uncertainty about specific acts, the solution to which was renewed individual effort and increased reliance on the mechanisms of the Church. The tendency of the devout early-modern Catholic was to ever greater wariness and prudence in wandering the "vale of tears." Here again, self-discipline paradoxically made the Church and its clergy more necessary than ever.

One might even argue that this cycle of frequent confession ultimately diminished the specter of sin. This trivialization was the thrust of the criticisms published in France by Blaise Pascal, who excoriated the laxness of confession as practiced by the Society of Jesus.[31] On the surface, he may have been right.[32] Frequent confession, however, did not simply permit an

---

[29] Delumeau has written, "No civilization had ever attached as much importance to guilt and shame as did the Western world from the thirteenth to the eighteenth centuries." Delumeau, *Sin and Fear*, p. 3.

[30] Ibid, p. 297.

[31] "Was it not enough to permit men so many forbidden things by means of the palliations you have introduced? Did you also have to give them occasion to commit the very crimes you could not excuse, by offering them absolution so easily and surely, by destroying priests' power to that end, and obliging them to absolve, more as slaves than judges, the most inveterate sinners, with no fear of God, no change of life, no sign of regret, apart from promises broken a hundred times; without penance, 'if they are unwilling to accept it'; and without avoiding the occasions of vice 'if they find it inconvenient'?" Pascal, *Provincial Letters*, no. 10, p. 161.

[32] Louis Châtellier has argued that the difference between Pascal's religion and that advocated by the Jesuits lay in the contrast between the communal and public form advocated in the Marian Congregations and the internal and introspective attitude advocated by the Jansenists and Pascal. *Europe of the Devout*, pp. 157–158. In terms of confession, I believe the disparity lay in the different aims of two forms of individual

An eighteenth-century confessional. The Church of Saint Johann Nepomuk, Munich, known as the Asamkirche. Author's photo. Here the confessional has achieved a fixed and prominent place in the church, with appropriate devotional statuary to awe the penitent.

and internal discipline. For Pascal, the objective was to examine the condition of the conscience itself, while his Jesuit opponents focused on a set of objective acts susceptible to correction by the dedicated Catholic.

easy way out for Catholics, but allowed them also to monitor and improve their consciences regularly. Although pervasive, sin could be readily dispatched, and the absolved sinner emerged from confession ready to try again. Forgiveness, in the form of the priest, was always just around the corner. For Catholics, confession was a way of measuring improvement over time while seeking to eliminate sins altogether. Indeed, this was precisely the goal.

From this program emerged a well-groomed conscience not only ready to seek absolution but, ideally, also able to withstand temptation and to pursue a virtuous life. The goal for most lay people was neither contemplation nor mysticism but an active life, single-minded in its dedication to "pure" Catholic religion and to spiritual perfection while living in the world. To achieve this, the external functions of penance gave way to internal and spiritual concerns. The devout Catholic appropriated the public, seasonal process of Lent and made it a private matter of the heart experienced at all times and in all seasons. The focus of piety also shifted from the public ritual of absolution to the internal preparation of the penitent, and the relations between layperson and clergy became at once more intimate and yet more circumspect, just as the local church, with its congeries of rites and festivals, gave way to the organized institution of international Roman Catholicism.

In the city of Munich today, the visitor can go from the Jesuit church in the center of commerce and activity to another church on the Sendlingerstrasse on the way to the Sendlinger Tor. This church of Saint Johann Nepomuk, known as the Asamkirche after the architect brothers who designed it, was built a century and a half after Saint Michael's. The church is a shrine to confession and to a confessor. Entering it, one immediately notes the original confessionals on either side of the vestibule. Open to the world, they provide only limited privacy and respite from the crowd. Continuing into the church, the visitor sees another set of confessionals. Above each stand massive sculptures to remind the penitent of the need to repent. The sinner sees the shortness of life and the consequences of impenitence represented in sculpted skeletal skulls on the door and walls around the confessionals. Within them, priest and penitent are suspended between hell and heaven, and the confessional, representing life on earth, offers escape from the former and hope of the latter.

## "Careful, Not Fearful"

The church of Nepomuk represents the changes in confession in seventeenth- and eighteenth-century Bavaria. Pessimistic perhaps about the world itself, Catholic confession assumed that human beings would fail, would fall short of perfection. Sacramental penance also assumed, however, that these same human beings could pick themselves up after falling and begin anew. In this sense, the Roman Catholic attitude toward confession was anything but pessimistic. In the seventeenth century, marred by war, plague, and a persistent sense of crisis, the relief offered by confession helped Roman Catholics to endure the seemingly unremitting grimness. Of course, endurance was the minimum. The most devout Catholics might even find sanctity in the world, perhaps even hope to triumph over it. Whether they did so is a secret no confessional will ever yield.

# Bibliography

## Unpublished Primary Sources

Bayerisches Hauptstaatsarchiv München.
  Blech Kasten 34: Geistliche Policey
  Geistliche Ratsprotokolle
  Jesuiten 101–135

## Printed Primary Sources

*Agenda Bambergensiis*. Ingolstadt, 1587.
*Agenda ecclesiae moguntinensis*. Mainz, 1551.
*Agenda ecclesiae trevirensis*. Trier, 1574.
Androtius, Fulvius. *Seelen Speiß unnd Communionbüchlein*. Dillingen, 1591.
*Articuli Reformationis, omnibus Parochis, Vicariis, Provisoribus, Cooperatoribus et reliquis Sacerdotibus Episcopatui ac Dioecesi Pataviensi*. Passau, 1590.
Beckmann, J. *Quellen zur Geschichte des christlichen Gottesdienstes*. Gütersloh, 1956.
*Beichtspiegel/ Kurzer und nothwendiger Bericht/ wie ein Christenmensch sich zu dem Sacrament der Buß schicken/ seine Sünde erkennen/ berewen/ beychten und büssen soll*. N.p., n.d.
*Bekenntnisschriften der evangelisch-lutherischen Kirche*. Deutsche Evangelische Kirchenausschutz, eds. Göttingen, 1967.
Bickell, G., ed. *Synodi Brixinenses saeculi XV*. Innsbruck, 1880.
Borromeo, Carlo. *Instructiones fabricae et supellectilis ecclesiasticae. Trattati d'arte del cinquecento*. Ed. Paola Barocchi, vol 3. Bari, 1962.
———. *Instructiones fabricae et supellectilis ecclesiasticae*. Trans. Evelyn Voelker. Ph.D. diss., Syracuse University, 1977.
Braun, Reiner. *Die bayerischen Teile des Erzbistums Salzburg und des Bistums Chiemsee in der Visitation des Jahres 1558*. Studien zur Theologie und Geschichte, vol. 6. St. Ottilien, 1991.
Braunsberger, Otto, S.J., ed. *Beati Petri Canisii Societatis Jesu Epistulae et Acta*. 7 vols. Freiburg, 1896–1923.
Brillmacher, Petrus Michaelus, S.J. *Catechismus, Das ist Christlicher Bericht von wahrer Religion und Gottes dienst/ Sampt einem andechtigen Bettbuch*. Cologne, 1587.

# Bibliography

Calvin, Jean. Antidote to the Council of Trent." In *John Calvin*, ed. John Dillenberger. Decatur, Ga., 1975.

——. *Institutes of the Christian Religion.* Trans. Henry Beveridge. Grand Rapids, Mich., 1953.

Canisius, Peter. *Beicht unnd Communionbüchlein, das ist, Kurtzer grundlicher und notwendiger Bericht von den zweien Sacramenten der Buß und des Fronleichnams Christi.* Dillingen, 1579.

——. *Catechismus. Kurze Erklärung der fürnemsten stuck des wahren Catholischen Glaubens.* Cologne, 1563.

*Catechism of the Council of Trent for Parish Priests.* Translated with notes by John A. McHugh and Charles J. Callan. 10th printing. New York, 1947.

*Catechismus und Praxis.* Trier, 1589.

*Catholische Fragstuckh uber den Catechismum.* Thierhaupten, 1592.

Chemnitz, Martin. *Handbüchlein der fürnemsten hauptstücke der Christlichen Lehre/ durch Frag und Antwort aus Gottes Wort einfeltig vnd gründlich erkleret.* Magdeburg, n.d.

Coster, Francis. *Schatzbüchlein Gottsäliger und Catholischer underweisungen/ der Christlichen jugent.* Cologne, 1579.

Cusanus, Nicolaus, S.J. *Christliche Zucht-Schul/ allen Seelsorgern/ und gemeinem Mann sehr nützlich.* Cologne, 1675.

Dalham, Florianus, ed. *Concilia Salisburgensia Provincialia et Dioecesana.* Augsburg, 1778.

Dietenberger, Johann. *Catechismus. Evangelischer bericht und Christliche unterweisung der fürnemlichsten stück des waren heyligen Christlichen glaubens.* Mainz, 1537.

Drees, Clemens, ed. *Der Christenspiegel des Dietrich Kolde von Münster.* Franziskanische Forschungen, vol. 9. Werl, Westphalia, 1952.

Drexel, Jeremias, S.J. *Nicetas das ist Ritterlicher Kampf und Sig Wider alle unrainigkheit, und fleischlichen wollust.* Trans. Christopher Agricola. Munich, 1625.

Eisengrein, Martin. *Beichtbuch.* Ingolstadt, 1579.

Erasmus, Desiderius. *The Essential Erasmus.* Ed. John Dolan. New York, 1964.

——. *Ten Colloquies.* Trans. Craig Thompson. New York, 1957.

Fabri, Johannes. *Ain Christenlicher, rainer Catechismus,* Augsburg, n.d., reprinted in Dillingen in 1558 and 1563. In Christoph Moufang, ed., *Katholische Katechismen des 16. Jahrhunderts in deutscher Sprache.*

——. *Ein Nuetzlich Beychtbuechlein wie der mensch sich seiner sünd erinnern unnd die bekennen soll.* Augsburg, n.d.

Falk, Franz, ed. *Drei Beichtbüchlein nach den zehn Geboten aus der Frühzeit der Buckdruckerkunst.* Reformationsgeschichtliche Studien und Texte, vol. 2. Münster, 1907.

——. *Die pfarramtlichen Aufzeichnungen (Liber consuetudinum) des Florentius Diel zu St. Christoph in Mainz (1491–1519).* Freiburg im Breisgau, 1904.

Franck, Sebastian. *Weltbuch: Spiegel und bildtniß des gantzen erdbodens.* N.p., 1533.

Franzen, August, ed. *Die Visitationsprotokolle der ersten nachtridentinischen Visitation im Erzstift Köln unter Salentin von Isenburg.* Reformationsgeschichtliche Studien und Texte, vol 85. Münster in Westfalen, 1960.

# Bibliography

Geffken, Johannes, ed. *Bilderkatechismus des fünfzehnten Jahrhunderts.* Leipzig, 1855.

*Geistlicher und heilsamer Unterricht/ ein general oder gemeine Beicht anzustellen.* Cologne, 1610.

Gerson, Jean. *Opusculum Tripartitum.* Trans. *Johannes Geiler von Kaysersberg.* Strassburg, 1510.

Götz, Johann Baptist, ed. *Das Pfarrbuch des Stephen May in Hilpolstein vom Jahr 1511.* Münster, 1926.

Greving, Joseph, ed. *Johann Ecks Pfarrbuch für U.L. Frau in Ingolstadt. Ein Beitrag zur Kenntnis der pfarrkirchlichen Verhältnisse im XVI. Jahrhundert.* Reformationsgeschichtliche Studien und Texte, no. 4–5. Münster in Westphalia, 1908.

Gropper, Johannes. *Hauptartikell christlicher Underrichtung zur gottseligkeit.* Cologne, 1547. In Christoph Moufang, ed. *Katholische Katechismen des 16. Jahrhunderts in deutscher Sprache.*

*Guldener Himmels-Schlussel. Das ist hoch-nothwendige Unterrichtung/ recht und volkommenlich zubeichten.* N.p., 1692.

*Handbüchlein der Bruderschafft vnser lieber Frawen.* Würzburg, 1610.

Hartzheim, Josef, and Joannes Fridericus Schannat, eds. *Concilia Germaniae.* 12 vols. Cologne, 1759–1790.

Hasak, Vincenz, ed. *Der christliche Glaube des deutschen Volkes beim Schlusse des Mittelalters, dargestellt in deutschen Sprachdenkmalen, oder 50 Jahre der deutschen Sprache im Reformationszeitalter vom Jahre 1470 bis 1520.* Regensburg, 1868.

——. *Herbstblumen, oder: Alter, ernste Wahrheiten. Zur Illustration des christlichen Volksunterrichtes in der vorreformatorischen Zeit.* Regensburg, 1885.

Helding, Michael. *Catechesis Das ist, kurtze Erklerung unsers h. Christlichen Glaubens.* Mainz, 1555. In Christoph Moufang, ed. *Katholische Katechismen des 16. Jahrhunderts in deutscher Sprache.*

Herolt, Joannes. *Sermones Discipuli in Quadragesima.* Venice, 1606.

Höhlbaum, Konstantin, ed. *Das Buch Weinsberg.* Kölner Denkwürdigkeiten aus dem 16. Jahrhundert. Leipzig, 1886.

Ignatius of Loyola, Saint. "Spiritual Exercises." In George Ganss, S.J., ed. *Ignatius Loyola: Spiritual Exercises and Selected Works.* New York, 1991.

Jacobson, Franz. *Geschichte der Quellen des Kirchenrechts des preußischen Staates.* (1837/1844).

Jedin, Hubert, ed. *Conciliorum Oecumenicorum Decreta.* Bologna, 1973.

Kolde, Dietrich. *Ein fruchtbar Spiegel, oder Handbüchelchen der Christenmenschen.* In Christoph Moufang, ed. *Katholische Katechismen des 16. Jahrhunderts in deutscher Sprache.*

*Kurzer Unterricht Recht und Wohl zu beichten. Von Einem der Societat JESU Priestern beschrieben.* Dillingen, 1677.

Landersdorfer, Anton, ed. *Das Bistum Freising in der bayerischen Visitation des Jahres 1560.* St. Ottilien, 1986.

Lautherius, Georg. *Drey christlich . . . Predigten . . . wie Buss zu wircken.* Munich, 1572.

Leisentritt, Johann. *Catholisch Pfarbuch.* Cologne, 1578.

Loserth, Johannes, ed. *Acten und Correspondenzen zur Geschichte der Gegenreformation in Innerösterreich unter Karl II und Ferdinand II.* 2 vols. Stuttgart, 1898–1907.

# Bibliography

Luther, Martin. "Articuli Christianae Doctrinae (1537)." *Die Bekenntnisschriften der evangelisch–lutherischen Kirche.* Göttingen, 1967.

———. *D. Martin Luthers Werke: Kritische Gesamtausgabe.* Weimar, 1883–.

———. *Luther's Works,* ed. Jaroslav Pelikan and H.T. Lehmann. St. Louis, Mo., 1955–.

Mai, Paul, ed. *Das Bistum Regensburg in der Bayerischen Visitation von 1559.* Beiträge zur Geschichte des Bistums Regensburg, ed. Georg Schwaiger, vol. 27. Regensburg, 1993.

Mayer, Georgius, trans. *Gemaine Beichtform. Wie der Sünder leychtlich zu erkantnuß seiner Sünden kommen/ und dieselben ordenlich Beichten kan.* Tegernsee, 1577.

Melanchthon, Philipp. "Apologia der Confession." In *Die Bekenntnisschriften der evangelisch–lutherischen Kirche.* Göttingen, 1967.

"Monita paterna Maximiliani, Utriusque Bavariae Ducis, S. R. J. Electoris et Archidapiferi, ad Ferdinandum, Utriusque Bavariae Ducem, Filium adhuctrimulum." In *Geschichte der Erziehung der Bayerischen Wittelsbacher,* ed. Friedrich Schmidt, pp. 105–142.

Moufang, Christoph, ed. *Katholische Katechismen des 16. Jahrhunderts in deutscher Sprache.* Mainz, 1881.

Müllendorf, R., and W. Scherer, eds. *Denkmäler deutscher Poesie und Prosa aus dem 8.–12. Jahrh.* Berlin, 1892.

Müller, Jacob, *Kirchengeschmuck, Das ist: Kurtzer Begriff der fürnembsten Dingen/ damit ein jede recht und wol zugerichte Kirchen/ geziert und auffgebutzt seyn solle.* Munich, 1591.

Nass, Johannes. *Handbuchlein des klein Christianismi.* Ingolstadt, 1570.

*Newer Beichtform. Das ist, Geistliche Underrichtung/ wie mennigklich leicht und ohne grosse Mühe/ ja ohn ainiges Schreiben/ in wenig Stunden/ sich von vilen verflossenen Jahren her/ zu einer vollkommen General, wie auch nicht weniger zur Ordinari-beicht/ so er zu Zeiten im Jahr/ als zur Oesterlichen Zeit/ und ander Festtagen zu thun pflegt/ sicherlich beraiten/ unnd solche mit Frucht verrichten könne.* Munich, 1635.

Ninguarda, Felicianus. *Manuale Parochorum et aliorum curam animarum habentium.* Ingolstadt, 1582.

Olin, John, ed. *The Catholic Reformation: Savonorola to Ignatius Loyola.* New York, 1992.

Pascal, Blaise. *Provincial Letters.* New York, 1967.

*Pastorale ad usum Romanum accommodatum in Dioecesi Frisingensi.* Ingolstadt, 1612.

*Pastorale ad usum Romanum accommodatum in Dioecesi Passaviensi.* Munich, 1608.

Pfeilschifter, Georg, ed. *Acta Reformationis Catholicae Ecclesiam Germaniae Concernentia Saeculi XVI.* 6 vols. Regensburg, 1960.

Pirckheimer, Caritas. *Denkwürdigkeiten.* In Marianne Beyer-Fröhlich, ed. *Deutsche Selbstzeugnisse,* vol. 4. *Aus dem Zeitalter des Humanismus und der Reformation.* Leipzig, 1931.

Polanco, Juan. *Breve Directorium ad confessarii.* Cologne, 1560.

Ribadeneira, Pedro de, S.J. *Leben Francisci Borgiae, dritten Generals der Societat IESU.* Trans. Conrad Vettern. Ingolstadt, 1613.

*Rituale sacramentorum Romanum Gregorii papae XIII Pont. Max. iussu editum.* Rome, 1584.

# Bibliography

Schilling, A., ed. "Die religiösen und kirchlichen Zustände der ehemaligan Reichstadt Biberach unmittelbar vor Einführhung der Reformation," *Freiburger Diözesansarchiv* 19 (1887).

Schmidt, Friedrich, ed. *Geschichte der Erziehung der Bayerischen Wittelsbacher von den frühesten Zeiten bis 1750.* Monumenta Germaniae Paedagogica, vol. 14. Berlin, 1892.

Schönfelder, Albert, ed. *Die Agende der Diözese Schwerin von 1521.* Liturgische Bibliothek. Paderborn, 1906.

Schornbaum, Karl, and W. Kraft. "Pappenheim am Ausgang des Mittelalters in kirchlicher Hinsicht auf Grund des Pfarrbuches des Pfarrers Stefan Aigner." *Zeitschrift für bayerische Kirchengeschichte* 7 (1932): 129–160, 193–220.

Schroeder, H. J., trans. and ed. *The Canons and Decrees of the Council of Trent.* Rockford, Ill., 1978.

———. *Disciplinary Decrees of the General Councils.* St. Louis, 1937.

Schwarz, W. E. *Briefe und Akten zur Geschichte Maximilians II,* vol. 2, *Zehn Gutachten über die Lage der katholischen Kirche in Deutschland (1573/1576) nebst dem Protokolle der deutschen Congregation (1573/1578).* Paderborn, 1891.

Scopper, Jacob. *Catechismus, Das ist/ Christliche Unterweisung und gegründer Bericht/ nach warer Evangelischer und Catholischer lehr.* Cologne, 1562.

Sehling, Emil, ed. *Die evangelischen Kirchenordnungen des 16. Jahrhunderts,* 5 vols. Leipzig, 1902–13.

Selgrad, Anton, ed. and trans. *Kanonische Visitationen der Apatiner Pfarrei im XVIII. und XIX. Jahrhundert.* Apatiner Beiträge, vol. 17. Straubing, 1979.

*Spiegel des Sünders* (Augsburg, ca. 1470). In Johannes Geffken, ed. *Bilderkatechismus des fünfzehnten Jahrhunderts,* Leipzig, 1855.

Strauss, Gerald, ed. "The Articles of the Bundschuh in the Bishopric of Speyer (1502)." In *Manifestations of Discontent in Germany on the Eve of the Reformation,* ed. Strauss. Bloomington, 1971.

*Underricht fur die Seelsorger und Pfarrherrn dess Stiffts Muenster, wie sie den Kindern unnd andern unwissenden den Catechismum nuetzlich furtragen sollen.* Münster, 1613.

Vogler, Georg, *Catechismüs in aüsserlesenen Exempeln, kürzen Fragen, schön Gesängern, Reymn und Reye für Kirchen und Schülen von newem fleissig aüsgelegt und gestelt.* Würzburg, 1630.

Waeber, L. "Constitutions synodales inédites du Prévot Schneuwly." *Zeitschrift für schweizerische Kirchengeschichte* 30 (1936).

Walasser, Adam. *Geistlicher und Weltlicher Zuchtspiegel. Schöne Christliche Lehr und Regeln/ wie sich allerlay Standts Menschen/ inn Geistlichen und Weltlichen sachen/ im hauß und darauß erbarlichen halten sollen.* Ingolstadt, 1572.

Wenzel, Horst, ed. *Die Autobiographie des späten Mittelalters und der frühen Neuzeit.* vol. 2, *Die Selbstdeutung des Stadtbürgertums.* Munich, 1980.

Wicelius, Georg. *Catechismus. Belehrung der Kinder der Kirche, ebenso gesund als kurz.* Mainz, 1542. In Christoph Moufang, ed. *Katholische Katechismen des 16. Jahrhunderts in deutscher Sprache.*

Wicks, Jared, ed. *Cajetan Responds: A Reader in Reformation Controversy.* Washington, 1978.

# Bibliography

## Secondary Sources

Abray, Lorna Jane. *The People's Reformation: Magistrates, Clergy, and Commons in Strasbourg, 1500–1598.* Ithaca, 1985.

Anciaux, P. "Le sacrement de pénitence chez Guillaume d'Auvergne." *Etudes de théologie et liturgie* (1948): 98–118.

Appel, Helmut. *Anfechtung und Trost im Spätmittelalter und bei Luther.* Schriften des Vereins für Reformationsgeschichte, no. 165. Leipzig, 1938.

Arendt, Hans Peter. *Bußsakrament und Einzelbeichte.* Freiburg, 1981.

Ay, Karl-Ludwig. *Land und Fürst im alten Bayern.* Regensburg, 1988.

Bahlmann, P. *Deutschlands katholische Katechismen bis zum Ende des sechzehnten Jahrhunderts.* Münster in Westphalia, 1894.

Bairoch, Paul, Jean Batou, and Pierre Chèvre. *The Population of European Cities from 800 to 1850.* Geneva, 1988.

Barnes, Andrew. "Religious Anxiety and Devotional Change in Sixteenth Century French Penitential Confraternities." *Sixteenth Century Journal* 19 (1988): 389–405.

Barth, Medard. "Beicht und Kommunionen im mittelalterlichen Elsaß." *Freibürger Diözesansarchiv* 74 (1954): 88–99.

Bauerreiss, Remouald, OSB. *Kirchengeschichte Bayerns.* St. Ottilien and Augsburg, 1955–1965.

———. *Pie Jesu – Das Schmerzensmann-Bild und sein Einfluss auf die mittelalterliche Frömmigkeit.* Munich, 1931.

Bäumer, Remigius. *Johannes Cochlaeus (1479–1552): Leben und Werk im Dienst der katholischen Reform.* Katholisches Leben und Kämpfen im Zeitalter der Glaubensspaltung, no. 40. Münster, 1980.

Baumgartner, Konrad. *Die Seelsorge im Bistum Passau zwischen Barocker Tradition, Aufklärung und Restauration.* Münchener theologische Studien, vol. 19. St. Ottilien, 1975.

Beck, Manfred. *Untersuchungen zur geistlichen Literatur im kölner Druck des frühen 16. Jahrhunderts.* Göppinger Arbeiten zur Germanistik, no. 228. Göppinger, 1977.

Becker, H. "Der Erfurter Domprediger Dr. Konrad Klinge und seine Stellung zur Reformation." *Franziskanische Studien* 10 (1923): 177–198.

———. "Dr. Konrad Klinge, der Fuhrer der Erfurter Katholiken zur Zeit der Glaubensspaltung," *Franziskanische Studien* 17 (1930): 273–297.

Benzing, Josef. *Die Buchdrucker des 16. und 17. Jahrhunderts im deutschen Sprachgebiet.* Walter Bauhuis, ed., Beiträge um Buck- und Bibliothekwesen, vol. 12. Wiesbaden, 1963.

Bezzel, Ernst. "Beichte III: Reformationszeit." *Theologische Realenzyklopädie.* Berlin, 1980. Vol. 5: 421–425.

Bilinkoff, Jodi. "Confessors, Penitents, and the Construction of Identities in Early Modern Avila." In Barbara Diefendorf and Carla Hesse, eds., *Culture and Identity in Early Modern Europe.* Ann Arbor, 1993, pp. 83–100.

Binterim, A. J. *Pragmatische Geschichte der deutschen National, Provinzial- und vorzuglichen Dioecesan-concilien,* 7 vols. Mainz, 1848.

# Bibliography

Bireley, Robert. *Religion and Politics in the Age of the Counterreformation: Emperor Ferdinand II, William Lamormaini, S.J., and the Formation of Imperial Policy.* Chapel Hill, 1981.

Black, Christopher. *Italian Confraternities in the Sixteenth Century.* Cambridge, Eng., 1989.

Bloomfield, Morton Wilfred. *The Seven Deadly Sins: An Introduction to the History of a Religious Concept, with Special Reference to Medieval English Literature.* East Lansing, Mich., 1952.

Bossy, John. "Blood and Baptism: Kinship, Community and Christianity in Western Europe, Fourteenth to Seventeenth Centuries." In D. Baker, ed., *Sanctity and Secularity. Studies in Church History,* vol. 10. Oxford, 1973: 129–143.

——. *Christianity in the West, 1400–1700.* Oxford, 1985.

——. "The Counter-Reformation and the People of Catholic Europe." *Past and Present* 47 (1970): 51–70.

——. "Essai de sociographie de la messe, 1200–1700." *Annales E.S.C.* 36 (1981): 44–70.

——. "The Social History of Confession in the Age of the Reformation." *Transactions of the Royal Historical Society* 25 (1975): 21–38.

Bouwsma, William J. "The Two Faces of Humanism: Stoicism and Augustinianism in Renaissance Thought." In Heiko Oberman and Thomas Brady, eds., *Itinerarium Italicum.* Leiden, 1975, pp. 3–60.

Boyle, Leonard. "The Summa for Confessors as a Genre and its Religious Intent." In Charles Trinkaus, ed., *The Pursuit of Holiness in Late Medieval and Renaissance Religion,* pp. 126–130.

Brady, Thomas, Jr. *Ruling Class, Regime, and Reformation at Strasbourg, 1520–1555.* Studies in Medieval and Reformation Thought, vol. 22. Leiden, 1978.

Braeckmans, Louis, S.J. *Confession et communion au moyen âge et au concile de Trente* Gembloux, 1971.

Brandmüller, Walter, ed. *Handbuch der Bayerischen Kirchengeschichte,* vol. 2. *Von der Glaubensspaltung bis zur Säkularisation.* St. Ottilien, 1993.

Brandt, August. *Johann Ecks Predigttätigkeit an U. L. Frau zu Ingolstadt (1525–1542).* Reformationsgeschichtliche Studien und Texte, no. 27/28. Münster in Westphalia, 1914.

Braun-Troppau, Edmund W., and Otto Schmitt. "Beichtstuhl." In Otto Schmitt, ed. *Reallexikon zur deutschen Kunstgeschichte.* Stuttgart, 1948.

Braunisch, Reinhard. *Die Theologie der Rechtfertigung im Enchiridion (1538) des Johannes Gropper: sein Kritischer Dialog mit Philipp Melanchthon.* Reformationsgeschichtliche Studien und Texte, no. 109. Münster in Westfalen, 1974.

Breuer, Dieter. "Absolutische Staatsreform und neue Frömmigkeitsformen. Vorüberlegungen zu einer Frömmigkeitsgeschichte der frühen Neuzeit aus literarhistorischer Sicht." In Dieter Breuer, ed., *Frömmigkeit in der frühen Neuzeit: Studien zur religiösen Literatur des 17. Jahrhunderts in Deutschland.* Amsterdam, 1984.

Briggs, Robin. "Sins of the People." In Briggs, *Communities of Belief.* Oxford, 1989, pp. 277–338.

# Bibliography

Brodrick, James, S.J. *St. Peter Canisius, S.J.* London, 1935.

Browe, Peter, S.J. "Der Beichtunterricht im Mittelalter." *Theologie und Glaube* 26 (1934): 427–442.

——. *Die häufige Kommunion im Mittelalter.* Münster, 1938.

——. "Die Kommunionvorbereitung im Mittelalter." *Zeitschrift für Theologie und Kirche* 56 (1932): 375–415.

——. "Die Pflichtbeichte im Mittelalter." *Zeitschrift für katholische Theologie* (1933): 335–383.

——. *Die Pflichtkommunion im Mittelalter.* Münster, 1940.

Brown, D. Catherine. *Pastor and Laity in the Theology of Jean Gerson.* Cambridge, Eng., 1987.

Buchner, Franz. *Die mittelalterliche Pfarrpredigt im Bistum Eichstätt.* Neumarkt, 1923.

Buxbaum, Engelbert Maximilian. *Petrus Canisius und die kirchliche Erneuerung des Herzogtums Bayern, 1549–1556.* Rome, 1973.

Cameron, Euan. *The European Reformation.* Oxford, 1991.

Casals, G. Eude. *La doctrina de la confesión integra desde el IV Concilio de Letrán hasta el Concilio de Trento.* Barcelona, 1967.

Châtellier, Louis. *The Europe of the Devout: The Catholic Reformation and the Formation of a New Society.* Cambridge, Eng., 1989.

Coreth, Anna. *Pietas Austriaca. Ursprung und Entwicklung barocker Frömmigkeit in Österreich.* Munich, 1959.

Cruz, Anne J., and Mary Elizabeth Perry, eds. *Culture and Control in Counter-Reformation Spain.* Minneapolis, 1992.

Dagens, Jean. *Bibliographie chronologique de la littérature de spiritualité et de ses sources, 1501–1610.* Paris, 1952.

Darnton, Robert. *The Kiss of Lamourette: Reflections in Cultural History.* New York, 1990.

Davis, Natalie. "From 'Popular Religion' to Religious Cultures." In Steven Ozment, ed., *Reformation Europe: A Guide to Research*, St. Louis, 1982, pp. 321–341.

——. "Some Tasks and Themes in the Study of Popular Religion." In Charles Trinkaus, ed. *The Pursuit of Holiness in Late Medieval and Renaissance Religion*, pp. 307–338.

Day, Dorothy. *The Long Loneliness.* New York, 1952.

Delaruelle, Etienne, E.-R. Labande, and Paul Ourliac. *L'église au temps du Grand Schisme et de la crise conciliaire (1378–1449).* In Fliche and Martin, eds. *Histoire de l'église depuis les origines jusqu'à nos jours*, vol. 14. Paris, 1964.

Delumeau, Jean. *Le catholicisme entre Luther et Voltaire.* Paris, 1971.

——. *Sin and Fear: The Emergence of a Western Guilt Culture, 13th–18th Centuries.* New York, 1990.

*Dictionnaire de spiritualité, ascétique et mystique.* Vol. 12, pt. 1, "Pénitence," by Pierre Adnes. Paris, 1984, pp. 943–1010.

*Dictionnaire de théologie catholique, contenant l'exposé des doctrines de la théologie catholique, leurs preuves et leur histoire.* Paris, 1938.
Vol. 1, part 2, "Attrition," pp. 2235–2262.
Vol. 3, part 1, "Confession," pp. 828–926.

# Bibliography

Vol. 3, part 1, "Contrition," pp. 1671–1694.

Vol. 12, part 1, "Pénitence," pp. 947–1056.

Vol. 14, part 1, "Satisfaction," pp. 1129–1210.

Dietterle, Johannes. "Die Summae confessorum (sive de casibus conscientiae)—von ihren Anfängen an bis zu Silvester Prierias—unter besonderer Berücksichtigung ihrer Bestimmungen über den Ablass," *Zeitschrift für Kirchengeschichte* 24 (1903): 35–374, 520–548; 25 (1904): 248–272; 26 (1905): 59–81, 350–362; 27 (1906): 70–83, 166–188, 296–310, 433–442; 28 (1907): 401–431.

Dolan, Jay P. *The American Catholic Experience: A History from Colonial Times to the Present.* New York, 1985.

Douglass, E. Jane Dempsey. *Justification in Late Medieval Preaching. A Study of John Geiler of Keisersberg.* Heiko Obermann, ed. Studies in Medieval and Reformation Thought, vol. 1. Leiden, 1966.

Duggan, Lawrence. "Fear and Confession on the Eve of the Reformation." *Archiv für Reformationsgeschichte* 75 (1984): 153–175.

Duhr, Bernhard. *Geschichte der Jesuiten in den Ländern deutscher Zunge.* 4 vols. Freiburg im Breisgau, 1907–1928.

———. *Die Studienordnung der Gesellschaft Jesu.* Freiburg, 1896.

———. "Zur Geschichte des Jesuitenordens. Aus Münchener Archiven und Bibliotheken." *Historisches Jahrbuch* 25 (1904): 126–167; 28 (1907): 61–83, 306–327.

Duval, André. "Le concile de Trente et la confession." *La Maison-Dieu* 118 (1974): 131–180.

Eberl, A. *Geschichte der bayerischen Kapuzinerprovinz 1593–1902.* Freiburg im Breisgau, 1902.

Eder, Karl. *Glaubensspaltung und Landstände in Österreich ob der Enns 1525–1602.* Studien zur Reformationsgeschichte Oberösterreichs, vol. 2. Linz, 1936.

Eisenhofer, Ludwig. *Handbuch der katholischen Liturgie.* 2 vols. Freiburg im Breisgau, 1932.

———. *The Liturgy of the Roman Rite.* Freiburg im Breisgau, 1961.

Engen, John van. "The Christian Middle Ages as an Historiographical Problem." *American Historical Review* 91 (June, 1986): 519–552.

Evans, R. J. W. *The Making of the Habsburg Monarchy, 1550–1700.* Oxford, 1979.

Evennett, H. Outram. *The Spirit of the Counter-Reformation.* Notre Dame, 1970.

Fazzalaro, Francis Joseph. *The Place for the Hearing of Confessions: A Historical Synopsis and a Commentary.* Catholic University of America Canon Law Studies, no. 301. Washington, D.C., 1950.

Feifel, Erich. *Grundzüge einer Theologie des Gottesdienstes: Motive und Konzeption der Glaubensverkündigung Michael Heldings (1506–1561).* Untersuchungen zur Theologie der Seelsorge, no. 15. Freiburg, 1960.

Feuerstein, Johann. *Lebensbild des heiligmäßigen P. Jakob Rem S.J. (1546–1618).* Bregenz, 1931.

Florey, Gerhard. *Geschichte der Salzburger Protestanten und ihrer Emigration 1731/1732.* Graz, 1977.

Flynn, Maureen. *Sacred Charity: Confraternities and Social Welfare in Spain, 1400–1700.* Ithaca, 1989.

# Bibliography

Forster, Marc. *The Counter-Reformation in the Villages.* Ithaca, 1992.

Frank, Richard. "Geschichte der evangelischen Privatbeichte in Sachsen." *Beiträge zur Sächsischen Kirchengeschichte* 19 (1905).

Friedberg, Emil. *Aus deutschen Bussbüchern: ein Beitrag zur deutschen Culturgeschichte.* Halle, 1868.

Geertz, Clifford. *Interpretation of Cultures: Selected Essays.* New York, 1973.

Götz, Johann Baptist. "Die kirchliche Festfeier in der Eichstätter Diözese am Ausgang des Mittelalters." *Zeitschrift für bayerische Kirchengeschichte* 9 (1934): 129–149, 193–236.

———. *Die religiöse Bewegung in der Oberpfalz von 1520–1560.* Erganzung und Erläuterung zur Janssens Geschichte des deutschen Volkes, vol. V, no. 3–4. Freiburg im Breisgau, 1907.

Greyerz, Kaspar von, ed. *Religion and Society in Early Modern Europe, 1500–1800.* London, 1984.

Grotefend, Hermann. *Taschenbuch der Zeitrechnung des deutschen Mittelalters.* Hanover, 1982.

Groupe de la Bussière. *Pratiques de la confession des Pères du désert à Vatican II.* Paris, 1983.

Guibert, Joseph de. *The Jesuits: Their Spiritual Doctrine and Practice.* Trans. W. J. Young. St. Louis, 1964.

Gy, Pierre-Marie. "Histoire liturgique du Sacrement du Pénitence," *La Maison-Dieu* 56 (1958).

———. "Le précepte de la confession annuelle (Latran IV, C. 21) et la détection des hérétiques." *Révue de science philosophique et théologique* 58 (1974): 444–450.

Hamm, Berndt. *Frömmigkeitstheologie am Anfang des sechszehnten Jahrhunderts.* Studien zu Johannes von Palz und seinem Umkreis. Tübingen, 1982.

Hantsch, Hugo. *Die Geschichte Österreichs.* Graz, 1959.

Harline, Craig. "Official Religion–Popular Religion in Recent Historiography of the Catholic Reformation." *Archiv für Reformationsgeschichte* 81 (1990): 239–262.

Harnack, Adolph von. *History of Dogma.* 7 vols. London, 1898.

Hausberger, Karl. *Geschichte des Bistums Regensburg,* vol. 2. *Vom Barock bis zur Gegenwart.* Regensburg, 1989.

———. *Gottfried Langwerth von Simmern (1669–1741), bistumsadministrator und Weihbischof zu Regensburg.* Georg Schwaiger, ed. Beiträge zur Geschichte des bistums Regensburg, vol. 7. Regensburg, 1973.

———, and Benno Hubensteiner. *Bayerische Kirchengeschichte.* Munich, 1985.

Headley, John M. "Borromean Reform in the Empire? *La Strada Rigorosa* of Giovanni Franceso Bonomi." In John M. Headley and John B. Tomaro, eds. *San Carlo Borromeo: Catholic Reform and Ecclesiastical Politics in the Second Half of the Sixteenth Century.* Washington, D.C., 1988.

Heinz, Andreas. "Die deutsche Sondertradition für einen Bussritus der Gemeinde in der Messe," *Liturgisches Jahrbuch* 28/4 (1978): 193–214.

Heydenreuter, Reinhard. *Der landesherrliche Hofrat unter Herzog und Kurfürst Maximilian I. von Bayern (1598–1651).* Munich, 1981.

Heynck, Valens. "Attritio sufficiens." *Franziskanische Studien* 31 (1949): 76–134.

# Bibliography

——. "Der richterliche Charakter des Bußsakraments nach Duns Skotus." *Franziskanische Studien* 47 (1965): 399–414.

——. "Untersuchungen über die Reuelehre der tridentinischen Zeit." *Franziskanische Studien* 29 (1942): 150–182.

——. "Die Verteidigung der Sakramentenlehre des Duns Skotus durch den hl. John Fisher gegen die Anschuldigungen Luthers." *Franziskanische Studien* 24 (1937): 147–170.

——. "Zum Problem der unvollkommenen Reue auf dem Konzil von Trient." In Georg Schreiber, ed., *Das Weltkonzil von Trient*. Freiburg, 1951, pp. 231–280.

Hilz, Anneliese. *Die Minderbrüder von St. Salvator in Regensburg, 1226–1810.* Georg Schwaiger, ed. Beiträge zur Geschichte des Bistums Regensburg, no. 25. Regensburg, 1991.

Hirschman, Adam. "Bilder aus dem Leben der Geistlichen der Diözese Eichstätt um die Mitte des 16. Jahrhunderts." *Archiv für Kulturgeschichte* 12 (1916): 380–400.

Hoeynck, V. *Geschichte der kirchlichen Liturgie des bisthums Augsburg.* Augsburg, 1889.

Hoffman, Philip T. *Church and Community in the Diocese of Lyon, 1500–1789.* New Haven, 1984.

Hofmann, S. "Der Rat der Stadt Ingolstadt und die Gegenreformation im Spiegel der Ratsprotokolle der 2. Hälfte des 16. Jahrhunderts." *Sammelblatt des historischen Vereins Ingolstadt* 73 (1964): 5–24.

Hopfenmüller, Annelie. *Der geistliche Rat unter den Kurfürsten Ferdinand Maria und Max Emanuel von Bayern (1651–1726).* Miscellanea Bavarica Monacensia, vol. 85. Munich, 1985.

Hörger, Hermann. "Organisational Forms of Popular Piety in Rural Old Bavaria (Sixteenth to Nineteenth Centuries)." In Kasper von Greyerz, ed. *Religion and Society in Early Modern Europe*, pp. 212–222.

——. "Stabile Strukturen und mentalitätsbildende Elemente in der dörflichen Frömmigkeit. Die pfarrlichen Verkündbücher als mentalitätsgeschichtliche Quelle." In *Bayerisches Jahrbuch für Volkskunde 1980/81.* Würzburg: Kommissionsverlag Karl Hart, 1982, pp. 110–133.

Hsia, R. Po-Chia. *Social Discipline in the Reformation: Central Europe, 1550–1750.* New York, 1989.

——. *Society and Religion in Münster, 1535–1618.* New Haven, 1984.

Hubensteiner, Benno. *Vom Geist des Barock: Kultur und Frömmigkeit im alten Bayern.* Munich, 1967.

Hübner, Karl. "Die salzburgischen Provinzialsynoden im 16. Jahrhundert." *Deutsche Geschichtsblätter* 12 (1910/1911): 97–126, and 12 (1912): 243–248.

Jedin, Hubert. *Geschichte des Konzils von Trient.* Freiburg, 1970.

Jungmann, Josef. *Die lateinischen Bußriten in ihrer geschichtlichen Entwicklung.* Forschung zur Geschichte des innerkirchliches Lebens, 3/4. Innsbruck, 1932.

——. *Missarum Sollemnia.* Freiburg, 1962.

——. "Rosensonntag." In Karl Rahner and Josef Hafer, eds. *Lexikon für Theologie und Kirche.*

# Bibliography

Kettenmeyer, J. B. *Die Anfänge der marianischen Sodalität in Köln 1576–1586.* Katholisches Leben und Kämpfen im Zeitalter der Glaubensspaltung, no. 2. Münster in Westfalen, 1928.

Kinder, E. "Beichte und Absolution nach den lutherischen Bekenntnisschriften," *Theologische Literaturzeitung* 77 (1952): 543–550.

Klaiber, Wilbirgis, ed. *Katholische Kontroverstheologen und Reformer des 16. Jahrhunderts: ein Werkverzeichnis.* Reformationsgeschichtliche Studien und Texte, no. 116. Münster in Westfalen, 1978.

Klee, Heinrich. *Die Beichte.* Frankfurt, 1828.

Knöpfler, Alois. *Die Kelchbewegung in Bayern unter Herzog Albrecht V.* Munich, 1891.

Kotter, Franz Josef. *Die Eucharistielehre in den katholischen Katechismen des 16. Jahrhunderts bis zum Erscheinen des Catechismus Romanus (1566).* Reformationsgeschichtlichen Studien und Texte, no. 98. Münster, 1969.

Krasenbrink, Joseph. *Die Congregatio Germanica und die katholische Reform in Deutschland nach dem Tridentinum.* Münster in Westfalen, 1972.

Kraus, Andreas. *Geschichte Bayerns von den Anfängen bis zur Gegenwart.* Munich, 1983.

Krautwig, N. *Die Grundlagen der Bußlehre des J. Duns Scotus* Freiburg, 1938.

Krieg, Michael, ed. *Bibliotheca Bibliographica*, vol. 5, part 1, *Bibliographie der deutschen Drucker des XVI. Jahrhunderts. I: Dillingen.* ed. Otto Bucher. Vienna, 1960.

Kuckhoff, Josef. *Der Sieg des Humanismus in den katholischen Gelehrtenschulen des Niederrheins 1525–1557.* Katholisches Leben und Kämpfen im Zeitalter der Glaubensspaltung, no. 3. Münster in Westfalen, 1929.

Kurtschied, Bertrand. *Das Beichtsiegel in seiner geschichtlichen Entwicklung.* Freiburg im Breisgau, 1912.

Lea, H. C. *A History of Auricular Confession and Indulgences in the Latin Church.* 3 vols. repr. New York, 1968.

Le Bras, Gabriel. *Introduction à l'histoire de la pratique religieuse en France.* 2 vols. Paris, 1942–45. *Institutions ecclésiastiques de la chrétienté médiévale.* 2 vols. Paris, 1959–1964.

Leisner, Otto. "Zum 400-Jahr-Jubiläum der marianischen Kongregationen im deutschen Sprachgebiet." *Freibürger Stimmen* 44 (1974): 142–150.

Lenman, Bruce. "The Limits of Godly Discipline in the Early Modern Period with Particular Reference to England and Scotland." In Kaspar von Greyerz, ed. *Religion and Society in Early Modern Europe 1500–1800.*

Loserth, Johann. "Die Salzburger Provinzialsynode von 1549: Zur Geschichte der protestantischen Bewegung in den österreichischen Erbländern," *Archiv für Österreichische Geschichte* 85 (1898): 131–357.

Lutz, Heinrich. *Reformation und Gegenreformation.* Oldenbourg Grundriß der Geschichte, vol. 10. Munich, 1982.

Martin, A. Lynn. *The Jesuit Mind: The Mentality of an Elite in Early Modern France.* Ithaca, 1988.

Mattes, Bernhard, C.S.S.R. *Die Spendung der Sakramente nach den Freisinger Ritualien.* Münchener theologische Studien, vol. 34. Munich, 1967.

Mauersberg, Hans. *Wirtschafts- und Sozialgeschichte zentraleuropäischen Städte in neuerer Zeit.* Göttingen, 1960.

# Bibliography

Mayer, A. "Liturgie und Barock." *Jahrbuch für Liturgiewissenschaft* 15 (1941): 67–154.

Mayer, Heinrich. "Geschichte der Spendung der Sakramente in der alten Kirchenprovinz Salzburg (Taufe, Firmung und Kommunion)." *Zeitschrift für katholische Theologie* 37 (1913): 760–804; 38 (1914): 1–36, 267–296.

McCue, James F. "Luther and the Problem of Popular Preaching." *Sixteenth Century Journal* 16 (1985): 33–45.

Mehring, Gebhart. "Stift Lorch." *Württembergische Geschichtsquellen* 12 (1911).

Meier, A. M. *Das peccatum mortale ex toto genere suo.* Regensburg, 1966.

Meier, Johannes. *Der priesterliche Dienst nach Johannes Gropper (1503–1559). Der Beitrag eines deutschen Theologen zur Erneuerung des Priesterbilds im Rahmen eines vortridentinischen Reformkonzeptes für die kirchliche Praxis.* Reformationsgeschichtlichen Studien und Texte, vol. 113. Münster in Westfalen, 1977.

Metzger, Wolfram. *Beispielkatechese der Gegenreformation: Georg Voglers "Catechismus in Außerlesenen Exempeln" Würzburg 1625.* Veröffentlichungen zur Volkskunde und Kulturgeschichte, no. 8. Würzburg, 1982.

Metzler, Johannes, S.J. *Der hl. Petrus Canisius und die Neuerer seiner Zeit.* Katholisches Leben und Kämpfen im Zeitalter der Glaubensspaltung, no. 1. Münster in Westfalen, 1927.

Meyer, Charles R. *The Thomistic Concept of Justifying Grace.* Mundelein, Ind., 1948.

Meyer, Hans Bernhard. *Luther und die Messe.* Paderborn, 1965.

Michaud-Quantin, Pierre. *Sommes de casuistique et manuels de confession au moyen âge (XII–XVI siècles).* Louvain, 1962.

Moeller, Bernd. "Religious Life in Germany on the Eve of the Reformation." In Gerald Strauss, ed. *Pre-Reformation Germany*, London, 1972, pp. 12–42.

Muchembled, Robert. *Culture populaire et culture des élites dans la France moderne (XVe–XVIIIe siècles).* Paris, 1978.

Müller, R. F., and W. Blankenburg. *Leiturgia. Handbuch des evangelischen Gottesdienstes*, vol 2. Kassel, 1955.

Nichols, Ann Eljenholm. "The Etiquette of Pre-Reformation Confession in East Anglia." *Sixteenth Century Journal* 17 (1986): 145–163.

Noonan, John T. *Contraception. A History of its Treatment by the Catholic Theologians and Canonists.* Cambridge, 1965.

Oberman, Heiko. *The Harvest of Medieval Theology.* Cambridge, Mass., 1962.

——. *Masters of the Reformation: The Emergence of a New Intellectual Climate in Europe.* Cambridge, Mass., 1981.

——, ed. *Forerunners of the Reformation.* Philadelphia, 1981.

Oestreich, Gerhard. *Neostoicism and the Modern State.* Cambridge, 1982.

O'Malley, John W., S.J. *The First Jesuits.* Cambridge, Mass., 1993.

Ortner, Franz. *Reformation, katholische Reform und Gegenreformation im Erzstift Salzburg.* Salzburg, 1981.

Oswald, Josef. "Der päpstliche Nuntius Ninguarda und die tridentinische Reform des Bistums Passau (1578–1583)." *Ostbaierische Grenzmarken. Passauer Jahrbuch für Geschichte, Kunst und Volkskunde* 17 (1975): 19–49.

Ozment, Steven. *The Age of Reform, 1250–1550.* New Haven, 1980.

——. *Protestants: The Birth of a Revolution.* New York, 1992.

# Bibliography

——. *The Reformation in the Cities: The Appeal of Protestantism to Sixteenth-Century Germany and Switzerland.* New Haven, 1975.

——, ed. *Reformation Europe: A Guide to Research.* St. Louis, 1982.

Parker, Geoffrey. *Europe in Crisis, 1598–1648.* Ithaca, 1979.

Pascher, J. *Das liturgische Jahr.* Munich, 1963.

Paulus, Nikolaus. *Indulgences as a Social Factor in the Middle Ages.* Trans. J. Elliot Ross. New York, 1922.

——. "Die Reue in den deutschen Beichtschriften des ausgehenden Mittelalters." *Zeitschrift für katholische Theologie* 28 (1904): 1–36.

——. "Die Reue in den deutschen Erbauungsschriften des ausgehenden Mittelalters. *Zeitschrift für Katholische Theologie* 28 (1904): 449–485.

——. "Die Reue in den deutschen Sterbebüchlein des ausgehenden Mittelalters." *Zeitschrift für Katholische Theologie* 28 (1904): 682–698.

Pelikan, Jaroslav. *Reformation of Church and Dogma (1300–1700). The Christian Tradition,* vol. 4. Chicago, 1984.

Pérez de los Ríos, J. M. "Confesión genérica, especifica y numérica en el Concilio de Trento." In *El sacramento de la penitencia.* XXX Semana Española de Teología (Madrid, 14–18 sept. 1970). Madrid, 1972, pp. 345–371.

Pfleger, Luzian. *Martin Eisengrein, 1535–1578: Ein Lebensbild aus der Zeit der katholischen Restauration in Bayern.* Freiburg im Breisgau, 1908.

Poschman, Bernhard. *Penance and Anointing of the Sick.* New York, 1964.

Rahner, Karl, ed. *Sacramentum Mundi.* New York, 1969. S.v. "Penance," by Karl Rahner, vol. 4, pp. 385–399.

—— and Josef Hafer, eds. *Lexikon für Theologie und Kirche.* Freiburg, 1957–1967.

Reinburg, Virginia. "Liturgy and the Laity in Late Medieval and Reformation France." *Sixteenth Century Journal* 23 (1992): 526–547.

Reinhard, Wolfgang. "Gegenreformation als Modernisierung? Prolegomena zu einer Theorie des konfessionellen Zeitalters." *Archiv für Reformationsgeschichte* 68 (1977): 226–252.

Reinhardstöttner, Karl von. "Volksschriftsteller der Gegenreformation in Altbayern." In his *Forschungen zur Kulture- und Literaturgeschichte Bayerns.* Munich, 1894, pp. 46–139.

Rößler, Hans. *Geschichte und Strukturen der evangelischen Bewegung im Bistum Freising 1520–1571.* Einzelarbeiten aus der Kirchengeschichte Bayerns 42. Nuremberg, 1966.

Roth, E. *Die Privatbeichte und Schlusselgewalt in der Theologie der Reformatoren.* Gutersloh, 1952.

Rublack, Hans-Christoph. "Lutherische Beichte und Sozialdisziplinierung." *Archiv für Reformationsgeschichte* 84 (1993): 127–155.

Ruggiero, Guido. *Binding Passions: Tales of Magic, Marriage, and Power at the End of the Renaissance.* New York, 1993.

Sabean, David Warren. *Power in the Blood: Popular Culture and Village Discourse in Early Modern Germany.* Cambridge, Eng., 1984.

Schauerte, Heinrich. *Die Bußlehre des Johannes Eck.* Reformationsgechichtliche Studien und Texte, vol. 38–39. Münster in Westfalen, 1919.

# Bibliography

———. "Zur Praxis der Osterbeichte im Mittelalter." *Theologie und Glaube* 12 (1920): 15–18.

Schellhass, Karl. *Der dominikaner Felician Ninguarda und die Gegenreformation in Süddeutschland und Österreich 1560–1583.* 2 vols. Rome, 1930.

Schilling, Heinz. *Konfessionskonflikt und Staatsbildung.* Quellen und Forschungen zur Reformationsgeschichte, vol. 48. Gutersloh, 1981.

Schlemmer, Karl. "Gottesdienst und Frömmigkeit in Nürnberg vor der Reformation." *Zeitschrift für bayerische Kirchengeschichte* 44 (1975): 1–27.

Schlombs, Wilhelm. *Die Entwicklung des Beichtstuhls in der katholischen Kirche: Grundlagen und Besonderheiten im alten Erzbistum Köln.* Studien zur Kölner Kirchengeschichte, vol. 8. Düsseldorf, 1965.

Schnürer, Gustav. *Katholische Kirche und Kultur in der Barockzeit.* Paderborn, 1937.

Schreiber, Georg. "Tridentinische Reformdekrete in deutschen Bistümern." *Zeitschrift der Savigny-Stiftung für Rechtsgeschichte, kanonische Abteilung* 38 (1952): 395–452.

———, ed. *Das Weltkonzil von Trient: sein Werden und Wirken.* 2 vols. Freiburg, 1951.

Schrems, Karl. "Der 'modus catechizandi' der katholische Kirchenkatechese in Deutschland im 16./17. Jahrhunderts." *Verhandlungen des historischen Vereins für Oberpfalz und Regensburg* 106 (1966): 219–241.

———. *Die religiöse Volks- und Jugendunterweisung in der Diözese Regensburg vom Ausgang des 15. Jahrhunderts bis gegen Ende des 18. Jahrhunderts (Ein Beitrag zur Geschichte der Katechese).* Veröffentlichungen des Vereins zur Erforschung der Regensburger Diözesangeschichte. Munich, 1929.

Schrott, Alois, S.J. "Das Gebetbuch in der Zeit der katholischen Restauration." *Zeitschrift für katholische Theologie* 61 (1937): 1–28; 211–257.

Schüller, Andreas. "Messe und Kommunion in einer stadttrierischen Pfarrel vor und nach der Reformation." *Trierisches Archiv* 21 (1913).

Schutzeichel, H. "Die Beichte vor dem Priester in der Sicht Calvins." *Dienst der Versohnung. Umkehr, Buße und Beichte — Beiträge zu ihrer Theologie und Praxis.* ed. Theological Faculty of Trier. Trier, 1974.

Schwaiger, Georg, ed. *Geschichte des Erzbistums München und Freising,* vol. 1. *Das Bistum Freising in der Neuzeit.* Munich, 1989.

Schwarz, Reinhard. *Vorgeschichte der reformatorischen Busstheologie.* Berlin, 1968.

Scribner, R. W. "Cosmic Order and Daily Life: Sacred and Secular in Pre-Industrial German Society." In Kaspar von Greyerz, ed. *Religion and Society in Early Modern Europe,* pp. 17–32.

———. *Popular Culture and Popular Movements in Reformation Germany.* London, 1987.

———. "Ritual and Popular Religion in Catholic Germany at the Time of the Reformation." *Journal of Ecclesiastical History* 35 (January, 1984): 47–77.

Soergel, Philip. *Wondrous in His Saints: Counter-Reformation Propaganda in Bavaria.* Berkeley, 1993.

Spindler, Max, ed. *Handbuch der bayerischen Geschichte.* 5 vols. Munich, 1969.

Spykman, Gordon. *Attrition and Contrition at the Council of Trent.* Kampen, Netherlands, 1955.

# Bibliography

Staber, Josef. "Die Predigt des Tegernseer Priors Augustin Holzapfler als Quelle für das spätmittelalterliche Volksleben Altbayerns." *Bayerisches Jahrbuch für Volkskunde 1960*. Munich, 1960, pp. 125–135.

———. "Ein altbayerischer Beichtspiegel des 15. Jahrhunderts (Cgm 632)." *Bayerisches Jahrbuch für Volkskunde 1963*. Würzburg, 1963, pp. 7–24.

———. "Die Teilnahme des Volkes an der Karwochenliturgie im Bistum Freising während des 15. und 16. Jahrhunderts." *Jahrbuch für altbayerischen Kirchengeschichte* (1964).

Stalla, Gerhard. *Bibliographie der Ingolstädter Drucker des 16. Jahrhunderts*. 6 vols. *Bibliotheca Bibliographica Aureliana*. Baden-Baden, 1971–1976.

Steinmetz, David. *Misericordia Dei*. Leiden, 1968.

Strauss, Gerald. *Law, Resistance, and the State: The Opposition to Roman Law in Reformation Germany*. Princeton, 1986.

———. *Luther's House of Learning*. Baltimore, 1978.

———. "The Religious Policy of Dukes Wilhelm and Ludwig of Bavaria in the First Decade of the Protestant Era," *Church History* 28 (1959): 350–375.

———. "Three Kinds of 'Christian Freedom': Law, Liberty, and License in the German Reformation." In G. Dunnhaupt, ed. *Martin Luther Quincentennial Conference*. Detroit, 1985, pp. 291–306.

Tambling, Jeremy. *Confession: Sexuality, Sin, the Subject*. Manchester, 1990.

Tentler, Thomas N. *Sin and Confession on the Eve of the Reformation*. Princeton, 1977.

———. "The Summa for Confessors as an Instrument of Social Control." in Charles Trinkaus, ed. *The Pursuit of Holiness in Late Medieval and Renaissance Religion*, pp. 103–125.

Thalhofer, Franz Xavier. *Entwicklung des katholischen Katechismus in Deutschland von Canisius bis Deharbe*. Freiburg im Breisgau, 1899.

Tomek, Ernst. *Kirchengeschichte Österreichs*. 3 vols. Innsbruck, 1949.

Trexler, Richard C. Review of *Sin and Confession on the Eve of the Reformation*, by Thomas N. Tentler. *Speculum* 53 (1978): 863–865.

Trinkaus, Charles, ed. *The Pursuit of Holiness in Late Medieval and Renaissance Religion*. Leiden, 1974.

Valentin, Jean-Marie, ed. *Gegenreformation und Literatur. Beiträge zur interdisziplinären Erforschung der katholischen Reformbewegung*. Amsterdam, 1979.

Vasella, Oskar. "Über das Problem der Klerusbildung im 16. Jahrhundert." *Mitteilungen des Instituts für österreichische Geschichtsforschung* 58 (1950): 441–456.

Veit, Ludwig Andreas. *Kirche und Kirchenreform in der Erzdiözese Mainz im Zeitalter der Glaubensspaltung und der beginnenden tridentinischen Reformation (1517–1618)*. Erläuterungen und Ergänzungen zu Janssens Geschichte des deutschen Volkes, ed. Ludwig von Pastor, vol. 10, no. 3. Freiburg im Breisgau, 1920.

———. *Volksfrommes Brauchtum und Kirche im deutschen Mittelalter*. Freiburg im Breisgau, 1936.

Veit, Ludwig Andreas, and Ludwig Lenhart. *Kirche und Volksfrömmigkeit im Zeitalter des Barock*. Freiburg, 1956.

Vorgrimler, Herbert. *Buße und Krankensalbung*, vol. 4:3 of Michael Schmaus et al., eds. *Handbuch der Dogmengeschichte*. Freiburg, 1978.

# Bibliography

Weissman, Ronald. *Ritual Brotherhood in Renaissance Florence*. New York and London, 1982.

Wenzel, Siegfried. *The Sin of Sloth: Accedia in Medieval Thought and Literature*. Chapel Hill, 1967.

Werner, Karl. *Geschichte der apologetischen und polemischen Literatur*. Regensburg, 1862–1865.

Widmann, Hans. *Geschichte Salzburg*. 3 vols. Gotha, 1907–1914.

Zeeden, Ernst Walter. *Katholische Überlieferungen in den lutherischen Kirchenordnungen des. 16. Jahrhunderts*. Katholisches Leben und Kampfen im Zeitalter der Glaubensspaltung, vol. 17. Münster, 1959.

Zimmermann, Charlotte. *Die deutsche Beichte vom 9. Jahrhundert bis zur Reformation*. Weida in Thüringen, 1934.

Zoepfl, Friedrich. "Adam Walasser. Ein Dillinger Laientheologe des 16. Jahrhunderts." *Jahrbuch des historisches Vereins Dillingen*. 72 (1970): 7–43.

Zöllner, Erich. *Geschichte Österreichs von den Anfängen bis zur Gegenwart*. 8th ed. Vienna and Munich, 1990.

Zumkeller, Adolar. *Erbsünde, Gnade, Rechtfertigung und Verdienst nach der Lehre der Erfurter Augustinertheologen des Spätmittelalters*. Würzburg, 1984.

# Index

# Index

# Index

# Index

# Index

# Index

Satisfaction, 6, 15–16, 18, 22, 65, 112, 145, 177, 200; Council of Trent, 112–113; Luther's opposition to, 66; Reformers and, 66

Savonarola, Girolamo, 37

Scopper, Jacob, 152

Scotists: necessity of confession, 17–18; attrition and absolution, 19–23, 26; Council of Trent, 108; pastoral success, 23

Scotus, John Duns, 17, 19, 24; influence in late medieval theology, 19

seal of confession: necessity of, 55; violations of, 55–56

secrecy in confession, 6–8, 52–53, 55–56, 72–73, 95, 97–98, 100, 102, 111, 116, 121, 134–135, 140, 142, 183, 186

*Seelen Speiß unnd communionbüchlein*, 147

Self-discipline, 12, 95, 200

Sens, 36

Setting of confession, 7–8, 10–11:
  in Bavarian visitations: conditions in the church, 98–100; crowding, 97–98; hinders secrecy, 97–101
  in Catholic Reformation, 115–116, 164, 186–187, 193: attempt to enhance solemnity, 132–133; confessional and changes in setting, 133–142; continued emphasis on public setting, 133; privacy not the original goal, 137–141; to reinforce judicial character, 132; traditional concerns, 133
  in medieval practice: absence of modern confessional, 48; *Beichtstuhl*, 48–49; ecclesiastical demand for open and visible setting, 47–48; hinders secrecy, 55; lack of fixed and permanent setting, 48; lack of privacy, 52–53; physical positions, 50–52; prohibition on confession in private houses, 47–49; public dimension, 47; in synodal legislation, 47; and women penitents, 48

Seven deadly sins, 112, 172

Sin, 17, 19–22, 25, 31, 42–43, 53, 59, 175, 192–200, 202

Social and spiritual burdens, 57–58; mitigated by seasonal character, 59

Social control, 30, 112, 117–118, 176, 192

Social factors in confession, 5, 7–9, 11, 56–58, 72–75, 82, 100–101

Society of Jesus, 10–12, 31, 61–62, 76, 78, 98, 100, 122, 135, 147, 151, 158, 189, 190–191, 200; Catholic Reformation piety, 191; in cities and sodalities, 189; examination of conscience, 174–178; frequent reception, 146–161; general confession of an entire life, 168–174; success, 187–191

Speyer, 160

Spindler, Christoph, 122

Spiritual care and voluntary confession, 28

*Spiritual Exercises*, 168

Spykman, Gordon, 24, 26

Staupitz, Johann von, 24–25, 63: and contrition, 25; and Gabriel Biel, 25; and Martin Luther, 63; and Thomas Aquinas, 24

Straubing, 81, 190

Strausdorff, 93

Styria, 48, 71–72, 74, 121, 122, 136, 139

*Summa Angelica*, 91

Tegernsee, 171, 175

Ten Commandments, 39, 67, 69, 112, 172, 174, 178

Tentler, Thomas, 29

Theology of penance:
  Council of Trent, 107–113; absolution and spiritual consolation, 108; annual obligation, 110; attrition and contrition, 108–109; attritionism upheld, 109; burdens and consolations, 109, 111; complete enumeration of sins, 108–111; defined, 108–109; indulgences, 112; necessity of confession, 109; rejection of Protestantism, 107; relation to medieval theology, 107; satisfaction, 112–113; satisfaction and discipline, 112–113; social discipline, 112–113; Treasury of Merits, 112; upholds private reception, 107
  in Luther and the Protestant Reformation, 63–66; annual obligation, 64; attrition and contrition, 63–64; certainty of absolution, 64–65; complete enumeration of sins, 65–66; Luther as basis for Protestant theology, 65–66; relation to medieval scholasticism, 63–64

# Index